AMERICA'S WAR IN AFGHANISTAN AND WORDS
FROM THOSE WHO SERVED

AT
WHAT
COST

J.J. AINSWORTH
FOREWORD BY MSG JOHN MELSON

FOREWORD

Having over 21 years of combined service between the United States Marine Corps and the United States Army, my exposure and experience from the last 20 years of war have given me insight and perspective that is unique in its way as having endured the brutality of combat — having embraced a true love for country and love for my brothers and sisters who have been sent off to fight beside me, fighting and surviving, being sent into harm's way. We do what we do for those to our left and right. We are not and have not been the ones to decide on war, but those who have gone know what the cost of war is for us.

I served in both Iraq and Afghanistan multiple times as an Infantry soldier on nine combat deployments. The opportunities to serve with what I consider some of the greatest Americans have been an incredible honor and privilege. Being introduced to Jessica and learning about her writing "*At What Cost,*" I was super intrigued and honored that she subsequently asked me to contribute and share my experience in her book and honored me by allowing me to write the foreword for her book. Jessica, having served, being a former service member, I feel she is a great person to put such a book together and give the contributing veterans the ability to share their stories in this way.

The outlook and perspective of every service member who has served in Afghanistan and what it means when asked what the cost was to them are unique, yet some aspects can be shared amongst them. When Jessica asked me for my perspective on "*At What Cost,*" answering what the cost of the war was for me was complex. However, those of us who have gone and served, regardless of how the war ended, need to remember this:

The way it ended did not take away an ounce of your hard work; it did not degrade, in any shape or form, your commitment. For those that lost their lives, it was not wasted. You and I do what we do for those to our left and right. You gave it your all, and you made your sacrifices to those serving beside you. Reading the experiences in Jessica's book is enlightening to know what our service members endured and the cost on them from 20 years of war. Thank you, Jessica, for such an honor, and thank you to Domenic for being my brother and serving our great nation.

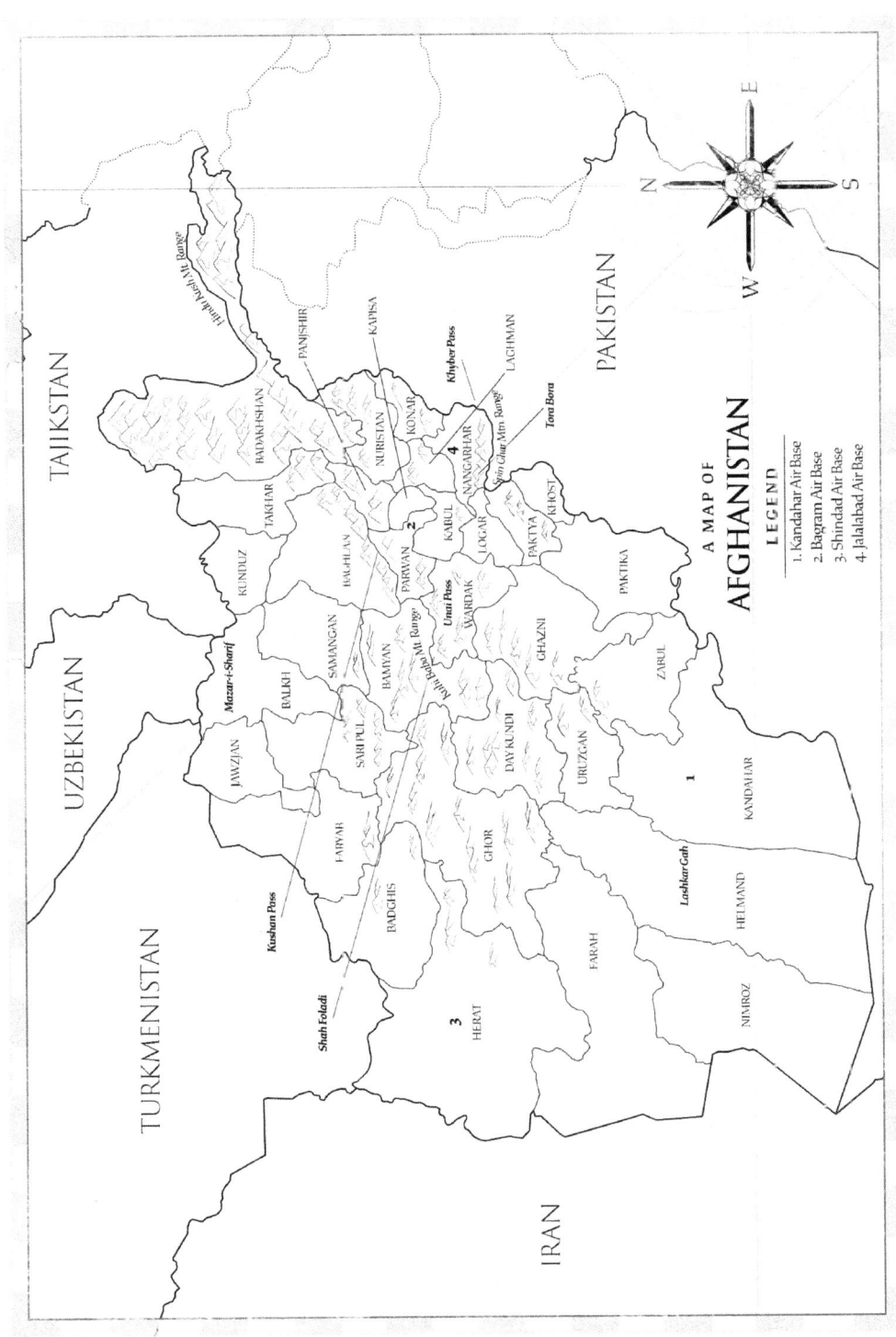

A MAP OF
AFGHANISTAN

LEGEND

1. Kandahar Air Base
2. Bagram Air Base
3. Shindad Air Base
4. Jalalabad Air Base

CONTENTS

INTRODUCTION

"Our response involves far more than instant retaliation and isolated strikes. Americans should not expect one battle, but a lengthy campaign, unlike any other we have ever seen. It may include dramatic strikes, visible on T.V., and covert operations, secret even in success. We will starve terrorists of funding, turn them one against another, drive them from place to place, until there is no refuge or no rest. And we will pursue nations that provide aid or safe haven to terrorism. Every nation, in every region, now has a decision to make. Either you are with us, or you are with the terrorists. From this day forward, any nation that continues to harbor or support terrorism will be regarded by the United States as a hostile regime."
—President George Bush

Twenty years after the war in Afghanistan began, it was over in the blink of an eye. There were talks of withdrawing from Afghanistan for a few years, but as 2021 ushered in a new U.S. president, so too would 2021 usher in the end of the "longest war."

In February of 2021, President Joe Biden had his administration review the U.S.-Taliban peace deal that began with the Trump administration. By April of 2021, that review had concluded, and President Biden announced the complete withdrawal of U.S. personnel from Afghanistan by September 11, 2021.

Before we had entirely—or even mostly—withdrawn, the Taliban began seizing control of districts and provinces throughout Afghanistan while the world watched in horror. Though I'm not sure, the full face of horror would become well known until around June/July, when our withdrawal was broadcast more prominently throughout the media.

By August 15, the Taliban had successfully seized control of Afghanistan, with then Afghan president Ashraf Ghani fleeing the country.

As we hastened our withdrawal, the media was rife with videos and images of Afghan civilians swarming the airport. They were desperate to flee; some even risked their lives holding on to departing aircraft. It was a scene straight from Vietnam—only this was Afghanistan.

Uproar across the nation had drastically increased after 11 Marines, one soldier, and one member of the Navy was killed in a bombing just mere days before the U.S. planned to be fully withdrawn from Afghanistan.

The U.S. completed its withdrawal on August 31, 2021.

In the face of this hasty and botched withdrawal, many questioned whether the end justified the means. Was it all worth it?

What was the cost of war?

It's easy to put a price tag on the war, but what about the human cost?

Approximately 1 million U.S. troops served in Afghanistan from 2001 - 2021, with about half of those having deployed more than once. However, that number does not account for the countless civilian contractors who had also served there.

A total of 2,448 U.S. Service Members died throughout the war in Afghanistan.

Approximately 21,000 U.S. Service Members were wounded in action (WIA).

Every day, approximately 22 veterans commit suicide—many of those combat veterans.

The war in Afghanistan may be over, but for many who served there, the battle still rages inside them. Anxiety. Depression. Anger. Guilt. Let's put a name to those battle scars—PTSD. One in five combat veterans has been diagnosed with PTSD. Unfortunately, that number does not reflect the number of combat veterans with undiagnosed PTSD.

Those numbers do not account for allied partners who were killed or wounded, nor the number of Afghan casualties.

The goal behind this book is to journey through significant events that occurred over the 20 years we were there and to see what it was like for our troops as they recount their time in Afghanistan.

When we think about the 20 long years we spent over there, we must also question at what cost? Did the end justify the means?

At the end of this book, you'll find a section called Roll Call, taken from the "final roll call." The final roll call is a military tradition to honor those that have fallen. In the Roll Call section at the end of the book, you'll find a list of every service member who died in Afghanistan. We will never forget their sacrifices. 'Til Valhalla.

Who am I? I'm one of the 1 million + veterans who had served in Afghanistan. I have deployed three separate times—Kuwait in 05 (yes, it was still technically a combat zone then), Afghanistan as a Soldier in the U.S. Army from 06-07, and lastly, Afghanistan again, this time as a contractor, from 14-15. My role for all of those deployments was as an intelligence analyst. While I did leave the FOBs (Forward Operating Base) over there a handful of times throughout each deployment, I certainly don't think I'm one of the "cool guys." I'm just a nerd with an affinity for research who is also just cool.

During my two tours to Afghanistan, I collectively spent two and a half years there. I met and interacted with some locals and interpreters, who were all very kind and welcoming. In addition, I was fortunate to see some of the country. Like all other veterans who served in Afghanistan, I have good memories and some bad ones.

Whether those memories were good or bad, Afghanistan was my home away from home for two and a half years. So, when the news of the Taliban seizing back control amid our hasty departure became headlines, I felt sick.

Watching the events unfold, I began questioning whether it was worth it. Did the end justify the means?

To find the answer to that, dear reader, has been my quest in writing this book. Many people I've spoken with about this—veteran and civilian alike—have also been asking themselves the same question. Was it all worth it? This is what compelled me to write this book.

To answer that question, you must understand the history of America's longest war and put yourselves in the shoes of those who served there.

As you journey with me throughout this book, I have kept opinions out of this historical retelling of events and limited them solely to the interview portions.

The stories shared in this book—I wish I had a way to include how emotional they were when recounting all of them. The tears and raw emotions, the joy and frustrations, all emphasized their memories in a way that absolutely gave me goosebumps. Their stories are relatively unedited to keep what they shared in their own words, so at times it may not flow as expected.

My goal in this book is not to sway you to believe it was or was not worth the cost but to help you understand what went on and decide for yourself if the end justified the means.

PART I

THE POLITICAL HISTORY OF AFGHANISTAN

Chapter 1
CULTURAL HISTORY OF AFGHANISTAN

Embroiled in one war after another, Afghanistan has a long history of turmoil. From internal strife to the Soviet-Afghan War, it's hard to imagine what a peaceful Afghanistan is like.

To understand the culture, which is elemental to finding your answer to whether it was all worth it in the end, we must first lay the foundation.

"Asia is a body of water and earth, of which the Afghan nation is the heart. From its discord, the discord of Asia; and from its accord, the accord of Asia."
- Allama Iqbal, an Urdu poet

Let's first start with the basics to give you a bit of background on Afghanistan.

Roughly the size of Texas, Afghanistan is a landlocked country bordered by several other countries, lying in the crosshairs of Central and South Asia.

The countries that border Afghanistan include Pakistan—to the east and South, Iran—to the West, Tajikistan, Turkmenistan, Uzbekistan—to the North, and China—to the Northeast.

Capital: Kabul

Population Size: approximately 39 million

Languages Spoken: Dari and Pashto

Major Ethnic Groups: Pashtuns, Tajiks, Hazaras, Uzbeks

Religion: Muslim—Sunni Islam (accounts for 90 percent), Shia Islam (accounts for 10 percent)

With traces of human occupation dating back 50,000 years, Afghanistan has ties to Alexander the Great and was even a part of the Silk Road.

Currently, the Taliban is in control of Afghanistan. Still, before that, the last president of Afghanistan was Ashraf Ghani, who, when elected, agreed to a power share with his rival Abdullah Abdullah. While Ashraf Ghani was serving as the president, Abdullah Abdullah was tasked with peace talks with the Taliban.

Just like the United States, there were (until the Taliban assumed control) three branches of the government: judicial, legislative, and executive.

There are 34 provinces in Afghanistan, and within each province, there are several districts. In total, there are 421 districts throughout Afghanistan. Of those provinces and districts, there was a provincial governor and a district governor. The president appointed the provincial governors, whereas the provincial governors chose the district governors. Before the Taliban took over, they operated with a "shadow government" that held the same roles as governors and police chiefs.

The Afghan Armed Forces consisted of the Afghan National Army (ANA) and the Afghan Air Force (AAF). The ANA also had a faction of their own Special Forces (ANSOF). As they are a landlocked nation, a naval force was not necessary.

The Afghan Armed Forces fell under the Ministry of Defense.

Afghanistan's police force was called the Afghan National Police (ANP), which fell under the Ministry of Interior Affairs.

The ANP consisted of the following sub-agencies—these are all acronyms/organizations you'll see mentioned throughout the book:

- Afghan Border Police (ABP)

- Afghan Highway Police (AHP)
- Afghan Local Police (ALP), later under ANP
- Afghan Uniform Police (AUP)
- Criminal Investigation Department (CID)

Like the military, the police also had their own District and Provincial Chiefs of Police. The president appointed Provincial Chiefs of Police. At the same time, the district chiefs of police were chosen by the provincial chief of police.

A pivotal figure to the people of Afghanistan—and Muslims worldwide—is the Prophet Muhammad.

Believed by Muslims to be the last prophet, Muhammad was born around 570 AD to the most powerful tribe in Mecca. Around the age of 40, the Prophet Muhammad began having visions and hearing voices. While meditating one day at Mount Hira near Mecca, the archangel Gabriel appeared to Muhammad. Gabriel's message to Muhammad was, "In the name of your Lord," which would be the basis for the Quran, the holy book of Islam. The revelations and messages that make up the Quran are said to have been revealed "in stages" to the Prophet Muhammad spanning the course of 23 years.

Muhammad began attracting followers while, at the same time, his message also angered many Meccan merchants. Part of his message and the revelations he'd received was that there was only one true God. Meccan merchants were worried that trade would suffer as, up until this point, they had worshiped and believed that pagan gods protected their trade and trade routes. However, Muhammad had created quite the stir by saying those pagan gods did not exist and that there was only one true God.

Fortunately, at least for a time, Muhammad was protected by his and his wife's family. However, once the family protecting Muhammad had passed away, Muhammad's situation became increasingly dire. So, Muhammad and his followers emigrated to Medina in 622, where they were assured they'd be able to practice their religion without persecution.

The significance of Muhammad's emigration from Mecca to Medina is that it is known as the hijra (the flight) and marks year one on the Islamic calendar.

Muhammad continued to receive revelations, spread the message, and grew his following.

After several years of violence, Mecca had fallen, and Muhammad and his followers had reclaimed the city, destroying all pagan idols.

The Prophet Muhammad died in the year 632 without having named his successor. The lack of a designated successor resulted in two factions of Islam: Shia and Sunni. The Shia believed that only direct descendants of the Prophet Muhammad were able to lead the Muslim community. In contrast, Sunni's believed that the Prophet Muhammad's successor should be selected by consensus.

To this day, the Muslim community remains divided into Sunni and Shia.

As mentioned above, the two major religions in Afghanistan are Sunni and Shia, both Muslim sects. While both sects have quite a few similarities, their differences formed what is known today as the Sunni-Shia Divide.

Their differences lie in doctrine, laws, and religious organizations, amongst a few other things. The conflict arises from the competitive aspect of "religious and political supremacy."[1]

While the crux of the divide is traced all the way back to the death of the prophet Muhammed, it wasn't until the late 20th century that the rift would result in widespread violence, particularly stemming from the Iranian revolution of 1979 when a radical Shia Islamist agenda rose. This radical Shia Islamist agenda was seen by conservative Sunni's as a challenge to them[2]. This trend of violence and religious persecution against one another continues to this day.

---

1   Sarah Pruitt, "Islam's Sunni-Shia Divide, Explained," History.com (A&E Television Networks, July 31, 2019), https://www.history.com/news/sunni-shia-divide-islam-muslim.

2   "Sunnis and Shia: Islam's Ancient Schism," BBC News (BBC, January 4, 2016), https://www.bbc.com/news/world-middle-east-16047709.

Regarding religion, the people of Afghanistan are very devout in their faith. The Quran is an incredibly sacred text to Muslims—similar to how the Bible is to Christians. To Muslims, the Quran is Islam's holy word and is considered "the word of Allah." They believe that the Quran is different from religious texts as the Quran is said to contain the literal words of God through the Prophet Muhammad.

Christianity sees Jesus as God's son, but Islam sees Jesus as just another prophet, along with Moses, David, and Noah. As mentioned above, the Prophet Muhammad is believed to be the last of the prophets.

After the Quran, the sayings of the Prophet Muhammad (hadith) and descriptions of his way of life (Sunna) are the most important texts amongst Muslims.

Chapter 2

THE POLITICAL HISTORY
OF AFGHANISTAN

You don't have to be a history buff to know that Afghanistan has been at war for a very long time—they fought against foreign adversaries (such as the Soviet invasion) and internally. Its most famous conquerors included Alexander the Great around 329 B.C., Mahmud of Ghazni around the 11th century, and Genghis Khan in the 13th century.

It wasn't until 1870 that Arab conquerors invaded what would later become known as Afghanistan. It was at this point that Islam took root.

Even past that point, nations had still tried to conquer Afghanistan. The British Empire attempted to annex Afghanistan in a series of skirmishes known as the British-Afghan Wars. These wars took place from 1838 – 1842, 1878 – 1880, and 1919 – 1921) until Afghanistan became an independent nation, which until this time had been a part of the British Empire.

In 1926 Amir Amanullah Khan declared himself King. He would go on to abdicate the throne a few years later, paving the way for Zahir Shah to become King. Shah would rule the country and offer stability for the next 40 years until the 1970s when he was overthrown due to a coup. The military coup was the paving stone leading to democracy.

The rise of democracy in the politics of Afghanistan can be linked to the country's 1963 constitution. Through this constitution, Afghanistan was said to become a modern democracy. Clauses supporting free elections, women's and civil rights, a parliament, and universal suffrage were all part of the democratic movement.

However, democracy has suffered many times in this nation. Just a decade after the new constitution was passed, Mohammed Zahir Shah's cousin Mohammed Daoud Khan staged a coup. Khan formed a republican regime and declared himself president. The republican regime made way for the unrest with neighboring countries and the rule of communist parties. Khan would later be killed in a communist coup.

While Afghanistan was struggling to build a democracy on the one hand, on the other, extremist groups were sprouting up as a result of the war with the Soviet Union. The Soviets had invaded Afghanistan to "support the Afghan communist government in its conflict with anticommunist Muslim guerrillas."[3] It was directly because of this war that the mujahideen (mujahideen translates from Arabic to "those who would engage in jihad") would form to rise against the oppressive government that had come about.

The mujahideen were backed by the United States. While some of those mujahideen fighters would go on to become well-known members of the Northern Alliance and politicians, others would later become members of an extremist organization, such as the Taliban.

Here's how the Northern Alliance got started.

In 1996, the Taliban seized power and formed a government after the Soviet-Afghan war and caused Mohammed Najibullah's, Afghanistan's last communist president, regime to fall. This would mark the beginning of several organized terrorist attacks against non-Pashtun ethnic groups (the Taliban are a Sunni, Pashtun ethnic group) in Afghanistan and foreign NATO countries. As a result of the violence caused by the fundamental-

---

3   "Soviet Invasion of Afghanistan," Encyclopædia Britannica (Encyclopædia Britannica, inc.), accessed July 12, 2022, https://www.britannica.com/event/Soviet-invasion-of-Afghanistan.

ist group, an Afghan Northern Alliance was formed under Burhanuddin Rabbani and Ahmed Shah Massoud in 1996.

In response, that same year, Ahmad Shah Massoud formed the Northern Alliance, alias United Islamic Front for the Salvation of Afghanistan (UIFSA). Their goal was to combat the growing violence and the strict interpretation of Islamic Law by the Taliban with the help of Al-Qaeda and ISIS.

Receiving support from several countries, including India, Turkey, Iran, Tajikistan, and Russia, most of the members of the UIFSA were from the Tajik ethnic group. However, by 2000, other ethnic groups had joined the Alliance.

Massoud was a legendary resistance leader, military commander, and politician from Afghanistan. Nicknamed the "Lion of Panjshir," he was involved in the Afghan mujahideen from the late 1970s until his assassination in 2001.

Ahmad Shah Massoud was born as "Ahmed Shah" to affluent parents from the Panjshir Valley of northern Afghanistan in 1953. He and his family lived in Panjshir shortly before moving to Herat and finally, Kabul, where he grew up.

Fighting for the country is seemingly in Massoud's blood — Dost Mohammad Khan, his father, served as a Royal Afghan Army colonel.

Massoud spent years as a freedom fighter. He started fighting for his beliefs and fellow Afghans when he was 21 and has since fought in war and politics.

Massoud first involved guerilla resistance fighting during the nine-year Soviet-Afghan War. Although only in his late 20s at the time, Massoud displayed efficient military organization, which attracted local guerrilla commanders to learn from him.

In 1979, he was able to take back control of and establish a base in his native province, Panjshir. Since establishing that base, Massoud and his men were able to fight the Soviet army occupying the country and the Afghan communist troops across Panjshir.

Massoud earned not only the loyalty of his men but also the recognition of other countries. The United Kingdom and the United States supported his efforts with funding, arms, and military instruction.

In 1992, Massoud was appointed the country's Minister of Defense under the Peshawar Accord. Massoud received criticism and praise for the cruelty of his military forces in Afshar and his creation of the Cooperative Mohammad Ghazali Culture Foundation to improve humanitarian assistance.

Massoud returned to fight in the mid-1990s as the Taliban rose to power and pushed for their fundamentalist view of Islam.

Massoud first approached the Taliban with an offer to join the nation's peace process in 1995. However, the Taliban declined the invitation, and the capital city of Kabul went through a siege and bombardment campaign for two years.

Since then, Massoud became involved in a tug-of-war with the Taliban forces over key cities of the country. In his years fighting against the Taliban, Massoud created the United Front. This alliance was made up of various Afghanistan forces and leaders. Together, they could defend and control almost 30% of the country's population until November 2001.

At a German conference in early 2001, Massoud had reportedly warned about Osama bin Laden. However, his warning would fall on deaf ears once more when he later learned of an attack planned by bin Laden against the U.S. The attack was set to be larger than the embassy bombings in Kenya and Tanzania.

On September 9, 2001, Massoud was assassinated while in Takhar Province. Two suicide bombers posed as interviewers before setting off explosives once they were granted an audience with Massoud.

The assassination was carried out only two days before the Taliban's attack on the United States. During one of his speeches, he was assassinated by suicide bombers posing as journalists. This use of suicide bombers in Afghanistan was a first but would not be the last. It is believed that Osama bin Laden ordered his assassination and that the suicide bombers were members of al-Qaeda.

Upon his death, Massoud left behind his wife, Sediqa Massoud, four daughters, and one son, Ahmad Massoud. Recently (2021), Ahmad established a resistance base in Panjshir to fight against the Taliban, following in his father's footsteps.

Ahmad Shah Massoud was honored posthumously as a National Hero of Afghanistan for his exemplary honor as a resistance leader and the country's defense arm.

The constant warring made Afghanistan a fertile breeding ground for strong, charismatic leaders who would become crucial in the fight to establish a democracy.

Throughout the political history of Afghanistan, three names have repeatedly proven to have a greater impact than others. The politics of Afghanistan would have changed drastically had it not been for the contributions made by Hamid Karzai, Ashraf Ghani, and Abdullah Abdullah. So, let's take a look at their brief political history.

Karzai would go on to be elected as a chairman of the interim government during one of the national Loya Jirga meetings for a stint of six months. Following the end of the six months, Karzai would be chosen during the 2002 Loya Jirga to be the interim president for a two-year term.

He made countless peacemaking efforts after being elected president of the country in 2004 and again in 2009. During his tenure, he maintained and strengthened relations with the NATO countries, and especially the U.S.

Towards the end of his regime, however, these ties started weakening. The change resulted from the casualties within the local communities during America's War on Terror. However, his efforts to maintain a good relationship with Japan led to reputable companies like Mitsubishi investing in the country. He made similar efforts to strengthen the India-Afghanistan friendship as well.

While Karzai certainly did some good during his time as president, his relationship with coalition forces became quite strained towards the end of his regime. Karzai had been accused numerous times of corruption.

Ashraf Ghani Ahmadzai assumed office on September 29, 2014. He was an academic and economist who was re-elected as president for a second time and sworn in for another regime in 2020. Much of Ghani's efforts have been focused on rebuilding the war-torn country.

The independent politician was also the finance minister between 2002 and 2004. As the finance minister, he carried out many operations to help build the country. For example, Ghani issued a new currency, introduced tariff reforms, and attempted to eradicate poverty in the country.

His ties with the Central Asian countries have helped developmental projects in Afghanistan and made way for stronger trade and business relationships.

Abdullah Abdullah was a medical doctor who became an advisor to the very same Ahmad Shah Massoud you just read about during the war with the Soviet Union. He arranged treatment and healthcare for civilians and fighters as an ophthalmologist and head of the health department. Abdullah Abdullah4 also made several notable contributions to the Northern Alliance. After the Taliban seized power of 90% of Afghanistan in the 90s, including the capital city Kabul, Abdullah was nominated as the United Front's (a.k.a. Northern Alliance) Minister of Foreign Affairs.

As the founding member of the Coalition for Change and Hope, Abdullah formed the largest opposing party against the Karzai regime—later in his political career. He challenged Karzai's presidency and regime on several occasions. He ran for the presidency again in 2014 and 2019, but Ghani assumed office both times.

---

4   "Biography of Dr. Abdullah Abdullah," Afghanistan Online, September 13, 2020, https://www.afghan-web.com/biographies/biography-of-dr-abdullah-abdullah/.

To every light, there is darkness, or yin and yang if you will, with the Northern Alliance representing the light and the Taliban (and other extremist organizations) representing the dark.

The word Taliban translates to "students" or "seekers," and it represents the vast majority of members who were students from Islamic schools. The extremist group has caused destruction and chaos not just in Afghanistan but around the world. To understand how the Taliban (Sunni-Muslim[5]) rose to power and sought allies, we need to look at the history of the Taliban and the peace negotiations that followed.

During the Soviet-Afghan war, women and children fled Afghanistan to seek refuge in neighboring countries such as Pakistan. Almost a decade in the making, the Taliban emerged after Madrasahs (Islamic teaching schools) indoctrinated and trained young Afghan refugees studying there. The organization would later seize power in all areas of Afghanistan, except a small portion in the northern region.

The founder of the Taliban was Mohammed Omar. He led the organization to seize power in the capital city, Kabul, in September 1994. (*Though they thought to seize power in Kabul, the Taliban had been formed in Kandahar.*) Omar formed the organization as a rebellion against the warlords after the end of the Soviet-Afghan war and the fall of Najibullah's regime.

Within just a short time, the Taliban numbers rose from a mere 50 to 1500 as students from a madrassa in Pakistan joined the Taliban. With the increase of recruits, they could secure more financing and militaristic support from Pakistan.

The Taliban began enforcing Sharia Law throughout the country, such as disbanding schools for children of both genders, excluding women from the workforce, and organizing many terrorist attacks across the country and abroad. What was once a movement, the Taliban had turned into a militia organization fighting against the Northern Alliance and later what would be-

---

5   "Whither the Taliban?," Foreign Military Studies Office Publications - Whither the Taliban?, accessed July 12, 2022, https://irp.fas.org/world/para/docs/990306-taliban.htm.

come the government along with coalition forces after the U.S. invaded in 2001.

Although the organization primarily consisted of Pashtun tribespeople from southern and eastern Afghanistan, some Tajik and Uzbek students were also involved in the consistent growth of the organization. Allegedly, the government formed by the Taliban between 1996 and 2001 was only recognized by four countries: Saudi Arabia, Pakistan, Turkmenistan, and the United Arab Emirates (UAE). Of note, Pakistan was accused of helping the Taliban by training students in Madrasahs located in Pakistan.

Yunus Khalis and Mohammad Nabi Mohammadi were the key players and the most influential figures that helped the Taliban rise to fame. In 1994, Mullah Omar led a team of fighters to various locations where warlords had allegedly been keeping young captives.

According to stories and legends, Omar formed the organization after a woman appeared in his dreams and asked him for help against crimes and corruption.

Al-Qaeda and the Islamic State of Iraq and Syria are two other extremist organizations mentioned throughout this book. They were said to be the core of the Taliban group. Without the support of these two extremist groups, the Islamic Emirate of Afghanistan would not have been able to adapt its interpretation of Islamic Law. Likewise, the history of the Taliban would have been short-lived without the two extremist groups' help.

Osama Bin Laden, the founder of Al-Qaeda, was exiled from Saudi Arabia and joined the Taliban. He would later organize several attacks against the opposing Tajik, Hazaras, and Uzbek ethnic groups and countries worldwide. His wealthy background helped the Taliban fighters, arms, and money from the Arab countries.

The Taliban have been using extreme violence in the name of Jihad to implement Sharia (Islamic Law) in Afghanistan and other Islamic countries. Although all U.S. troops deployed in Afghanistan after the 9/11 attacks have since departed from Afghanistan, with the last few leaving on August 31, 2021, many had predicted it would lead to more violence and organized crimes in the future, as seen in the history of the Taliban—and they were right.

The Center for Security Policy (CSP) considers and defines Sharia as a military doctrine with both legal and political aspects. However, a Muslim would not agree with this definition.

Although there is still an ongoing debate on how Islam should be practiced in the modern world, most academics studying the religion agree that: The interpretations and applications of Sharia have changed and continue to do so; Sharia is not understood as a single term; Various Muslim communities have their own interpretations of the religion; It prioritizes religious observances such as fasting and prayer rather than national laws.

The positive aspect of Sharia is that it is adaptable and responsive to the needs of its followers. The negative part is that its laws demand severe punishments for certain crimes.

But what made Sharia even more infamous was how Osama Bin Laden applied the law during his reign of terror.

Let's talk about Osama bin Laden for a moment.

Perhaps most well known for being the mastermind behind the September 11 terrorist attacks, Osama bin Laden was the founding member of the terrorist group al-Qaeda. But his story doesn't start there.

Born to wealthy parents in 1957, bin Laden was born and raised in Saudi Arabia. While his mother was more middle-class, his father was a millionaire who had built a successful construction company. It would only be a few years before bin Laden's father would divorce his mother.

Osama bin Laden would leave home in 1979 at the age of 22 to join Abdullah Azzam[6] and the mujahideen in Pakistan, fighting against the Soviet Union in Afghanistan. His role helped him

---

6   *Abdullah Azzam, known as the father of the global jihad, was bin Laden's mentor and reason for joining the mujahideen.*

gain credibility and influence, as his role in the fight against the Soviet Union was to funnel weapons, manpower, and money to aid the mujahideen. Using money and equipment from his construction company, he poured loads of resources into the fight against the Soviet Union.

Together with Abdullah Azzam, Wa'el Hamza Julaidan, and Ayman al Zawahiri, bin Laden founded Maktab al-Khidamat in 1984, also known as the Afghan Services Bureau. This organization aimed to secure funds and foreign recruits to continue supporting the mujahideen in Afghanistan.

In 1988, just a few short years later, bin Laden founded al-Qaeda. It was right before the formation of al-Qaeda that bin Laden would split from al-Khidamat.

At this point, the war in Afghanistan with the Soviet Union was still going but was winding down as it would end in early 1989. As a result, Azzam and al-Zawahiri began to have different opinions regarding Maktab al-Khidamat and the direction it would move in since the war ended. Azzam wanted to stand up for a "pure Islamic government" in Afghanistan. In contrast, al Zawahiri wanted to use the wealth and connections the organization had secured to fund global jihad.

Perhaps not so surprisingly, Abdullah Azzam would be assassinated soon after that. On November 24, 1989, Azzam, his father, and his brother were assassinated by a car bomb while on their way to prayer. While there were several suspects, including al Zawahiri and bin Laden and even the CIA—there is still no information on who assassinated Azzam.

Notably, however, bin Laden was swayed to the side of al Zawahiri over the dispute about Muktab al-Khidamat—hence the speculation of bin Laden playing a part in his assassination.

Why did Osama bin Laden split from Abdullah Azzam? Well, as I mentioned a moment ago, bin Laden, like al Zawahiri, believed that the Arab fighters and the funds secured through al-Khidamat should be used to fund jihad in other places. But on the other hand, Azzam held firm to the belief that the Arab fighters and the funds should be used in Afghanistan.

Despite this friction, al-Qaeda was founded by Osama bin Laden and Abdullah Azzam. Quite a strange dynamic there, isn't it?!

After Azzam's death, bin Laden assumed control of al-Khidamat, which would become integrated with al-Qaeda.

Fast forward a bit here.

When the Iraqi invasion of Kuwait occurred, and King Fahd of Saudi Arabia accepted the support of the United States, Osama bin Laden would go on to publicly denounce the Saudi government's dependence on the U.S. government. Bin Laden had approached Saudi royalty, including King Fahd, to offer up the assistance of al-Qaeda. When asked how he would defend the country, bin Laden responded, "We will fight him with faith." The King refused and turned to the U.S. for support. Bin Laden had argued that the Quran prohibited non-Muslims from setting foot in the Arabian Peninsula, particularly the two holiest shrines of Islam: Mecca and Medina.

In 1990, the FBI raided the home of El Sayyid Nossair, an associate of al-Qaeda operative Ali Mohamed, and found plans to blow up New York City skyscrapers. In addition to those plans, they also found plans for other terrorist attacks in the United States. This was the earliest known discovery of al-Qaeda's terrorist plans in non-Muslim countries.

With bin Laden publicly criticizing the Saudi government for their alliance with the U.S., bin Laden was eventually expelled from the country in 1991. Following the expulsion, bin Laden and his followers had initially moved to Afghanistan for a brief period before settling in Sudan. While in Sudan, he established a new base for the mujahideen in Khartoum. He had found success by working respectable jobs and investing in agriculture, infrastructure, and various businesses. In addition, he was known for being generous to the poor and was quite popular amongst the people there.

Even though he worked hard to build himself up in Sudan, he continued publicly criticizing Saudi Arabia, which led to them stripping him of his Saudi citizenship. The Saudi government even went so far as to convince his family to cut off his $7 million a year stipend. (Did I mention his family was wealthy?!)

Later the U.S. State Department, with good reason, accused Sudan of "being a sponsor of international terrorism" and of allowing bin Laden to operate training camps. After some secret and not-so-secret meetings, Sudan would be the next country to expel bin Laden in 1996.

It didn't just end with expulsion from Sudan, though. It is estimated that bin Laden lost between $20 million to $300 million as the Sudanese government seized his construction equipment. In addition, bin Laden was forced to liquidate his assets, including his businesses, land, and horses.

Given the choice of which country to turn to, bin Laden chose to return to Afghanistan—Jalalabad, Afghanistan in particular.

Enter Mullah Mohammed Omar, founder of the Islamic Emirate of Afghanistan and leader of the Taliban.

After his move to Afghanistan, bin Laden formed close ties with Omar.

As if he had an almost "I told you so moment," bin Laden declared war on the United States, citing that the U.S. was meant to have vacated Saudi Arabia after the Iraq threat had ended, yet they were still there. As a result, Osama bin Laden declared war on America.

Over the next few years (1990's), bin Laden's al-Qaeda members participated in jihads in Algeria, Egypt, and Afghanistan.

The Northern Alliance, founded in 1996, stood up to defend against the Taliban after they had taken Kabul. I'll talk about the Northern Alliance here as they play a significant role throughout this book.

When Jalalabad was threatened to be overrun by the Northern Alliance, bin Laden was forced to flee his home there. After another attack on the Taliban by the Northern Alliance in Mazar-i-Sharif, bin Laden secured his relationship with the Taliban by sending al-Qaeda reinforcements to support them.

Fast forward two years to 1998. The U.S. was still in Saudi Arabia, resulting in Osama bin Laden upping his declaration of war. His declaration of war included a declaration of a fatwa against the U.S.; He wasn't alone in his fatwa. Bin Laden and al-Zawahiri cosigned the fatwa against the U.S. This fatwa declared that killing North Americans and their allies was an "individual duty for all Muslims," claiming Americans were "very easy targets."

Later in 1998, bin Laden and al-Zawahiri would form an al-Qaeda congress. Shortly after that, al-Qaeda launched the 1998 U.S. Embassy bombings on August 7, 1998, targeting U.S. Embassies in Dar es Salaam, Tanzania, and Nairobi, killing hundreds of people.

In retaliation for this, in August of 1998, President Bill Clinton launched a series of cruise missiles targeting Osama bin Laden in Sudan and Afghanistan.

Just a few short months later, in December of 1998, the Director of Central Intelligence, Counterterrorism Center briefed President Clinton on the plans al-Qaeda made to attack the United States, including the fact that they had been training personnel to hijack aircraft.

On June 7, 1999, the FBI named Osama bin Laden one of the Top 10 Most Wanted.

Intertwined through the events we walked through above, Osama bin Laden was continuously building new connections, bringing in more money, weapons, and manpower in the name of jihad and supporting al-Qaeda. There were many conflicts that bin Laden had directly or indirectly (as the head of al-Qaeda) played a role in. They are not all mentioned in this section, nor will they be throughout this book. This chapter is just to give you an overview of the events leading up to the September 11 terrorist attacks that would catalyze our war in Afghanistan.

As you can guess from here, his plans and efforts against the United States continued leading to the events that took place on September 11, 2001.

Osama bin Laden followed an extreme form of Islamism and believed that restoring the law of God would fix all of the problems in the Muslim world. Moreover, he was convinced that Afghanistan was the only Islamic country in the Muslim world during Mullah Omar's Taliban reign.

However, the country suffered the most during Osama bin Laden's time there and when the Taliban was in power prior to the U.S. invasion in late 2001. For instance, under the enforced Sharia Law, the Afghan people were forbidden to practice sports and watch television. Sharia also carried over to children receiving an education as the children of Afghanistan were not allowed to receive formal education—neither boys nor girls were allowed an education.

Osama bin Laden believed that non-Islamic believers should be killed when it was done in the name of jihadism.[78]

Sharia is one of the most confusing laws in the world because of how its leaders have changed it over the years and how it continues to change. The Muslim religion became even more infamous after Osama bin Laden enacted Sharia Law during his time in Afghanistan.

The people of Afghanistan were the ones who suffered the most during his reign, especially considering that it forbade many essential things that are necessary for human beings.

Afghanistan wouldn't become truly democratic until 2004 when Hamid Karzai became the democratically elected president. He ruled over the seat for a whole decade before Ashraf Ghani assumed office in 2014. Historically, the transition of power from Karzai to Ghani marked the first peaceful transition of power for the government of Afghanistan.

After the 9/11 attack on the World Trade Center, the U.S. formed an alliance with anti-Taliban leaders of Afghanistan to eradicate the terrorist military organization and remove it from power. The formation of an interim government (emergency government) was planned to replace the existing government in

---

7   *Jihad is an Arabic word that means "to strive or struggle."*

8   "What Does the Term 'Jihad' Mean?," Islam Ahmadiyya, accessed July 12, 2022, https://www.alislam.org/question/what-does-jihad-mean/.

December of 2001. Remember Hamid Karzai from the Northern Alliance?

Hamid Karzai was elected as chairman of the interim government. The interim government consisted of a chairman, five vice-chairmen, and 24 individuals. Each of them would head a separate department of the interim government. The structures and the head of the interim government were decided at the Bonn Conference held at Hotel Petersburg by prominent political figures of Afghanistan. The Northern Alliance, the Rome Group, and the Peshawar Group were in attendance.

Hamid Karzai formed a cabinet of 30 members, with half of the posts given to members of the Northern Alliance.

This interim government was formed after the fall of Kabul as a peacemaking effort to ensure the city's security. The Bonn Agreement and the alliances were also endorsed by the U.N. Security Council Resolution 1383. Karzai would lead Afghanistan

Afghanistan abounds with numerous insurgent groups. However, none have had the same destabilizing effect as the Haqqani Network. The Haqqani Network is an insurgent group founded by Jullaladin Haqqani. The Pushtun-led group is under the command of the founder's son, Sirajudin Haqqani.

With active operational bases in Pakistan and Afghanistan, the insurgent group's scope of control extends to either side of the Pakistan-Afghanistan border. For years, the group has launched coordinated attacks from its active bases.

Along with the Haqqani group's capture and detainment of U.S. Soldier Bowe Bergdahl from 2009 to 2014, the attacks have cemented the group's reputation as one of Afghanistan's most sophisticated and deadliest militant groups for over two decades. Here's some background on the Haqqani group.

Jullaladin Haqqani began his military career in 1978 when he became a senior military leader. Under the Hezb-e Islami resistance movement, Haqqani was one of the major military figureheads to counter the Soviet presence in Afghanistan.

Haqqani then branched out of the resistance group, forming his faction in the early 80s. Receiving support from the CIA, Haqqani was able to foster relationships with other foreign agencies, including the Pakistani Inter-Service Intelligence (ISI).

The surplus of support later emboldened Jullaladin Haqqani, who took the helm of a Mujahadeen for over a decade.

The Haqqani Network's relationship with Al-Qaeda began with the latter group's founding in the 1980s. The relationship was strengthened further as the Taliban, the Haqqani Network, and Al-Qaeda collaborated throughout the Afghan-Soviet campaign.

The relationship between Al-Qaeda and the Haqqani Network was strengthened even further as the Network provided safe havens for Al-Qaeda militants. Many of these safe havens were in neighboring Pakistan, one of the countries where the Haqqani Network was based.

One influential government member made it his mission to disrupt the insurgents and seek revenge. His name was Abdul Raziq Achakzai.

As a result, of its rapid growth, the Taliban were able to seize the town of Spin Boldak, an area that lies on the border with Pakistan. The Taliban would soon go on to conquer and seize Kandahar City by November 1993. Over the next year, they would secure an additional 10,000 members and seize 12 more provinces.

Born in 1979 in Spin Boldak, Afghanistan, Abdul Raziq Achakzai would become both a warlord and war hero. Eventually, he became the top police commander in Afghanistan before his death in October of 2018. Something to keep in mind as you're reading through this is that Raziq was illiterate.

As Raziq and his family were residents of Spin Boldak, they had been there at the time the Taliban had seized Spin Boldak and Kandahar. Only his story gets worse. As prominent members of Spin Boldak, his father and uncle were assassinated by the Taliban. As a result, Raziq and his family fled the area, finding safety in Pakistan.

Abdul Raziq and his family returned to Afghanistan after the U.S. invasion. After his return, he joined the anti-Taliban forces under Gul Agha Sherzai and helped eradicate the Taliban from Kandahar.

While in 2001, he was pretty much unknown in terms of influence and power, which wouldn't last long.

He worked his way up from working as an Afghan National Policeman (ANP), particularly as a border policeman on the Afghanistan-Pakistan border, to eventually become the provincial police chief in Kandahar and, later, the top police commander in Afghanistan before his death in 2018. He was considered an ally to the U.S. and a fierce Taliban fighter.

While it sounds as if he may be a war hero to be celebrated, and certainly that is true to a point, there was also a dark side to his rise to power.

Described by Human Rights Watch as Kandahar's "torturer in chief," it was alleged that Abdul Raziq Achakzai had committed numerous human rights violations. Those alleged violations ranged from extrajudicial killings to forced disappearances and even tortured at allegedly secret detention centers. But, of course, he denied all of this.

According to the Human Rights Watch report, his torture at the secret detention camps included "suffocation, crushing the testicles, water forcibly pumped in the stomach and electric shocks."[9]

The United Nations Committee against torture claimed the allegations were "numerous and credible" and that Abdul Raziq was "widely suspected of complicity, if not of personal implication, in severe human rights abuses, including extrajudicial killings and ...secret detention centers."[9]

Despite requests for Raziq to be relieved from his position of power and even to stand trial for those crimes, the Afghan gov-

---

9   "Will Afghanistan Prosecute Kandahar's Torturer-in-Chief?," Human Rights Watch, October 28, 2020, https://www.hrw.org/news/2017/05/17/will-afghanistan-prosecute-kandahars-torturer-chief.

ernment refused all requests, shielding Raziq from facing any consequences.

Though that is not the full extent of his crimes/corruption, Raziq made millions by collecting "tolls" from trucks passing through the Spin Boldak crossing at the Afghanistan-Pakistan border. This was confirmed by U.S. military officials testifying before members of Congress. He was also accused of drug smuggling, with one report estimating he made around 5-6 million each month from drug smuggling alone.

However, that was what the media outlets were reporting. Those who had worked with Raziq and the people of Afghanistan considered him to be the "Robin Hood of Kandahar." Raziq was known to be a very caring and generous individual, which you'll come to see in the interview below from COL (Ret.) Nick Crosby, who worked hand-in-hand with Raziq for a year.

During his rise to power until the day he died, there had allegedly been around 30 known assassination attempts on his life. And in October of 2018, an assassin working on behalf of the Taliban disguised himself as the governor's bodyguard and assassinated Abdul Raziq Achakzai.

As Abdul Raziq Achakzai had been the primary controlling force in Kandahar, the birthplace of the Taliban, this was a huge victory for the insurgents.

COL (Retired) Nick Crosby

I joined the Army at the age of 21. I convinced my brother to go "buddy platoon" because they were going to pay for school. We walked by a VHS tape machine on one of the booths at Washington State University, and I was like, "Dude, we could do this. We're country boys. We could be infantry." That's sort of how we grew up—rugged and rough. We wanted to join as mechanized infantry. And that's why we joined—it paid for college and looked really cool.

On September 11th, I was in Medford, Oregon, on an ACRC assignment and was 35 years old. We were getting ready to push one of the enhanced brigades to the Sinai, so we were working with the Oregon National Guard, and I remember that morning very vividly. Waking up, getting ready to go to work, and watching the news. I saw the first plane strike, and then while we were watching the news, the second one hit. I immediately contacted my father-in-law, who was also in the military; he was stationed in Hawaii at the time. With the time difference, it was 6:00 AM for me and 3:00 AM for him. Seeing my call at that time of the morning, he panicked and asked, "What's wrong?" I said, 'Turn on your television. Something's going on."

For the rest of the hours, days, and weeks that followed, we all sat around watching our favorite news channel as things started to unfold while taking orders from higher headquarters. We were in disarray for a period of time but started figuring it out, and getting things together. I would say it took at least about 48 to 72 hours. But yeah, Medford, Oregon. Crazy.

Throughout my career, I did two long tours to Afghanistan in '06-'07 and then '14-'15, and then I also did a very short tour with the National Guard over to Iraq. We went to Camp Liberty and did a long/short haul out of Saudi Arabia. It was only like a month.

When I left for Afghanistan this time ('14-'15), I was 46/47, married with three kids. My kids were ages 13, 10, and 7 at the time.

Excited. That's how I would describe how I felt about going there this time. I had been in contact with Tony, my predecessor, the SFAAT team's commander. Tony and I have known each other our entire lives. We were in the same platoon at Fort Benning as Lieutenants when we went through the infantry officer basic course, and later we were Captains together in Hawaii. He talked to me about the mission coming up. With it being an election year, he advised me on everything they were doing to prepare the police to secure the city. It was an exhilarating time. You have tons of things running through your head about how you can assist and what you know.

Tony and I were infantry officers, not police officers. So, I questioned, how do you take the information and all the resources you've gained over the years, apply it, and continue the same programs he had implemented? In one of our after-action reviews, we identified something key: "They're tired of us changing the priority every year."

So, I maintained what Tony had done, primarily on my mind, ensuring a smooth transition between us as he departed.

I was primarily based in Kandahar throughout this deployment. We would go to several smaller FOBs, fire bases, and all around Kandahar, but the primary base we were on... It was terrible. While on one of the smaller ones, we were connected to the one next to Lieutenant General Abdul Raziq.

In terms of describing Kandahar Airfield (KAF) and the morale there... I will remember the other base (not KAF) because the other one has many more fond memories. It was rustic, but it allowed us to walk through a single door to access the Afghan National Police headquarters. So, in my daily interaction, we could go across and literally go hourly. Vice versa. Raziq would walk with his entourage to my side. And so, my headquarters was a two-and-a-half-foot wall away from his headquarters.

As we passed through that steel door back and forth—it was the most ideal situation you could be in as an SFAAT commander—you could communicate with your partner as you're trying to advise and assist, per the name. Of everything they were trying to do within, the twist we were putting on it was to support the American values and what we wanted the Afghan government to do. We also tried to get the Afghan forces away from some of the techniques they'd used in the past. So, it was like, "Hey, the rule of law."

My role in Afghanistan was Security Force Advise and Assist Team (SFAAT) Commander. At one point, we had deployed with just over 30 soldiers. Maybe it was a little less than that, but then over time, we grew. Some didn't see the value in some of these third-party civilian teams, and I said, "You're stupid. You're literally stupid." So, we integrated them into our team. As we continued to grow, we were moved from our FOB onto the main Kandahar FOB, the airfield. We had our own office space there and suddenly, you realize you have like 70 people working for you.

During our nightly meetings, we talked about how we could network, things that someone would hear, or different perspectives some civilians would provide their perspective on. Beside Lieutenant Colonel Barney, my right-hand man, everybody else was captains and below on our team. These kids had been in the Army for about five years or less, and we're trying to teach them to interact with someone who fought the Russians and the Taliban for years, with 30 years of war under their belt. These young troops are going out there with the mentality of, "Let me tell you how you're supposed to run logistics."

Whenever anyone offered to send us any new personnel, I said, "I'll take them. I'll happily take him, and we'll integrate him into the team because they can do well here in the South." And so, I got people from Kabul and Herat. When they started closing things down in Herat, we started pulling them in.

Colonel Chaloner and I understood that for the police and the Army to interact properly, Raziq and Hamid had to get along, and that became one of our personal missions, to put them together as much as possible. And hats off to COL Chaloner and his team. They did a phenomenal job. The Australian advised us his team is working with us. We wouldn't have been as successful as we were without the SFAAT and COL Chaloner's leadership to assist us with Raziq.

There were so many happy memories there. I was part of General Raziq's promotion ceremony, where I got to pin on his third star; that was incredible. I got to meet all of Raziq's kids.

Being with the team when the governor's mansion got attacked and being able to pin Combat Infantry Badges (CIBs) on the entire Sturdy Platoon is definitely one of my highlights from my entire tour. That was an incredible feeling, not only for the person they protected but for them asking me to do that. It was very humbling.

The variety of visitors we had was another highlight. There was this interest in General Raziq and the folklore that went with him. Being able to travel around and allow people access, because he trusted me quite a bit towards the middle of the tour to bring people, was great. Raziq would say, "Why am I meeting with this person?" And we would tell him, "This person is going to tell your story. This person is trying to assist you in doing this part of your mission." So, we had this variety of reasons we would allow access to him to assist him because he had a pretty bad rap and had done a lot of things in the eyes of the U.S. government that they did not approve upon. However, he did so much good for the community. He was the underlying tone known as the Robin Hood of Kandahar.

Being able to tell his story, I think, is what really helped him to understand that we were looking out for him and the best interest of the Afghan police. It was like don't take money at border checkpoints. Don't just go out and behead a bunch of Taliban; You can arrest them. You can bring them in and make your laws work. And we did that. It wasn't clean by any means, but he definitely gave back stuff that he had confiscated. He gave back up-armored Humvees. He gave up some heavy equipment that he had confiscated. So it was more about the relationship that we'd gained that allowed us to sort of bringing him into the understanding that if you allow us to tell your story correctly, you'll come out of this as a hero and not as the villain that people are painting you into a corner as.

One day, an attack at a southern border police station occurred, and several were killed. General Raziq was trying to get assistance to go down and extract some of his people from there. Initially, we were trying to assist, but we immediately came across the wall on our side. He was like, "I need help now. I need a helicopter now." For reference, the Afghan police didn't have any helicopters. Only the Afghan National Army had helicopters. And it came to the point where I was in his office, and all of a sudden, these three Afghan National Army pilots came in. He laid $3,000 on his desk, three stacks of $3,000 apiece.

He laid it on his desk and said, "I want to rent your helicopter. I need you to go to the South, and I need you to help us extract these people." And they did. Which turned into just this huge shit storm with the Army leadership and the U.S. When the helicopter came back, there was blood being washed out of their helicopter, all over the tarmac. The stench, seeing the dead bodies of all these police officers that were attacked and hearing the stories, it's like—was it a drug deal gone bad? Was it just the Taliban attacking the police station? That didn't really matter to me. What mattered is you're looking at 14 dead bodies, and more wounded inside of a helicopter just getting dragged off, and that's how we were treating people. We didn't help them, and this was the result.

We had the ability to help that day. We really did. I struggled with that one for a long time. It brings back some not fun memories of how I interacted with my leadership after the fact. But we could have done something, and we didn't, and that's probably my worst day.

What was it like going outside the wire? Normal. It's just normal. In probably the first 30 days, your anxiety level is high because you train, you do all these things back at home station to prepare you for that, but when you get outside the wire, things are going on around you. Everybody's looking at you. Once you get past that, it becomes very normal. Then all of a sudden, an event will occur, and you adjust to the event. You put in mitigations, or more security, or change how we do our convoys and the times for the day. Then it all gets back to this normalcy of daily operations.

I was one of the extremely lucky people who could work with both Brian Pearl's brigade and the special forces units because they were interested in using Raziq's intelligence network. And so, having them work with me and getting out of the wire, taking a helicopter when we had to go out to wherever was just amazing.

I don't know if I would have felt that I accomplished anything if I hadn't gone outside the wire. So, normalcy is an odd word. It was more of a sense of accomplishment daily because we were interacting with the locals.

On one of the days I was in Afghanistan, the governor's mansion got hit by an attack. After it got hit, my argument to my leadership was, "Don't show them we're scared." Let's go back and have a meeting the next day. And we weren't allowed to do that, so I was like, "Okay, meeting next day." So, after meeting with resistance, I had to find my own way to carry on the mission, and that's where it wasn't circumventing; it was just a different mission set. I could go with some of the special forces units, interact immediately with the Afghan National Police again, and go to the training headquarters.

So, they saw that at least a contingent of the U.S. Army was not scared to go back out, and it had nothing to do with our headquarters. I think everyone realizes now if you have one soldier on the ground, that soldier represents the United States Armed Forces. It doesn't matter how many. It's like as long as one soldier is there, they understand that the United States will take care of that soldier, and if that soldier's there, he'll take care of the Afghan Police and the Afghan Army. And being able to represent that single soldier or team, our SFAAT team with our security forces on the ground, those kids that were with me were so proud. I still maintain contact with some of them.

With the exit from Afghanistan, all my interpreters that I got out of Aghanistan contacted me. Some still have family there trying to maneuver and get out through different avenues. The platoon leader reached out and contacted me as well. We deal with it in our own way because we did a lot of good. And I said, "It doesn't matter what happened today. What matters is what we did in 2014-15."

I did a lot of soul-searching before communicating with those I've served with and my interpreters. What's the right command message? It still goes back to that. It's like, "Hey, look. Don't worry about what's in the news today. Look back at your pictures. Think back on the stories that we had." We were there. We made a difference. And we did the best we possibly could every day to ensure that our mission was accomplished when we got up and flew out of there. Anyway, it worked for us.

When Raziq was a child, I believe he told me he was 12 or 13, the Taliban had captured his father and mother and hung them right in front of him. From that day forward, his vengeance and wrath on the Taliban, no matter what, was definitely going to take revenge. You could see it in his eyes when he talked about it. And the network that he had was amazing. We used to laugh. This is no exaggeration—he'd have, between his aids that he always had around and his security force, he must have had nine phones that I actually witnessed. There was probably more. But he had access to Taliban operatives. He had access to the Hawaladar network. He was dealing with Taliban money.

So, he was very interconnected to make sure he could hit them where it would hurt—be it in the pocketbook or operations on the ground. Raziq and I talked about the money, and he told me he had tons of money, millions of dollars. I don't know how much money he actually had, though.

The police headquarters got attacked. As you know, they're all surrounded by 10, 12-foot walls. One of his police officers, a younger kid, walked on top of the wall, dropped a hand grenade, and killed the Taliban guy that was killing lots and shooting things around him. And the next day, we're all sitting in his office, and he brings the soldier in. He had included me in several of these events, but he handed this kid $10,000. That kid wouldn't make $10,000 in the next 50 years of his life, but Raziq was not stingy with money.

When we traveled together anywhere in the South, he would see people and parade; much like when we would have someone step forward to give out an Army Commendation medal or something. Raziq would say, "Hey, here's $1,000 because your commander just said you did an outstanding job." It was always a reward of money. I don't think they valued the bangles and the ribbons as we do. It's more like he just knew that would change their life and their lifestyle, being able to give money. These guys didn't take the money for themselves. They gave it to their family, their extended family, and that way, everybody gets wealthier.

I saw that over and over, his generosity to people, his kind-ness to people. And I also saw the other side of him, where there were between 24 or 26 Taliban he beheaded outside the city and then took pictures. We (the U.S.) got bent out of shape because they were advertising it on the local television, and I asked him about it. He said, "Well, how will their families come to collect the bodies?" So, it wasn't disrespectful. It was very respectful in nature if you understand their religion and their values on what they do. They prayed before every meeting we had. It was a very religious and honorable culture. They don't see a beheading the same way we see a beheading. It was more of recognizing, "you've done me very wrong here." However, the family can still come to collect and identify the body so they can follow religious burial procedures.

So, I saw the worst. I saw the best. I understood in many ways why because of Raziq's history with his mom and dad. He was a goodhearted man. I truly believe that to this day. I've talked to several people about him over my time in Southern Afghanistan, and they sort of know all the folklore about him but opening their eyes and telling his story is really important. Now, obvi-ously, after his murder, it's very important to me that I get the story right.

When Raziq was murdered, it felt like he was a family member. I'd grown so close to him over that period. COL Chaloner reached out because he knew I really liked General Raziq, so we had this great conversation. My interpreters—one's in Australia, and we have five here in the U.S.—several of them had reached out be-cause they were suffering. After all, we had lunches together, and we had dinners together with Raziq. He (Raziq) didn't need to, but he brought us to meet people. He was just this overly gener-ous, overly friendly person in those settings. And it hurts; It hurt many of us deeply, and we all wanted to understand why. I don't know if we ever got the real story. Still, reportedly, it was one of his security guards that actually assassinated Raziq and the governor or one of the governor's security guards. We knew the governor very well, holding meetings with him weekly. And to understand that both of them were killed almost instantly was heartbreaking. It really was.

While over there, my assignment was to work with Raziq. We were bringing all of these people all over RC South to Kandahar to train them how to be police officers. So, that sergeant major and that two-star general are good friends, too. We went out and visited them at least once a week, and there were always complaints like, "You see Raziq more than you see us." And it was like, "Yes, I do."

We integrated a third-party team of civilians into our team. While teaching them different techniques on how to train, I said, "Hey, this is your guys' mission. We'll monitor and assist you. I'll take the heat whenever there's a problem, but I need you out there helping them train." And they did a phenomenal job of taking what needed to be done, not because they were doing it incorrectly on purpose, but trying to teach a bunch of people how to train properly. We've (the U.S.) got a couple hundred years of doing it in a very specific way, and a process, and a procedure of putting a soldier through to get trained.

In their eyes, they go to training for four weeks, and now they're a police officer. They never go back. I said, "You can't have that mentality." There's always this reintegration back to the schoolhouse. And so, we were trying to build the non-commissioned officer corps.

In one of my bigger missions, we did a weapons repair facility in the South, and every week I walked up as the soldier, I'd be like, "My weapon is broken." And we'd hand it to the person. He would take down the serial number, the problem, and my name, and they (the Afghans) would watch. It accelerated the learning curve, but we'd watch them go through the entire process and show us what it was like until it got back and fixed, back to the front, and then how we would contact the unit to get the weapon back.

And we had a weapon loan program. It was so successful. While we never saw one weapon repaired during my nine months there, my replacement texted me and was so excited. He goes,

"Nick, it finally worked." So, they were repairing weapons daily. You just have to be patient. These projects don't happen overnight, but things will get better if you're persistent and don't change the mission or priorities.

Under Brian's command ('06-'07), while we were in Kandahar, we had soldiers killed in a roadside bomb. While I was not on that mission, I did see the bodies going to the plane. Brian did it right; It was a very respectful ceremony. We sort of took a pause to make sure that those soldiers were remembered properly. It was a very humbling experience.

The Colonel in charge of reforming Afghan prisons in Kabul had pulled up to the gate one day, as he had done daily like we all go out and interact with our counterparts. One of the guards up on top of the walls opened fire, and sadly, I didn't know the other people that day. More than just the Colonel had died. I left about a week before that. I think I was sitting in Kuwait, out processing, when I heard the news, and I just didn't know what to do. It was like, "I just talked to that guy." I shook his hand when I left because I had interacted with him almost on an every-other-day basis. It was a very odd feeling.

But you know, I'm not alone. Obviously, in my position, I was very shielded from many personal relationships because we worked inside a building, inside of headquarters, et cetera. In the South, on my second deployment, we were very lucky that we were able to make sure everyone survived and was fine. Even after the attack on the governor's mansion. We had one soldier that was evacuated because of head trauma due to the explosions at the back gate, but other than that, we were lucky. On my second tour to Afghanistan, we came out okay.

There is one unique story that I picture if people ask me what it was like in Afghanistan and what they would do, to the extent of being proud of something. So, we had flown down somewhere—I don't remember where—but we were touring a very small village, and we all had lunch sitting on the dirt floor, drinking what tasted like formaldehyde out of a can, and we were introduced to the village elder. The village elder had just voted. So, if you're not aware, the Afghans had to dip their finger in ink when they voted. After everyone had voted, the Taliban came in and chopped the village elder's finger off right at the end.

Photo Credit: COL (Ret.) Nick Crosby

The wound was fresh, with just a blood-soaked white bandage. So, I stopped, and we talked to him. To him, it wasn't about his finger; it wasn't about the Taliban. All he could talk about was how proud he was to have voted personally in an election. The guy looked like he was 30. He could have been 55. I was shocked that this person totally disregarded the personal dismemberment of his hand. For him, it was more about "I just participated in something I'd never done in my life." Not to get political, but we've lost that in the U.S. about what it means to be able to go to a ballot box and vote and the freedoms that we just take for granted, and the Afghans don't. They've lived under many different rules, from Russia to the Taliban. You may remember pictures from the '50s and '60s. The Afghans were in suits and had cars. They would drive from event to event. Afghanistan back then looked similar to the U.S.

Afghanistan was the number four fig trader in the world. All these things were going their way back then, which changed so much. And those older guys remember that time. But that was one of those days that you sat in amazement of, "We suck as a country." Look at these guys; how much they appreciate a bottle of water, being able to vote, and living in a village that literally is surrounded by 50 miles of nothing. And this is how they thrive. They're like, "We get attacked all the time. Okay, it doesn't matter to us." That was a memorable day for me.

Another Raziq memory—Raziq had gone out to Herat, and he came rolling up that day, jumping out of his vehicle, and gave me a big hug. I'm looking at the side of his truck, which was an up-armored SUV with blast marks on it. I mean, there was embedded metal in the windows and the side of his truck. And I said to him, "Dude, what the hell?" He goes, "Taliban. They cannot kill me." He was always proud. And I would—not to my leadership's approval—show off our connection. We'd have lunch together, and he'd talk me through these stories, and I got to talk to his family.

We were in Herat and flew in Chinooks on a Special Forces mission. We took them hundreds and hundreds of pounds of potatoes, and oil, and rice, and some ammunition in there too, but humanitarian ammunition, and we unloaded it. Raziq was sitting there with this boy he had brought to the front. This boy was one of those beautiful children that got green eyes, and he's telling Raziq this story of how his parents were killed by the Taliban. General Raziq being all emotional about it, just goes to what I knew about him as a good person.

Photo Credit: COL (Ret.) Nick Crosby

And you may say what he has done to bad people goes against him, but we don't understand the society; we don't abide by their laws. It's different. But those are the kinds of stories I hope he is remembered as, and people will reflect on his life. He's the one who did make a difference for so many years. Not just during the time I was with him, but all those years, he made a real difference in Afghanistan. He fought on hilltops as a young independent soldier against the Taliban. Surrounded. And fought through it. And gained a name for himself as this warrior. It was all just very moving.

Here's another memory. Right next to Kandahar Airfield, there was another Afghan-connected base by a wall, but no doorway between those two. We had to go all the way around to access it. Shaq, my primary interpreter, and I were there for a meeting. It was after the elections, and there were tons of U.S. personnel and Australian personnel on that compound. They all left and were all taking off in convoy, after convoy, after convoy. I had stayed behind to talk to Raziq about some things that were happening the following week, and so I got left behind. They left me there and were like, "Hey, we'll come back for Colonel Crosby."

So, we go from daylight to dusk. The sun is down now, and I'm just walking outside. It's pretty much the same area where everything happens throughout the day. All of a sudden, a soldier starts yelling at me—an Afghan National Police soldier. He starts advancing on me very quickly, and Shaq's trying to interpret what's going on. He's like, "Calm down. Calm down." And so, long story very short, I didn't know the night-time password. Shaq didn't know the password either. So, two more police came over, and I've got one directly in front of me standing about 10 feet away, with two more on each side of me. Obviously, I have my M-4 and my pistol here, and the ANP soldiers are all locked and loaded, pointing their weapons directly at my head. Shaq was trying to get in front of me. I said, "Shaq, sit down. Calm down. We're going to sit down." What is the most non-aggressive stance you can be in? Besides on your knees, of course. I wasn't going to do that.

But I sat down, put my hands back behind me, and just stayed like that. I didn't want to touch the sling or webbing on my rifle because it was attached up here, and I didn't want to take my pistol out and lay it to the side, so we just sat back. We sat there for what felt like an hour, but it was probably only like two or three minutes as they got closer and closer. By the end of that episode, they were within about four or five feet of us, pointing their weapons at us. I just kept thinking, "It's going to work out. I've got faith in God. Things are going to work out." Raziq had come out of the building in his convoy, and he started to pull up. He said something to the police, and they went from this aggressive stance to suddenly shaking my hand.

I'm checking my underwear like, "Okay. We're good." But again, it's not the power Raziq had, but how you can take anyone with this emotional high of getting ready to shoot someone and bring them down. Raziq's like, "Hey, man. I'm really sorry." So, that was a very memorable moment, I will tell you.

Photo Credit: COL (Ret.) Nick Crosby

When I think about our goal in Afghanistan, I believe that our goal was in the interest of the U.S.; it was a strategic base. If you look at all the "stans," Uzbekistan, and Pakistan, occupying that space gave us a strategic foothold in a very, very bad part of the world. So, it's like we need to align with the Army and police so the U.S. could have a bigger hand in touching the police. When we did that, it was very clear to so many people. It's like we're here, just like we're still in Korea. Why would we stay here?

And so, not to belabor my point about why we pulled out, but our mission with the Afghan security forces was primarily to assist them in establishing a legitimate government that was looking out for the people, along with security forces that would give them relative security.

I learned the term "relative security" on my first deployment because I was very lucky in my position. During that first deployment to Afghanistan, I was able to listen to Karzai in smaller rooms, and he would ask very, very simple questions. He said,

"Do you have murder in the U.S.?" Yes. "Do you have people that get raped in the U.S.?" Yes. "Do you have people that are beaten?" Yes. "And you have crime?" All over the U.S., "people take money from people." Yes. He goes, "Well, we have what the U.S. has. We have relative security."

And Karzai continues, "It's not purely secure, but it's relative enough where the people trust me that if something goes so bad, I have a police force that will go out and handle that." Back then, the idea was that anything in the city was handled by the police, and anything outside of the city was handled by the Army. I think we sort of stuck by those rules over time. But you started thinking through what we live in, especially over the last couple of years and what's going on with the movements in the U.S. we barely live in relative security. Being able to walk outside your home and feel safe, especially if you're in a few of the unique cities that have become lawless. We laugh and say, "Oh, they're a third-world country." It's like, sometimes, they have better insight into what the world really operates as. We should listen once in a while.

I say that story a lot to people, as we live in the same type of security that Afghanistan did daily before the Taliban assumed control again.

Did we accomplish that goal? Obviously, as a strategic stronghold, no. We gave that up. We'd achieved it. We did. It was there. Bagram was a Russian base before we occupied it; It was very strategic in nature. If we had maintained Bagram, Kandahar, and maybe Herat... Herat's unique with its sort of commerce back and forth with Iran, which people haven't addressed. But because of the Pakistan border, we had those three. The soldiers died all the time. Soldiers have been dying in training exercises this year, as well. But maintaining a worldwide footprint for strategic purposes is necessary. Are we the world police? Come on, we are. We are the world police. And being able to maintain a police station in somewhere like Afghanistan, in a very bad part of the world, we had it, and we gave it up.

Did we accomplish our mission with the Afghan Security Forces? We did while we were there. It's as simple as that. It's like,

"Here's the deal. You guys can open up the arms rooms, you can open up the Army flow of ammunition, or we're going to kill your family." Oh, well, you can have that. And people don't understand, especially with the news showing all the equipment left there. We didn't leave anything. When you leave a base, you pretty much leave a base. We left all of the M-16s, M-4s, all the 240 machine guns, Humvees, and helicopters to the Afghan National Army; that's what they (the Taliban) took. We didn't have helicopters sitting on tarmacs with U.S. flags painted on them.

The news did a really poor job of explaining what was happening in Afghanistan, but we did our mission while there. I think the security forces always considered the mission accomplished with our assistance. They did phenomenally; It just takes time. And you need to remember: How many decades does it take to change attitudes? I don't know, but we were only there for two, and then we left, so guess what? We won't be able to do that again for a long time because there's no trust. We lost all the trust.

So, yeah, we gave up the first goal, and then we abandoned the second one.

I thought about the question of how I felt about us pulling out of Afghanistan. I knew I would be asked that question by my interpreters. It's embarrassing. I mean, I was literally embarrassed that our country abandoned these people. A good number of those we left behind had no problem picking up a rifle. My interpreter, Shaq, picked a rifle up and engaged the enemy, and then we said, "You know what? Thanks for participating, but we're leaving." And we don't have a reason for why we left. Does anybody know why we left? Really? We were there too long. What the hell does that mean? We've been in Korea since the '50s. We've been in Germany since the World War. It doesn't make any sense. But I think embarrassment is the right word because that's what I felt when I talked to people who mattered.

I think if you look at some of the things they highlighted in the news as we were pulling out, you have women and girls who said, "I can no longer go to school." And you think only people like us, who were there, would understand that statement. For people who don't understand what it's like in Afghanistan, that may seem ridiculous. But okay, you don't know the history of the Taliban, why they want to maintain this uneducated fighting force. When you see those stories, it's heartbreaking because you know how many schools were full of girls that could do the math, that could speak English? They were learning English. And they're learning Pashto, Dari, and all kinds of things. It was emboldening to them. It's like they have taken back their country. And we gave it up overnight. We just literally gave it up overnight.

The Taliban wasn't resurging. It was almost like, "Oh, everybody's leaving? We've got an opportunity here." I think that was the most telling when I saw a couple of stories about that. I saw the hospitals that I toured, the teachers left, the doctors leaving all over the news. They just collapsed back to what they had when the Russians invaded Afghanistan. That's what happened.

One of our interpreter's mother and father are still there; they're very, very simple people. He also had two brothers; one brother actually ran and was the provider of the school for girls, and he and his wife would teach all these girls. They had like 30 girls in the school, and he closed it down. All of the awards that we've given to AJ were prominently displayed inside the house but were since burned. The mother and father, the two brothers, and the one brother's wife are now on the move.

I've written letters to humanitarian assistance. I've written to my senator, Senator Hawley, and Governor Abbott in Texas. AJ, one my interpreters, is from Houston. I'm trying to get all the avenues out there to help them figure out how to get his family out. Because of his family, if his brothers are arrested, they take them, put them on buses, most likely the U.S. buses that we left, and arrest them. They send them into pockets where the Northern Alliance still exists up in the North and part of Central Afghanistan, and they make them get off the bus and fight. So, the sentence is, "You're going to fight for us, or we'll kill your family." That's their situation, so why wouldn't you help a family like that get out?

The word is abandonment; abandonment of the people that mattered and what they believed we would do for them.

When I left Afghanistan, I was able to get all five of my interpreters out. So, Shaq moved to Australia, where they allowed families. Dash is in Washington, D.C., and AJ is in Houston. Nazir is, I think, still in California. There's one more, but all five of them were able to get out. We saw the writing on the wall back in '14. I was like, "I've got to get you guys out now."

One of our interpreters' fathers was beheaded because he supported the U.S., and we worked through that with him. And despite that, he still wanted to be one of the team members. We provided him security, obviously, but that was the punishment. It's like, "Hey, you want to work with the U.S.? That's fine. We'll just kill your family."

What was my own cost of war?

You lose a year with your family. And so, the teenage years for your daughter, your son moving into that, it's a cost. Still, I would tell you right now, hats off to my wife and what she does with our children, and understanding the resiliency the Army gave everyone in those circumstances. The community it had created at home, the groups my wife was a part of, and even school with the kids that they were able to participate in alleviated a lot of the cost, I would say. It becomes where dad has deployed so many times in his career, not all overseas, but I'd go to the National Training Center for 30 or 40 days, so they were used to the absence. Obviously, that one was a lot longer, but with the assistance of Facebook and being able to video call them, that helped. Kandahar had a great area where you could call pretty much anytime you wanted to, phone banks, and everything. It really helped. You start to be able to write again. It's like, "My hand has arthritis." Postcards.

So, the cost was just lost time. Did it cost me anything with my relationship with my wife or my children? I can't say yes, and I can't say no. It's more of an expectation of having a military career and what you did over that timeframe. My kids were way too young for my first deployment. My daughter was like four. My son was a baby. They don't remember anything. My wife does, though. Sort of abandoning your wife with a baby for a year.

You'd get on Facebook, and all you'd hear in the background is screaming, but the cost for me was worth it. I got to do something I could tell you probably only a handful of people in the entire Army only had the opportunity to do. I mean, I got to meet and engage daily for an entire year of my life with General Raziq. You can't replace that. Brian Pearl, Brett Chaloner, all of these people, allowed me to come together. I got to experience first-hand and tell people what it was like to see Karzai handing the reins off at the presidential election. I got to see how they conduct their elections and their really weird techniques. We got to plan security for an election.

Some of the crazy stuff that we got to do, it's like it was well worth the absence that was mitigated by my wife and what the Army did. But what I got to participate in and experience, I loved it. I loved every day that I was deployed. It made you feel like you accomplished something while you were over there.

So, there's my cost.

PART II

THE EARLY YEARS

Chapter 3

THE EARLY YEARS

"More than two weeks ago, I gave Taliban leaders a series of
clear and specific demands: Close terrorist training camps;
hand over leaders of the Al-Qaeda network; and return all
foreign nationals, including American citizens, unjustly
detained in your country. None of these demands was met. And
now, the Taliban will pay a price."
—President Bush, October 7, 2001

A common misconception about the war in Afghanistan is
that the war began on October 7, 2001. However, on September 17, President Bush authorized the CIA to conduct operations in Afghanistan against al-Qaeda and the Taliban. The CIA
would be the first boots on the ground in Afghanistan for the
War on Terror on September 26.

Within just 15 days of the 9/11 terrorist attacks, the CIA was
able to rapidly deploy a number of operators to Afghanistan,
following President Bush's order. This team of individuals was
known as the "Northern Alliance Liaison Team," code-named
Jawbreaker. They were the first "boots on the ground."

This wasn't the CIA's first time in Afghanistan. However, thanks
to their operations supporting the Northern Alliance, they were
relatively well-prepared in terms of knowledge about Afghanistan's language, territory, history, and culture. I'll cover that a bit
more shortly.

As soon as their boots hit the ground, they began doing what they do best—intelligence gathering. The sheer volume of intelligence they had reportedly gathered is simply stunning.

As the U.S. military would shortly set boots on the ground, Operation Jawbreaker would continue alongside Operation Enduring Freedom.

Thanks to that intelligence gathering and the efforts of those early forces, the troops coming in under Operation Enduring Freedom were able to hit the ground running by eradicating terrorism and disrupting terrorist networks.

Dubbed the "opening salvo" to our war on terror, U.S. and U.K. forces began conducting an aerial bombardment in Afghanistan on October 7, 2001—the start of Operation Enduring Freedom (OEF).

When the U.S.-led coalition began bombing, they targeted al-Qaeda and Taliban strongholds, including Kabul, Kandahar, Jalalabad, Kunduz, and Mazar-e-Sharif.

To go along with the U.S. and U.K.'s entrance into Afghanistan, logistical support was provided by Germany, Australia, and Canada. Later, troops had also been provided by the Northern Alliance.

Recognizing the hardships of bombing Afghanistan, coalition troops began air-dropping humanitarian supplies for Afghan civilians.

Seeking to rally others to their cause, the Taliban would go on to make a statement aired before the public that these actions were "an attack on Islam." Osama bin Laden would also make a prerecorded statement shared with the world calling for **war on all** non-Muslims worldwide.

After weakening the Taliban defenses and strongholds, coalition troops went from conducting pure aerial bombardments to a ground invasion on October 19th/20th. The majority of the troops conducting this ground invasion would be the Northern Alliance, with the U.S. and other coalition troops providing air and ground support to them.

With more than 100 CIA members, approximately 300 U.S. Special Forces personnel, local & tribal forces, and those from the Northern Alliance, they were able to divide and conquer. While some focused on intelligence gathering, others served as the door kickers. The invasion was in full swing.

In the coming days, the joint efforts resulted in the Anti-Taliban Northern Alliance being able to wrestle control from the Taliban and topple their regime on November 9. From that point, the results would be swift and in our favor. Kabul was the next to fall when the Taliban unexpectedly fled the city on November 13.

As the Northern Alliance and coalition forces kept advancing, the Taliban was forced to flee repeatedly, losing control of one city after another.

On November 26, we (the Northern Alliance with coalition support) successfully captured Kunduz, the last city the Taliban held in the North.

While many Taliban members had fled to Pakistan, there were still a number of them gathered in the South.

Forward Operating Base (FOB) Rhino, the first U.S. and coalition forces ground base, was established in Afghanistan in November 2001.

Herat would soon fall from the grasp of the Taliban as well.

Kandahar, the last remaining Taliban-held city, would meet a similar fate in December 2001. However, to leave it at that would be a disservice as this battle would be one in which some of our big-name players would have their shining moment.

And so, we enter now the battle of Kandahar.

Even in December, the temperatures were hot. There were no cold days in Kandahar. With the Arghandab River flowing through the area, Kandahar is still to this day one of the most agriculturally prominent areas in the country. The region is known for producing pomegranates and grapes and is a major source of marijuana and hashish.

Kandahar is the second-largest city in Afghanistan and is the most culturally significant city to Pashtuns. Kandahar has been their traditional seat of power for more than 300 years.

Being strategically located along several trade routes, Kandahar has always been the center of conflict, dating back to Alexander the Great in the 4th century B.C.

Knowing this, it should be no surprise that the city is also one of the largest trading centers for sheep, wool, silk, felt, food grains, fresh (and dried) fruits, and tobacco.

With Kandahar having ties back to the 4th century B.C., making it one of the oldest known human settlements, there's an incredible amount of history here. To stick to our storyline, we'll start at the point where the mujahideen defeated the Soviets and took back Kandahar.

During the Soviet occupation, the Soviet Army used Kandahar International Airport for their 10-year occupation. Then, in 1992 as the Soviet occupation collapsed, Kandahar fell to local mujahideen commander Gul Agha Sherzai—though his reign over Kandahar would be temporary, for now.

Two years later, in 1994, the Taliban seized control of Kandahar with allegedly little to no fight from Mullah Naqib.

With control over this major city and its people, the Taliban began enforcing Sharia Law.

Sharia Law, also called Islamic Law, is a religious law derived from religious perceptions from the Quran and the Hadith (essentially, the sayings and deeds of the Prophet Mohammed). We did cover Sharia Law pretty well already, so I'll leave it at that for now.

In Kandahar, when the Taliban seized control in 1994 and began enforcing Sharia Law, some actions included forbidding boys and girls from attending school and banning any and all forms of formal education. In addition, they were also forbidden from T.V., films, music, and sports, among other things.

Fast forward to October of 2001, when a couple hundred U.S. and coalition forces set boots on the ground and established

FOB Rhino. Once established, U.S. Special Forces reached out to Anti-Taliban commander Gul Agha Sherzai in November of 2001 to take back Kandahar.

While Gul Agha Sherzai had approximately 800 fighters under him, his force was still outnumbered and poorly equipped. Therefore, shortly after receiving supplies, Gul Agha Sherzai and his forces set off for Kandahar.

As they began their journey, they ran into the Taliban in Takht-e-pol. Unfortunately, it was an ambush, and the journey to Kandahar almost didn't happen.

With the help of U.S. forces, Gul Agha Sherzai and his men could drive back the Taliban and continue their path to Kandahar. The Taliban suffered such a crushing defeat at Takht-e-pol that they fled from Takht-e-pol altogether. Nevertheless, their defeat served as just another victory along the path to justice.

Along a similar timeline, Hamid Karzai (remember that name from earlier?), leader of the Anti-Taliban Eastern Alliance, and his men found victory in the Battle of Tarin Kowt. After delivering a crushing blow to the Taliban, Karzai spent several weeks recruiting for the Eastern Alliance, building up his troops to around 800 men.

With the size of his force rebuilt and his army resupplied, Karzai and his 800 men began their journey to Kandahar.

On November 30, Karzai and his forces began advancing on Petaw. After meeting with no resistance from the Taliban and seizing control of Petaw, they continued. But, like any other journey here, they would again meet with Taliban resistance at the Sayd Alim Kalay bridge.

It was a brutal two-day battle that had almost ended Karzai's journey. Finally, despite stiff resistance from the Taliban, Karzai and his troops were able to take the bridge. The next day, however, a stray American bomb detonated, leaving several U.S. Special Forces killed and Karzai wounded.

Karzai and his troops held firm through it all and began negotiations with the Taliban over Kandahar.

Gul Agha Sherzai and his men, not far behind Karzai, began their assault on Kandahar on December 7. Sherzai and his troops were met with little resistance as, by then, the Taliban had already surrendered to Hamid Karzai.

Karzai and Sherzai had successfully taken Kandahar from the Taliban.

Hamid Karzai was named chairman of the interim government on December 5. He would also go on to be named President of Afghanistan. Gul Agha Sherzai was named Governor of Kandahar after the battle. Coalition forces had finished securing Kandahar on December 9.

While providing support to our Afghan allies during the Battle of Kandahar, through our fault, we lost some of our own U.S. service members.

The very first casualties of the war in Afghanistan were not a result of the enemy. On December 5, 2001, the U.S. had mistakenly dropped a bomb too close to our friendly forces while executing an operation on Taliban members with mortars at the Sayd Alim Kalay bridge. As a result, three U.S. Special Forces soldiers were killed and another 19 injured. Their names are MSG Jefferson Donald Davis, SFC Daniel Henery Petithory, SSG Brian Cody Prosser.

The first American soldier in Afghanistan to be killed by enemy combatants was Sergeant First Class (SFC) Nathan Ross Chapman with the 1st Special Forces Group.

On January 4, 2002, while directing troop movements near the town of Khowst, SFC Chapman was shot by enemy fire and would later die.

SFC Chapman's death may have been the first (by an enemy), but it would certainly not be the last.

While the Battle of Kandahar drew down, the Battle of Tora Bora began.

From December 6 through the 17th of 2001, the Battle of Tora Bora occurred in the Tora Bora cave complex in Eastern Afghanistan. The objective? Kill or capture Osama bin Laden. After receiving credible intelligence regarding the whereabouts of bin Laden, this was our moment for revenge.

The Tora Bora cave complex is located near the Khyber Pass, which leads into Pakistan. The United States believed that Tora Bora was the al-Qaeda headquarters and, at the time, the current location of bin Laden.

The media had portrayed the Tora Bora caves as an intricate and elaborate cave system housing approximately 2,000 al-Qaeda fighters. They believed the impenetrable fortress contained hospitals, a hydroelectric power plant, offices, a hotel, a weapons cache, roads, and even a ventilation system. Secretary of Defense Donald Rumsfield said, "This is serious business; there's not one of those. There are many of those."10

This battle had been widely anticipated. On December 3, the CIA and U.S. Special Forces were inserted into Jalalabad for Operation Jawbreaker with a mission to kill or capture bin Laden.

On December 5, the Northern Alliance fighters seized control of the low grounds. Following their success, the U.S. began an aerial bombardment to "take out targets," which lasted approximately 72 hours.

That's three days of non-stop bombings.

Al-Qaeda fighters had dug into the mountains and moved to higher, more fortified grounds.

About a week later, Delta Force troops, Air Force STS, and two British Special Forces (embedded with the Delta Force troops) began a ground assault on the Northern Alliance troops.

Facing the possibility of defeat, al-Qaeda turned to local leaders to negotiate a truce with them at a time in which they would surrender their weapons.

Do you smell a plot hole here?

We can all recall the date on which Osama bin Laden was killed, and this was not it.

---

10   Josh Rothman, "Bin Laden's (Fictional) Mountain Fortress," Boston.com (The Boston Globe), accessed July 12, 2022, http://archive.boston.com/bostonglobe/ideas/brainiac/2011/05/bin_ladens_fict.html.

Looking back on the events at Tora Bora, it seems probable that the al-Qaeda fighters were simply stalling for time to allow bin Laden and other key al-Qaeda members to escape to safety.

But the Battle of Tora Bora wasn't over just yet.

By December 17, the Northern Alliance, with local militias and coalition forces, had taken the last cave complex in Tora Bora. The U.S. would continue searching the area for bin Laden and al-Qaeda leadership but would turn up empty-handed.

Osama bin Laden and the al-Qaeda leadership believed to be there had vanished, and it would be many more years until we would find bin Laden again.

And the caves that were thought to house more than 2,000 al-Qaeda fighters and consisted of all sorts of hospitals, power plants, hotels, and weapons caches turned out to be a small cave system with nowhere near the number of fighters believed to be there.

The Battle of Tora Bora is shrouded in controversy for more than one reason. First, we had him within our grasp, and yet, he was able to escape.

Gary Bernstein, the former CIA officer who had led the team tasked with locating bin Laden said that had the Bush administration committed more troops earlier, the outcome may have been different. We might have been able to either kill or capture bin Laden.[11]

The request to proceed in just that way had been submitted and subsequently rejected by the Bush administration as they believed that if bin Laden were to flee to Pakistan, Pakistan would detain him.

Had Osama bin Laden been killed or captured during the Battle of Tora Bora, the War on Terror may have ended quicker.

And sure enough, in 2009, the United States Senate Committee on Foreign Relations investigated the Battle of Tora Bora. It con-

---

11   Gary Berntsen and Ralph Pezzullo, *Jawbreaker: The Attack on Bin Laden and Al-Qaeda: A Personal Account by the CIA's Key Field Commander* (New York: Three Rivers Press (CA), 2006).

cluded that Secretary of Defense Donald Rumsfield and General Tommy Franks had not committed enough troops to the Battle of Tora Bora. Based on the information they were privy to, they further concluded that they believed that bin Laden had been in Tora Bora but had since fled to Pakistan.

It's always hard going down that shoulda, woulda, coulda road.

If things had been different and we had had enough troops, would we have successfully killed or captured bin Laden? Would the War on Terror have ended? Or would another al-Qaeda leader have stepped in to fill bin Laden's shoes?

Chapter 4

ESTABLISHING DEMOCRACY

A fghanistan's history in politics is quite turbulent but relevant to understanding the War on Terror.

The Bonn Agreement, also known as the Agreement on Provisional Arrangements in Afghanistan Pending the Re-Establishment of Permanent Government Institutions, was a series of agreements made on December 5, 2001, following the U.S. invasion of Afghanistan. It was meant to re-create and rebuild Afghanistan.

Until this point, there had been no nationally recognized government in Afghanistan since the 1970's when the Soviets forced their way into the country. And after the Soviets were toppled, the Taliban came in and declared themselves the new government. So, while determining a way forward, they had decided that a transition period would be prudent, hence the interim government.

It had been decided on this day and at this very conference that Hamid Karzai would be the chairman of this interim government, but that before a permanent government could be established, there needed to be at least one Loya Jirga. Remember the Loya Jirga from earlier?

"The agreement sought to establish a new constitution, an independent judiciary, free and fair elections, a centralized security sector, and the protection of rights of women and also minorities, such as religious and ethnic groups."12

Attending this international conference in Bonn, Germany, were 25 politically prominent Afghans. Notably absent was the Taliban, which some believe led to their resistance. U.N. negotiator Lakhdar Brahimi called this their "original sin"13 a few years later, in 2006.

In addition to determining the way forward politically, the Bonn Agreement also envisioned the International Security Assistance Force (ISAF), which the United Nations formally established through Resolution 1386 that same month.

ISAF was the NATO-led military mission that was built on multiple prongs of support to Afghanistan: 1) Engage in the War on Terror against the Taliban and al-Qaeda, 2) train and assist Afghan National Security Forces (ANSF), and 3) assist in the rebuilding of Afghanistan. ISAF conducted operations in Afghanistan until December 2014, when they ceased operations and disbanded.

While the war is raging on throughout the country, politicians in Kabul begin making strides toward stabilizing the government.

Loya Jirga was first formed in Afghanistan in the 18th century when the Hotaki dynasty rose to power, followed by the Durrani Dynasty. It is a traditional legal assembly that was formed to address issues, such as the sudden death of the head of state.

Other legal issues, such as constitutional change or war settlements, are also discussed in a Loya Jirga. The Loya Jirga is often considered the Islamic Consultative Assembly, which consists of a summit and a rural council. Like a town hall meeting, many tribal leaders in Afghanistan still use the Loya Jirga system for internal and external clashes.

---

12   Dr. Rajkumar Singh, "Chasing Peace in Afghanistan: Dynamics and Dilemmas," Daily Outlook Afghanistan, the Leading Independent Newspaper., July 12, 2021, http://outlookafghanistan.net/topics.php?post_id=29792.

13   Dr Anna Larson and Astri Suhrke, "Afghanistan," Lessons from Bonn: Victors' peace? | Conciliation Resources, June 1, 2018, https://www.c-r.org/accord/afghanistan/lessons-bonn-victors%E2%80%99-peace.

King Amanullah Khan first institutionalized this traditional assembly and later expanded it to include ethnic groups, such as the Hazaras and Tajiks, other than the Pashtuns. More recently, the Loya Jirga meeting was organized to extend a peacemaking treaty with the Taliban.

In 2020, another Loya Jirga was formed to come to a conclusion regarding the fate of some 400 prisoners. The prisoners in question were of the Taliban and were accused of major crimes. The traditional assembly was to decide whether or not these criminals could be freed as part of the peacemaking process.

Now that we've covered the Loya Jirga and some political contexts, let's dive a bit deeper.

By 2001, the alliance had power over approximately 30% of the population in several cities of Afghanistan. Following the 9/11 attacks, U.S. troops were deployed in the country, who provided aid for the alliance and helped them remove the Taliban from power in December 2001.

After a 2003 Loya Jirga, a 502-member assembly in Kabul has just approved the latest version of the constitution of the Islamic Republic of Afghanistan. The constitution established a presidential system similar to that of the United States, dividing power amongst the three branches of the government: executive, legislative and judicial.

Before the 502-member assembly, approximately 35 individuals, including Afghans and foreign legal experts, spent around a year working on the draft of the constitution.

The constitution, as it stands, included 162 articles. While it's easy to assume that the 35 members who drafted the constitution and/or the 502-member assembly were the ones who created the 162 articles on their own, this was not necessarily the case. The constitution and the 162 articles were more or less created by the people, for the people. Half a million Afghans were asked what they felt should be included in the constitution.

Let's not delude ourselves here and think that all people were represented in that half a million. This is just speculation, but this author believes that those with wealth and/or influence were likely asked their opinion. The lower-class citizens were likely excluded from this discussion.

With the constitution's immediate effect, the next thing on the agenda would be formally electing the president.

The presidential elections were initially planned for July 5, 2004, but they had to be postponed due to security concerns (go figure).

Until this point, Hamid Karzai had been acting as interim president of Afghanistan since 2002 and the chairman of the interim government before that (and since December 2001).

This was a historic time for the people of Afghanistan. This was their first-ever presidential election.

Altogether, at the onset, there were 23 presidential candidates; however, by the time the campaign began, five hopefuls had dropped out of the race. There were 18 solid contenders, one of which was a female.

Vowing to disrupt the elections, members of the Taliban set out to strike fear in the hearts of those seeking to cast their ballot. Coalition forces provided security in support of Afghanistan's first democratic election—and would also provide support for later presidential elections.

To further assist the people of Afghanistan, the Joint Electoral Management Body (JEMB) helped oversee the elections.

Election day was October 4, 2004. There were approximately "4,900 polling centers with 22,000 polling stations operational in all districts of Afghanistan's 34 provinces."[14] In addition to those polling stations, there were also "2,800 polling stations [which] served refugees in Iran and Pakistan."[15]

Despite the very real threats of violence, 8,128,940 Afghans voted, accounting for 70% of all registered voters in Afghani-

---

14   Anusha, "Iec.org.af Election Types : Independent Commission of Afghanistan," www.electionin.org, accessed July 12, 2022, https://www.electionin.org/2639.html.

15   "Results Leave Karzai One Step from Victory," The Guardian (Guardian News and Media, October 25, 2004), https://www.theguardian.com/world/2004/oct/25/afghanistan?CMP=gu_com.

stan. Approximately 60% of voters were male, and the remaining 40% were female.

Why do I mention gender here? Oppression, of course. Remember that under the Taliban, women and children were faced with some particularly gruesome atrocities. So the fact that there was a woman presidential candidate AND 40% of the voters were women was a big deal!

The elections further angered the Taliban and al-Qaeda, though. They viewed the presidential elections as Americans trying to exert their dominance over the region.

Election day did not come and go with no bloodshed.

During the elections, five Afghan National Army (ANA) soldiers died in skirmishes, 15 Joint Electoral Management Body staff members were killed, and a further 46 were injured in various other attacks.

Within a few days, the numbers were in, and the new president was announced. With 55.4% of the votes in his favor, President Hamid Karzai was the first-ever president of Afghanistan.

Was there voter fraud in the 2004 presidential election? Absolutely. It's a widely known fact. Karzai himself would even admit to it later on.

With the presidential elections being such a historical moment, and with how much the Taliban and al-Qaeda blamed and despised the U.S. for it, is it really any wonder that Osama bin Laden made an unexpected appearance after disappearing for the last three years?

On October 29, 2004, al Jazeera broadcast a prerecorded message from Osama bin Laden to America. During this 18-minute video, bin Laden confesses to orchestrating the 9/11 terrorist attacks in the United States and condemns the Bush administration for its response.

During the video, bin Laden goes on record to say, *"God knows it did not cross our minds to attack the Towers, but after the situation became unbearable—and we witnessed the injustice and tyranny of the American-Israeli alliance against our people in*

Palestine and Lebanon—I thought about it. And the events that affected me directly were that of 1982 and the events that followed—when America allowed the Israelis to invade Lebanon, helped by the U.S. Sixth Fleet. As I watched the destroyed towers in Lebanon, it occurred to me to punish the unjust the same way: to destroy towers in America so it could taste some of what we are tasting and to stop killing our children and women."

"We want to restore freedom to our nation, just as you lay waste to our nation,"16 bin Laden said.

There was speculation that the video was released at a time in which it was intended to influence the U.S. presidential elections that were to be held just days after the video was released.

President Bush and Senator John Kerry, presidential hopeful, were united in their stance against his words.

Bush's response was, *"Let me make this very clear: Americans will not be intimidated or influenced by an enemy of our country. I'm sure Senator Kerry agrees with this. I also want to say to the American people that we're at war with these terrorists, and I am confident that we will prevail."17*

United with President Bush's remarks, Senator John Kerry remarked, "Let me make it clear, crystal clear: as Americans, we are absolutely united in our determination to hunt down and destroy Osama bin Laden and the terrorists. They are barbarians, and I will stop at absolutely nothing to hunt down, capture, or kill the terrorists wherever they are, whatever it takes. Period."18

16   Al Jazeera, "Full Transcript of Bin Ladin's Speech," News | Al Jazeera (Al Jazeera, November 1, 2004), https://www.aljazeera.com/news/2004/11/1/full-transcript-of-bin-ladins-speech.

17   "President Bush on Friday: 'We Will Not Be Intimidated'," National Archives and Records Administration (National Archives and Records Administration), accessed July 12, 2022, https://georgewbush-whitehouse.archives.gov/news/releases/2004/10/text/20041029-18.html.

18   PaolaFarer, "Kerry Statement on Bin Laden Tape," KUSA.com (KUSA, October 29, 2004), https://www.9news.com/article/news/kerry-statement-on-bin-laden-tape/73-344859151.

The video influenced our presidential elections, as President Bush's popularity shot up in the polls after the video had been released.

Despite the timely release of this video, we were still unable to locate Osama bin Laden.

In May of 2005, Bush and Karzai entered our two countries into a partnership by signing a joint declaration. This partnership allows the U.S. to continue using the military bases established in Afghanistan.

Karzai raised some significant concerns that were left unanswered through this partnership. For example, he wanted more control over U.S. forces, Afghan prisoners returned from U.S. custody, and answers for alleged abuses of Afghans while in U.S. custody.

Bush gave no quarter to control U.S. forces, reinforcing that U.S. forces would only answer to the United States. The release of prisoners would remain controversial, but perhaps the alleged abuse would be taking center stage. Two Afghan prisoners being detained at Bagram Airfield reportedly died while in custody, and the Pentagon had investigated the incidents as murder.

More abuse scandals are coming, folks. This is just the start.

Although we focused here primarily on the negative, there was a positive to this agreement. The goal behind this partnership was to "strengthen U.S.-Afghan ties and help ensure Afghanistan's long-term security, democracy, and prosperity."

Chapter 5

MAJOR OPERATIONS

Operation Anaconda was the first large-scale military operation since the Battle of Tora Bora. This operation set out to eliminate and capture the remaining organized al-Qaeda and Taliban resistance.

From March 2 to March 16, 2002, approximately 2,000 coalition troops and approximately 1,000 "pro-government" Afghan militia battled somewhere between 300 to 1,000 al-Qaeda and Taliban fighters in the Shahi-Kot valley.

That's a pretty wide range of numbers there, right?

Initially, U.S. forces estimated that there were between 150 – 200 fighters in the Shahi-Kot valley. Still, it was later determined that the actual number of insurgents had swelled to around 500 to 1,000.

The U.S. estimated that during this battle, they had killed approximately 500 insurgents; however, journalists had later relayed that there had only been 23 bodies found. So perhaps the truth lies somewhere in the middle there?

Do you smell a controversy? Well, you're not wrong.
The battle took place in the Shahi-Kot Valley and Arma Mountains southeast of the city of Zurmat. With difficult terrain, this operation was the first to involve American forces in a prolonged ground battle since Operation Enduring Freedom began.

Overall, Operation Anaconda was considered a success. General Tommy R. Franks, U.S. Army Commander, U.S. Central Command (USCENTCOM), stated that Operation Anaconda succeeded in clearing the enemy in the valley and the hills of the battlefield. He added that this operation achieved what many other operations failed to get done.

This operation also served as a strategy lesson for the U.S. military. The rugged terrain gave the enemy the advantage of the environment. This factor became an example for the military to consider complex planning and executing rapid air support for ground operations.

Operation Anaconda worked around four primary objectives: (1) Capture and kill al-Qaeda key leaders, (2) Destroy al-Qaeda Foreign Fighters, (3) Prevent the escape of al-Qaeda Foreign fighters, and (4) Defeat Taliban forces that continue to resist.

March 2, 2002, was the formal beginning of Operation Anaconda. The military prepared by having Special Operations Forces (SOF AKA SF) surveying the battlefield in late February. The SOF teams also set up positions and assisted Afghan military forces in getting into formation.

By 6:00 AM on March 2, three CH-47 helicopters arrived, and 125 men from the 1/87th Infantry Regiment assembled as the 10th Mountain Division. Within ten minutes, al-Qaeda fighters fired at the division. The enemy was familiar with the rugged terrain and had all the advantages, causing the battle's first injuries.

However, U.S. forces tightened their control over the battle later on. A 24-hour battle occurred between March 3 and March 4, where U.S. soldiers reportedly killed hundreds of al-Qaeda forces that attempted to control an isolated hilltop position.

The battle for the hilltop position established a new observation post that overlooked al-Qaeda's supply and escape route. Within this timeframe, the U.S. suffered its major casualties: seven of eight American deaths in this battle (more about this to come).

As U.S. forces extracted fallen comrades, they began re-strategizing. This time, they considered enemy forces much stronger than initially anticipated. Thus, they intended to renew the attack by bringing more helicopters, reactivating Afghan support, and resupplying forces to keep up with a prolonged battle.

By March 9, the U.S. troops secured one of the two most significant battle zones, Objective Ginger. With extensive air support between March 9 and March 10, the U.S. dropped more bombs from aircraft than other days during Operation Anaconda.

The surviving al-Qaeda and Taliban troops withdrew their forces by March 16. U.S. CENTCOM officially declared the battle over on March 19, once the U.S. completely took control over the Shahi-Kot Valley, Objective Ginger, the Whale (a major point of high land that meets water), and nearby ridges.

Ultimately, the U.S. military met its initial priorities in Operation Anaconda despite the battle taking longer than expected. As such, the military took note of the several issues that extended the battle to apply in subsequent efforts.

Among the problems highlighted in Operation Anaconda was the lack of collaborative efforts. Joint forces must be present in the planning stages to effectively deploy commands. Thus, the military needed to improve its unity of command, clear authoritative lines, and points of responsibility.

Eight Americans died, and 80 were wounded during Operation Anaconda. Of the eight deaths, five were from the U.S. Army, two from the United States Air Force (USAF), and one from the U.S. Navy Sea, Air, and Land (SEAL) Team.

Seven deaths also occurred on March 4, when a Special Forces team attempted to rescue them. The team had brought a helicopter to enter the Takur Ghar ridgeline to reinsert a U.S. Navy SEAL team.

However, the helicopter crashed after the opposition launched three rocket-propelled grenades (RPGs) at the vehicle. This casualty highlighted the necessity of close involvement between ground operations and air support during the planning phase.

Following Operation Anaconda, U.S. officials believed major combat was over; however, we would soon learn otherwise.

President Bush, U.S. Central Command Chief Gen. Tommy Franks, and Afghan President Hamid Karzai *"have concluded that we are at a point where we clearly have moved from major combat activity to a period of stability and stabilization and reconstruction and activities."* —Secretary of Defense Donald Rumsfeld announcing that the major combat in Afghanistan was over.[19] He appeared at this conference with the president of Afghanistan, Hamid Karzai.

By May 1, 2003, 83 Service Members had been killed in support of Operation Enduring Freedom. Looking ahead, there were 2,400 Service Members killed in support of OEF. So, I think it's safe to say that the major combat was far from over.

Over the next few years, the United States, coalition forces, and Afghans would work to reconstruct Afghanistan. From rebuilding infrastructures to implementing a transitional government, Afghanistan was changing.

Through it all, the Taliban and members of al-Qaeda did not relent in their attacks. However, there was no further word on Osama bin Laden. The last known communication from him had been in 2001.

U.S. and coalition forces continued to conduct missions to eradicate terrorists and help to bring stability to a country long devoid of it.

Improvised Explosive Devices (IEDs), mortars, rocket launchers, and all sorts of weapons had become even more commonplace. For those going "outside the wire" (meaning leaving the base), there was a constant threat of violence and a constant fear of death. And the more our technology advanced to aid our missions, the cleverer the enemy got alongside us.

There was still a threat, even for those who did not leave the base. The enemy planned attacks in which they would launch

---

19   "Timeline: U.S. War in Afghanistan," Council on Foreign Relations (Council on Foreign Relations), accessed July 12, 2022, https://www.cfr.org/timeline/us-war-afghanistan.

mortars at the bases. Suicide bombers would detonate at the front gates of our bases. Small arms would be fired at helicopters taking off and landing.

Being in a combat zone is almost a constant adrenaline rush, and it should be. The moment you get comfortable and complacent is the moment you lose.

When you're on a deployment, it almost feels like time stops, or maybe it feels more like you're in some kind of a twilight zone. Your family and friends are all moving on without you while you're stuck living the same day over and over, like in the movie Groundhog Day. You get up, conduct personal hygiene, report to duty, conduct physical fitness somewhere in there, and do personal hygiene again before you pass out in your bunk for the night. If you're lucky, you might get to sleep through the night. The base sirens would interrupt other nights, signaling you to grab your gear and get in a bunker.

Your friends and family back home don't understand this. They don't understand the fear, the adrenaline rush, the twilight zone effect, and it sometimes seems pretty lonely. But you're not alone. No matter what walk of life you've come from, you're not alone. Everyone out there is in a similar situation and understands what it's like. They become your new family during the deployment.

While deployed, there's a good chance you'll see and/or experience things that will haunt you. Some learn to detach themselves from those situations and almost experience them from a bird's eye view, somehow making them seem less real.

Often, soldiers cope by making light of a bad situation. As a result, dark humor runs rampant amongst Service Members. While those on the outside may see that dark humor as cruel, it is just another way that you learn to deal with the atrocities of war. I digress. Let's get back into it.

Enter Operation Red Wings.

To those who have watched the film or read the book, Lone Survivor is the true story of Marcus Lutrell and his fellow soldiers. Marcus Lutrell was a member of the four-person direct action team that pursued Ahmad Shah on June 27, 2005. The pursuit resulted in an ambush that led to the deaths of Luttrell's three other SEAL teammates.

The story was set against the background of what, to many, was one of the most infamous operations in U.S. military history — Operation Red Wings.

Operation Red Wings was a joint military operation. It was executed with one goal in mind — the apprehension or elimination of Ahmad Shah, an insurgent leader from East Afghanistan, not to be confused with Ahmad Shah Massoud, the war hero, or his son, Ahmad Shah.

Planned to take place in five phases, the infamous operation was executed by a direct-action team consisting of four Navy SEALs, of which Luttrell was part.

Operation Red Wings was a joint military operation that was said to have been four years in the making. However, the events that prompted its execution in 2005 began as early as 2001.

2001 was the year when the United States, with the Afghan military, went on the offensive against insurgents. The counter-insurgency operations involving the coalition continued until 2004 when the goal of nation-building became the new priority.

Democratic elections in many parts of the country were pushed. In the interest of legitimacy, the United States was to play no hand in deciding the outcome of elections. However, with insurgents hampering elections in areas outside the nation's capital, like Kunar, a military presence and action were necessary.

Insurgent leader Ahmad shah, who controlled the Eastern Afghanistan mountains, terrorized villages in Kunar and nearby rural parts of Kunar province.

To the Afghan government and the United States military, stopping Ahmad Shah would facilitate at least a portion of the nation-building outcome envisioned by the coalition.

On the night of June 27, 2005, the four-person direct action team was to insert a fast rope into an area between Sawtalo Sar and Gatigal Sar. The drop point was selected for its conduciveness and concealment.

Upon reaching the landing zone (L.Z.), the team of Navy SEALs made their way to an overwatch position. En route to the predetermined location, the team was spotted by locals. As per the operation's rules of engagement, the locals were not attacked or detained.

Unfortunately, the locals gave away the team's position to men led by Ahmad Shah. As a result, between 10:50 pm and 1:00 am, the team was pinned down by insurgents armed with rocket-propelled grenades (RPGs) and AK-47s.

The team fought for hours. Finally, one of the team members called in for support but could only notify the command of being under attack. As a result, the team's location remained unknown to their command. All of their team members died except for Luttrell, who was severely injured after the firefight.

Luckily, a resident took Luttrell and hid him. Luttrell would have died if the locals had not intervened, given the severity of his injuries from the firefight.

The brave men who participated in Operation Red Wings were Navy Lieutenant Michael P. Murphy, Petty Officer 2nd Class Danny Dietz, Petty Officer 2nd Class Matthew G. Axelson and Navy Hospital Corpsman 2nd Class Marcus Luttrell.

Back at the command center, ex-fil plans (plans to conclude the mission and return to base) were being drafted to extract Luttrell and any other survivors. The extraction plan required insertion into Sawtalo Tar. Insertion was to be manned by a quick response team (QRT) consisting of marines and members of SEAL Team 10. The extraction mission was called Operation Red Wings II.

The QRT boarded two Chinook helicopters escorted by Black Hawk helicopters. Escorting the two Chinook helicopters were AH-64 Apache attack choppers to provide air support during transport and insertion.

When the team was about to reach Sawtalo Tar, one of the Chinook helicopters carrying around half of the QRT went down. One of the insurgents fired an RPG at the Chinook, which hit the transmission below the rear rotor assembly. The helicopter immediately plummeted to the ground, killing everyone on board.

With air insertion compromised, the search for Luttrell had to resume other ways. This time, a ground search approach was favored before moving to aerial surveillance. Eventually, search teams could locate the bodies of the 16 men who made up the QRT.

It was not long after that Luttrell was also found hidden by the Afghan, who pulled him a kilometer from Sawtalo Tar.

The service members that were on board the Chinook during Operation Red Wings II were Machinist Mate 2nd Class (SEAL) Eric S. Patton, Senior Chief Information Systems Technician (SEAL) Daniel R. Healy, Quartermaster 2nd Class (SEAL) James Suh, Chief Fire Controlman (SEAL) Jacques J. Fontan, Lt. Cmdr. (SEAL) Erik S. Kristensen, Electronics Technician 1st Class (SEAL) Jeffery A. Lucas, Lt. (SEAL) Michael M. McGreevy Jr., Hospital Corpsman 1st Class (SEAL) Jeffrey S. Taylor, Staff Sgt. Shamus O. Goare, Chief Warrant Officer Corey J. Goodnature, Sgt. Kip A. Jacoby, Sgt. 1st Class Marcus V. Muralles, Maj. Stephen C. Reich, Sgt. 1st Class Michael L. Russell, Chief Warrant Officer Chris J. Scherkenbach, and Master Sgt. James W. Ponder III.

We've covered several major combat operations to this point, but here's something to warm your heart—Operation Sleigh Ride.

It was Christmastime in a war zone, and the troops deployed to Afghanistan were a long way from home. In addition, there was almost no downtime to celebrate the holidays as the mission there was continuous. Between the grueling hours and being under a near-constant threat, the holidays were indeed not what you're used to.

In December of 2005, looking to bring a little joy and magic to those deployed to some of the more remote FOBs in Afghanistan, Operation Sleigh Ride was conducted.

While traditionally, Santa rides a sleigh, Santa flew in on a chinook helicopter with packages from loved ones and special treats from the big man himself for troops deployed to Southeastern Afghanistan.

With stops at Orgun-E, Sharona, Salerno, and Ghazni, Santa delivered goodies, posed for pictures, and spread lots of cheer. To say it was a much-needed morale boost would be an understatement. Photos and videos show troops posing with Santa—and even sitting on his lap—grinning from ear to ear.

MSG John Melson

One day, around my 18th birthday, I came home from high school to my mom telling me someone was there to see me. I walked in, and there was this guy in his khakis—which I would later come to know as his Charlie's. He introduced himself as Sergeant Pearlman, saying he wanted to talk to me about some opportunities in the Marine Corps. I looked at my mom and asked, "Why are you doing this?" To which she responded, "You're about to graduate. You don't have a job; you didn't get signed to play professional hockey. So, just like your uncles who went in the Marine Corps, guess where you're going?" I cursed her up and down. Every day in the Marine Corps was horrible while I was at Bootcamp. Despite that, it was one of the best things my mom ever did for me. It set me in the right direction. That was 1989.

My mother was the catalyst for my joining the military. However, so many Marines in my family had all been very successful in life that I didn't have a leg to stand on to argue with her. Looking back now, that was my introduction to becoming a man. I wanted to be a kid still, but it was time to grow up, and my mom brought me to that crossroads. I served as a truck driver in the Marine Corps. After serving in the Marine Corps for a few years, I got out and took a break for a few years.

When the towers got attacked on 9/11, I was at MassBay community college. I was taking classes to work towards a radiologic science degree to be an x-ray technician. I was on lunch break and had just walked into the cafeteria to grab a sandwich and a drink. I sat down and was watching on the T.V. on the wall, and I saw the one tower smoking. And then I saw the second tower get struck while it was on live T.V. Unfortunately, at the moment, I didn't know that it was *live* T.V. I thought it was some action movie. So, I looked at one of the younger students beside me and was like, hey, is this some Bruce Willis movie or something? And he looked at me like I was crazy. He was like, no, that's life right now in New York City. And I was like, oh, no, this is really bad.

MassBay Community College in Wellesley, Massachusetts, just outside of Boston, started making announcements over the loudspeaker. Everyone was to leave and go home due to the current threat. There were a lot of people rushing out to leave. I just kept thinking this is not good if we're being attacked. I got in my car, and I turned on the radio. The radio started making some breaking news flashes, and it was becoming more and more apparent that we were under attack.

So, I drove a few miles down the road and walked right into a Marine Corps recruiting office because I had been in the Marine Corps years ago, and I told him I wanted to re-enlist. I got out as a lance corporal, and I wanted to go back in. He asked me what made me want to come back in, and I responded, "You're not paying attention to the news. We're being attacked right now. And if someone's going to come and start a fight with us, I know the Marines are going. I want to be a part of it." And so that's where my second journey in the military after a 15-year break began.

The Marine Corps tried to put me in and started going through the process. I went through M.E.P.s but was disqualified because I had been arrested during my 15-year break of service from the Marine Corps. They weren't willing to give me a waiver. So, my ability to go in was crushed. And then I just started watching how the United States started responding to the attacks on September 11th. But I didn't give up; I kept trying to go in. I tried to go into the Army and got the same result: disqualified.

One of the guys I had gotten to know through my part-time job in downtown Boston, he was a recruiter for the National Guard. He approached me and said, "Hey, I think we might be able to do

something for you in the National Guard if you want to get in."
I expressed my concerns to him about wanting to go overseas
since the National Guard typically remains a stateside force. He
responded that the National Guard *was* being sent to fight this
war. This was now in 2003.

Despite being previously disqualified, this recruiter had sent
me to M.E.P.s, where I was able to make it through to the physical
at this point. However, as fate would have it, I was disqualified
medically. During the physical, they found a lump in my neck
and sent me to Boston University Medical Center, where they
did an ultrasound and X-rays on my neck. They determined that
I had a tumor on my carotid artery, stopping the blood flow to
my brain. I had cancer.

So, I left there and went that day to the Veterans Administration hospital and insisted on talking to my primary care doctor
because I had been complaining about this lump—even before
this point. The lump had been growing inwards; it wasn't something that was showing outwards, so he couldn't see it. Once I
was able to sit down with my doctor that day, he did an initial
check with his stethoscope and found that there was no pulse
above where that tumor in my neck was. The tumor stopped the
blood flow to my brain and other points in my body.

The next day I had to go back into the doctor's office for a follow-up, which led to a scope being sent through my thigh, going
up to my artery. Long story short, I was in for surgery in less
than two weeks. Without the surgery, they had given me a five-
year life expectancy. My daughter had just been born that September—September of 2003—and I didn't want to risk her not
having a dad. So, I opted for surgery. They removed eight inches
of my carotid artery where the tumor had been growing and replaced it with the saphenous vein from my leg.

At this point, I figured my chances to return to the military
were done. Who would approve me to go in? However, the Guard
recruiter didn't give up on me. He was determined.

After a few months of speech therapy and learning how to talk
and swallow again, the recruiter asked if I still wanted to join.

My answer was yes. So, we went back through the medical process, but the doctor determined he wasn't an expert in this area, so he wanted to send it up to higher echelons to allow those that *were* experts the chance to decide whether or not I was medically cleared to join. And I left there that day with hope.

For me, if they deemed me fit to serve, it meant I had a better chance at a higher survival rate.

When I got the call from the Army, I worked at my business. I answered the phone thinking it was a customer, but it turned out to be a Colonel regarding my medical waiver to join the military. He said, "Son, you understand we're a country at war right now?" And I responded, "Yes, sir." He said, "You understand the surgery you went through and that you're lucky to have survived that surgery?" To which I replied, "Yes, sir, I understand." The Colonel continued, "You still want to come in knowing that we're at war?" Without hesitation, I answered, "Yes, Sir. That's why I did this." After that, he told me I'd be hearing from my recruiter shortly, saying I'd been cleared for full duty.

I was shocked. I couldn't quite grasp the idea of being fully cleared, so I asked him to clarify—was I cleared to be a cook? Sew buttons? What? With my enlistment packet in front of him, he told me I was fully cleared to go in the infantry, which I had requested.

Not even two minutes after hanging up with the Colonel, my recruiter called, telling me to get down there. So, I drove down and swore into the Massachusetts Army National Guard. After handing me my drill packet and training schedule, they asked me if I wanted to volunteer for overseas deployment, and I said yes, that's why I joined. I wanted to be a part of the fight.

I was in the Massachusetts Army National Guard for about a month before being picked up for deployment. When I went in, I could do maybe three push-ups because of the atrophy from all the nerve damage—that was when I went in; I can do way more than three now, though.

That first deployment took me to Sinai, Egypt. We were in the country for about six and a half months and had several terrorist attacks during our time there. I ended up leaving Egypt on emergency leave because my daughter, my little girl, had a seizure and had gone into a coma. They rushed me home to see her. She came out of it, and she's good now. She's currently about to graduate high school and set off for college.

I'm jumping around in time a bit, but when I look back, time went so fast; one minute, she's this little peanut, and now she's as tall as me and is an athlete.

After my emergency leave to be with my daughter, I went back to deployment in Egypt. I was back for about a month before we left theater.[20]

We arrived back at Fort Dix, New Jersey, and they brought us to the chapel to welcome us all home. The Sergeant Major walked in and announced that there were units in Iraq that weren't currently at 100% manning strength and needed volunteers to join them. So, I raised my hand.

While I was deployed to Egypt, the glass business I had owned had gone out of business. But, as a dad and committed to fighting the war, I had to keep a paycheck coming in. So, yeah, I went back overseas.

I went to Iraq and served with the Mississippi Army National Guard 1/155 BCT. They had already been in theater when I arrived, but I was there with them for about nine months. We finished that deployment, and I got back to Camp Shelby, Mississippi, to out process so I could head back to Massachusetts. As I'm out processing, this Colonel was in processing. We were both at the same desk as a traffic jam. Both of us tried to be polite and allow the other to process first, so we started talking. He was with the National Guard Bureau Headquarters and remarked about how we took a lot of casualties and abuse while in Iraq. It was a challenging deployment, for sure.

And this is how I ended up in Afghanistan.

---

20   Theater is another way to describe the country you're deployed to. For instance, arriving in theater means the same as arriving in the country on a deployment.

In the midst of our conversation, the Colonel asked how I felt about bringing my combat experience with me to join his team leaving for Afghanistan. I was like, "Wow, that's another year of employment for me, and now I get to see Afghanistan." So, I said, "Okay, Sir. I've been fighting in Iraq's urban environment and want to see what those mountains have. Let's see how much we can clean up over there. I'm your guy."

They brought me into another office, talked to another Colonel, and told me to stop out processing and that they would change my orders to deploy to Afghanistan.

I had to stop them at this point. My son was born while I was in Iraq; at this point, I still haven't been able to see him yet. After telling them this, they told me they'd send me home on a four-day pass so that I could see my son. Thinking it would be a couple of months before I'd leave for Afghanistan due to training, those Colonels quickly refuted that thought, saying it would be a mere three weeks until I'd be out there. At the end of the day, I still needed a paycheck and wanted to fight in the war, so I agreed.

During my four-day pass, I got to see my son for the first time and was also able to spend some time with my daughter before returning to Camp Shelby to begin the process of leaving again. While going through the process of shipping out to Afghanistan, I was allowed to attend Air Assault and Airborne school. Not as a part of the deployment but separately. The Colonel asked, "Well, what if I send you when we return from Afghanistan?"

I had reservations; What if I didn't make it back, and then I never would have had the chance to go?

The Sergeant Major with us during this discussion didn't want me to go. Looking back, that Colonel and Sergeant Major had a great relationship. I think the Sergeant Major knew how to push the Colonel. To the Sergeant Major's dismay, the Colonel agreed to let me go to Fort Benning to attend the schools. After attending Air Assault and Airborne schools, I returned to Camp Shelby. They got me on the first smoking bird out of there to Afghanistan. The main body of the team had already departed two weeks prior.

When I deployed to Afghanistan, I had already completed two other deployments, so the idea of going through the process for me was not shocking this time. I was motivated and amped on this deployment, hoping nothing got in the way. I wanted to be a part of this. We would run around Afghanistan, hunting down and fighting the Taliban and the people responsible for attacking the U.S.

For the mission in Afghanistan, I was embedded with the Afghan Army. I was a part of a four-person ETT (embedded training team). After learning what I'd be doing over there, I was stoked. We were in the Day Chopin Valley at FOB Lane in Zabul province. We worked with the ANA and the ODA Special Forces from the 3rd Special Forces Group. For me coming into it as a young Sergeant in the Army—when I say young, I was in my mid-30s, I had only been a Sergeant for a year and a half—I was like, wow, I'm going to be living and training with the Afghan Army fighting the Taliban. To me, this was an incredible opportunity to make a big difference. They would see that Americans aren't so bad; one, because I was out there training and living with them, and two, because we were out there killing bad people who want to do bad things. It was a very busy year.

Our living quarters over there was this wooden hut with a concrete slab floor. The wood was super dry like if a spark got on that wood, it would probably have burnt up quickly. We had these wall-mounted air conditioning units that sometimes wouldn't even work. For a bathroom, we had these tubes that would stick up out of the ground; we'd have to pee in the tubes. There was also a wooden shed that you'd poop in. Under that wooden shed, there was this cut in half 50-gallon drum your poop would go in. We would have to pour diesel in that 50-gallon drum and burn the poop. You'd have to stir it up to get it all to burn. Pretty gross.

There were only four of us and then an entire ODA team. When we had to do anything internally, like classes with the ANA, it was always like, "oh, here we go." So, despite those frustrations, morale wasn't terrible; no one was desperate to go home. I think the morale amongst the guys with us and the ODA was high. But the ODA guys had beards—everyone knows the ODA have beards. When a new Sergeant Major came in, the ODA guys were forced to shave, so their morale went down briefly.

We stayed pretty busy. Anytime we had to go out on a mission, everyone was always pumped and excited to go out. I don't want to say war junkies, but we were guys who would make them (insurgents) regret it if they wanted to start trouble. No one wants to sound scared, right? But in the back of everyone's mind, everyone was just hoping to make it home. So, in my opinion, morale was always good.

I have to say that some of my happiest memories from deployment came from this tour. One time, we were driving in this dry riverbed, and I was up in the turret. I turned for a moment to see how close everyone else was when I felt the truck jerk. I saw the headlight coming up, and I yelled "roll-over" and jumped down inside the turret. The sun had been in the driver's eyes, so he lost sight of the riverbed and kept driving. He stepped on the gas pedal, making the truck tip over and land on its side. On top of the radio mount in our vehicle, we had a couple of bandcliers with preloaded magazines for our M-4s. Probably 10 or 12 of them were preloaded, but they weren't secured in the vehicle; they were just in pouches up there, so you could pass them around to anyone who needed them.

Anthony was in the driver's seat, and I was in the turret, trying to scrunch down as the truck rolled over. Our interpreter was in the backseat, screeching in pain, and I couldn't figure out why. I looked, and it turned out my foot was on his face, pressing him against the window. He was like, "You're on my face!" I was like a spider on a spider web trying to get pushed out of the gunner's hatch from the roll-over.

It seemed like a long pause between when the truck went up and landed on its side. And then my interpreter tries to tell me to get off his face. Then, suddenly, my buddy Kevin, sitting in the front as the truck commander, started yelling. After checking if he was okay, we found out the ammunition sitting on the radio mount slid off and hit him. He ended up breaking a tooth.

So, we all start climbing out of the truck sideways, waving at the other trucks to come to hook us up and pull us out. Kevin didn't even help me tie up the truck. I love this guy. He was pacing back and forth in a way that reminded me of the cartoons when they cussed, but it came out "frickin, frackin." He's just dropping every swear word there is, pacing back and forth with a cigarette in his mouth. I swear he must have smoked a pack while he was pacing. He was so mad that his tooth was broken. It could have been a terrible situation, and someone could have been hurt much worse, but looking back now, it's just a really funny memory, remembering how it all played out.

Another story from that deployment... The Colonel who asked me to go on that deployment needed to meet with the Afghan commander and his staff and wanted me to drive him. He also wanted me to come in and sit with him through the meeting and dinner. Well, we get there, and everyone sits on the blanket, on the floor, and they come in with this big plate of rice and food. There was meat, but it was a leg of lamb, not even cut. The lamb was just all shredded meat sticking up. In Afghan culture, if you refuse to eat, they see it as an insult. I tried my hardest to plead with the Colonel to get out of eating, telling him I'd already eaten before the mission, but it was no use. All I'm thinking about is how I will fill that 50-gallon drum with diesel because of what will be coming out of me after I eat this. I'm watching them use their bare hands to dig into the food, and my stomach is turning.

From there, the rest of the time I was in Afghanistan, I always took the diarrhea medicine before sitting down to eat because it's going to get you—I'd always tell my soldiers that, too. I used to laugh because that Colonel got it bad. He was in and out of the bathroom for like three days. I think that may be why he later submitted me for Ranger school—out of revenge.

When we were near the end of that deployment, the same Colonel had asked me if I would consider attending Ranger school. At that point, I had no interest in attending. I'm in my mid-30s at this point and have already served in the Marine Corps. I just wanted to do my part in the war and felt that I was a bit late in the game for Ranger school. However, the Colonel kept trying to convince me, advising that if I planned to stay in the infantry, it was important for me as a leader to earn my Ranger tab. I put my foot in my mouth when I responded to him, saying that while I was more interested in pursuing work stateside, if the challenge arose, I would accept it.

Lo and behold, the next day, I got an email notification that I was reserved for attending Ranger school in the following months.

So, I went to his room and started banging on the door, saying, "Sir, Sergeant Melson here. I need to talk to you." After telling him about my reservation for Ranger school, he congratulated me, telling me it was fantastic news.

I had looked up the requirements for Ranger school, and one of them was a five-mile run. I'm out here running around with Afghans in the mountains. How am I supposed to pass a five-mile run? With every bit of confidence in me, the Colonel said, "If I didn't think you could figure it out and pass, I wouldn't have had them submit your name."

Every chance I had, I was either running on a treadmill or running laps around the perimeter of the FOB. I did like a million circles to try to work on my run. I hate going into anything half-stepping and failing. So, I was going to put my best effort forward.

When I returned from that tour to Afghanistan, I was supposed to go to Ranger school. However, as a Massachusetts National Guardsman, my leadership in Massachusetts put the brakes on it. They were curious how I got the Ranger school slot and who was supposed to pay for it. So, they pulled my slot at Ranger school. Now, being left without work or a paycheck, I resubmitted my name to volunteer for another deployment.

And I was off, like a week later, to Iraq again.

From 2007-2008, I was with the Maryland National Guard in Iraq. I met some fantastic Americans, great people. The Battalion commander of that unit had a Ranger tab. He liked how hard I was as far as training and making sure guys understood their

S.O.P.s[21], mission planning, and not letting complacency kick in. He appreciated that. One day, he sat down in the chow hall with me and asked what I wanted to do in the Army. I pointed to his Ranger tab. I told him about the opportunity stripped from me in attending Ranger school and said I wanted the chance to go. Now that the opportunity had been taken from me, I wanted to go.

He advised me to work through my channels to secure space but knowing my command likely wouldn't send me, I tried to strike an agreement with him. I suggested he keep me on with this unit for some follow-on orders if I could secure a space in Ranger school. I told him that I'd be willing to train some of his soldiers to take with me. He took the bait.

I reached out to the Colonel who had initially gotten me the spot in Ranger school and said I think someone's willing to support this. I was at the Battalion Commander's office the following day. He took me up on my offer to not only send me to school but to train some of his people to attend school with me. In between missions, we would all get together, and we would do training to work on that five-mile run because I knew that five-mile run was coming.

These soldiers worked hard and got in excellent shape. They were good at mission planning and understanding the importance of your role as a leader.

After all that preparation, we returned from deployment together and went to Ranger school. As I'm lining up for the five-mile run, my biggest hurdle, I hear someone call my name. It was a Lieutenant I was in Afghanistan with two years prior. We ended up graduating from Ranger school together. After graduating from Ranger school, I went back to Massachusetts, where I was slotted to attend Pathfinder school.

I had this group of buddies in Massachusetts with whom we'd all made a pact. Our pact was to wait until we were all back together and volunteer to deploy so we could all go together. Well, when I got back, my buddies had already volunteered and were

---

21   S.OP stands for Standard Operating Procedures.

set to ship out in about a week. They had volunteered without me saying they weren't sure how long I would be at Ranger school. So, I reached out to someone I had deployed with previously who worked at the National Guard Headquarters and asked if they had any info on this deployment to Afghanistan. They said they were still looking for more volunteers to go, asking if I had gotten my Ranger tab. Well, thank goodness I got my Ranger tab because it allowed me to go out on this deployment.

While waiting to ship out on this next deployment, I had the opportunity to attend Pathfinder school at Camp Edwards in Massachusetts. I was there for maybe three days and failed the sling load test. After they processed me, I drove home since I was only about 30-40 minutes from my house.

It was a nice summer night, and knowing that I'd be leaving for Afghanistan again soon, I took my motorcycle out for a ride. Something happened while I was driving down to Marina Bay for the evening. I was driving across the bridge from Boston into Quincey headlights were coming straight at me on the wrong side of the highway. I saw another motorcycle in front of me; it was a head-on collision. A drunk driver had been driving down the wrong side of the highway. As I pulled up, I saw the driver's front tire was smashed off. I checked on her quickly; She was in a daze but was okay.

The first thing I saw when I looked over, though, was the motorcycle in pieces. Next, I saw the guy lying on the side of the road. I got off my bike, and another S.U.V. pulled up; the people in the S.U.V. jumped out to try to help the guy. As I walked up, I could see a big piece of flesh, like in combat. It was a part of his body lying on the road. I looked, and I'm pretty sure it was his calf muscle. At that point, I realized, okay; I've got to switch modes. What am I about to walk up on?

When I walked up, an older couple was on the phone with 911 and had placed a blanket over him, covering him from the waist down. They started talking to the guy lying on the ground. He said his name was Mark, who is actually a great guy. I started talking to Mark as well, asking him where he was coming from, and while he was answering, I looked at the older lady and asked under my breath, "how bad is it?". I didn't want to say it where he could hear it so he wouldn't panic. The lady shook her head and lifted the blanket; his leg was gone.

Now, I'm looking for something I can use as a tourniquet. When I looked down, he had a belt on, so I took his belt off and made a tourniquet on his leg. The emergency services finally showed up and got him out of there.

Mark ended up living. He's a father of five who now has a prosthetic. He's a great family friend now.

Looking back, everything is connected. I was meant to enlist so they could find the cancer. I was meant to deploy because of all the incidents I got to be a part of, to fulfill what I wanted to do and have my kids be proud of me. And I failed out of Pathfinder school to be there for Mark.

I deployed not long after to Afghanistan again. After I'd left for this deployment, the governor and state police had invited my kids to the State House. He gave my kids a medal from the state police for me, but they wanted to present it to my kids.

My mission to Afghanistan this time was the same ETT mission I had done previously in Afghanistan, embedded with the Afghan Army again. As I mentioned earlier, I was in Zabul Province the first time I went to Afghanistan. This time, I was in Herat, which is in Western Afghanistan.

I was there for maybe 24 hours when the Colonel for all RC-West had pulled me into his office to counsel me and set expectations. After looking at my paperwork and seeing that I had served in the Marine Corps, he decided to send me to work with a Marine Special Operations Unit in Farah. This Marine Special Operations unit was embedded with a weapons company from the Afghan Army. Since I had already completed a mission working with a weapons company in the ANA, he thought I would be a great fit for this mission. I would essentially bridge the gap as I'd been in the Marine Corps and previously worked on that particular mission with the ANA before.

So, we were at FOB Rescorla, which held a lot of meaning. Rescorla was one of the men that died in the Twin Towers trying to save people. So, the FOB was named after him. That struck a nerve with me. Here I am trying to make an impact.

The FOB was a small camp. There were only maybe eight of us on the camp, and it was attached to where the Marine Special Operators were. We saw a lot of action out there. It was great and brought a lot of fulfillment, just like all my deployments. You don't do it for the money.

People in my family would always ask why I kept going, saying I could probably make more money working stateside. It's not about the money. It's that sense of fulfillment that gives you purpose. I joined while we were at war to serve in wartime and contribute to what I call the win. I wanted to contribute to the win as long as the United States was still standing and our enemies were dying. To me, that means winning, right? But there is a cost with that. We lose a lot of good young men and women in the process. But, as sad as it is, that comes with our line of work, right?

How I look at it is this: Throughout my time as an NCO 22, I have never wanted to be that guy that loses sleep because of PTSD or survivor's guilt. There are a lot of people that suffer from it. I don't want survivor's guilt, or any type of guilt, because my soldiers didn't make it home or I didn't train them enough. So, when I was in training (before deploying), I'd see other platoons, squads, and companies, with their soldiers getting pizza, playing video games, or goofing off. I just thought, man, we can't get more time back once time has gone by. I wanted to take advantage of every opportunity to train those that are going to serve with me, to give them a better fighting chance, and to understand that my life was in their hands like their life was in my hands. So, if I'm willing to work this hard to keep you alive, I need you to work just as hard to keep me alive. It's a shared, reciprocal relationship.

It's better to sweat now and complain now in training so that being deployed isn't as hard. Right? It's a sweat more in training, bleed less in battle type of mentality. And I've always been that

---

22   Non-Commissioned Officer

way. I've tried to instill that in my soldiers and junior leaders. To me, it's helped a lot—and to their families as well. They come home and struggle less because they understand that more. It helps strengthen and build more inner resiliency because they know that this is what they've got to do.

So, I try to explain to people that I'm not up late at night feeling guilty because of soldiers we've lost in battle because I know there was nothing more that I could have done. I trained them with every ounce of energy I had in my body, shared every bit of experience I've acquired through my previous times being overseas, and to know that sometimes, bad things happen. But when bad things happen, is there a way to avoid them? Well, it couldn't have been avoided with training because I've shown them everything.

I've tried to make sure that point was driven home to my junior leaders by saying, "You're going to be in a bad spot if you're soft on your soldiers. And you lost them because you were being soft. You can't go back in time, bring them back, and train them the right way. Let's not waste this opportunity." That's how I've always been.

Years later, when I got to teach at Ranger school, that was still one of the biggest things people would remember about me. The same mentality. I will instill the same stress and chaos you would experience in the worst of times on the battlefield. I know I jumped ahead a bit here.

Going back to FOB Rescorla. During this deployment, we had a Humvee flip over. I'll tell you, the relationship between the Master Sergeant that was in the flipped over truck and I—I love him to death. During that deployment, though, he was on active duty, and I was in the National Guard, so I think there was some animosity. I believe that I was this young punk Staff Sergeant in his eyes. He was always trying to flex on me, so there was a lot of bantering back and forth.

When the Humvee got stuck on its side, I climbed back in, and he told me to go save myself. He kept telling me to get out while he was stuck inside holding this thermite grenade. He was planning to blow the truck so the enemy wouldn't get it. I'm looking at him, knowing he's a dad; he's got two kids. I can't stand this S.O.B. I told him no, I wasn't going to leave him. They're (the insurgents) going to snatch the thermite grenade and kill us both. So, the truck was up on its side, and I threw it out of the turret. I told him, "I'm not leaving you." He kept trying to push me out, truly believing we weren't going to make it out.

I jump out and wave up another Humvee. I hook up the Humvee, jump back into the driver's seat, and get the wheels unstuck from the mud. We got the truck back up on all four wheels, out of the irrigation canal, and onto the road. I looked over at him, and he was just sitting there in shock. I asked, "Hey, are you okay? Are you good?" That's my thing. I always ask everyone if they're good. Needless to say, despite the shock, he was good. We had stuff to do. So, I jumped up on the .50 cal and brushed off the mud.

I'll never forget that night when we broke contact, and the Marines came out to help us get out of there. He was sitting on the side of the truck, and I was up top cleaning up the brass and re-oiling and lubricating the .50 cal. I looked down, and he was looking up at me, and I said, "What? You're making me feel weird. What are you staring at me for?" He responded, "You came in and saved me today." I told him, "Don't give me any of that malarky. I don't want to hear any of that stuff." He continued to say, "No, man. If I make it home, I'm going to get to see my kid graduate high school and play football because of you."

Alright, now he's starting to piss me off. So, I jumped off the truck and stood before him, and we hugged each other. We've been best buds ever since. Even though we had that love-hate relationship, I would never have turned my back on someone like that.

So, I returned from my deployment, and my buddies who volunteered to go while I was at Ranger school returned about the same time. What's next? Well, they came back from their deployment asking what I thought about going to the Special Forces with them. I was like, yeah, let's go for it. This would be both a good and bad choice for me. Good for trying to take up the challenge, bad for going with some of my best friends. Why? Well, despite knowing the rules and regulations, when my buddy got lost while doing land navigation, I helped him, and we got caught. That was that. For helping him, I was sent home. But he was my best friend, and there was no way I would turn my back on him.

It's now January of 2010, and I was offered a promotion. I was number one on the promotion list, and they had asked if I would volunteer to go back to Afghanistan and train a platoon to go to Kunar. So, I trained up a platoon of about 55 soldiers to prepare for this deployment. Now I'm in Eastern Afghanistan in Kunar Province. This was my third time in Afghanistan.

During this deployment, we would be faced with O.P.23 Nevada, but I'll come back to that. The kids who were with me were so good at their job. I've been fortunate. I'm hard on them in training, but they're so good at their job that they make me look great. When such good quality people and soldiers surround you, they make your job easier. However, I'm getting ahead of myself because our relationship at the beginning was a horrible welcoming relationship. There was work to be done and a lot of bad habits. It was pretty hard to get a bunch of Guard guys to buy into my mentality because I just deploy, deploy, deploy, but I was like, it could be your ass.

Our platoon was short-staffed. We had maybe 30 people at that point. After finding out I had a platoon now, people who had been on previous deployments from other states started volunteering and transferring over to us. So, the next thing you know, I had 13 people in my platoon who had been on previous deployments. One of them was Sergeant Wood, who was at OP Nevada. He was also with me in Farah, Afghanistan.

The Massachusetts Guard had trouble filling the ranks, so I ended up with a cook, mechanic, and two supply clerks—not everyone in my platoon was infantry. When it came time to deploy, though, you would never know the difference because those mechanics, cooks, and supply clerks were just as badass as the regular infantry guys. They were just that well trained and that awesome.

On that deployment, we saw a lot of action. Everywhere I've gone, I've always seen a lot of action. It's like I'm cursed or a magnet or something. It always spirals into something; I've never had a deployment where we just deployed, worked out, and came home. However, this was an extremely fulfilling tour to watch those young soldiers change from when I first got there to after I trained them. Their tactical prowess grew, their confidence and their effectiveness as a team grew, and I was in awe. They didn't necessarily need me anymore, and that's when I felt like I'd accomplished my job. Of course, I worked myself out of a job, but that's what you're supposed to do. Right? In the civilian world, you're homeless and unemployed if you work yourself out of a job. But in the Army or any military branch, you advance when you make people good enough to replace you. So I felt really proud of those guys.

I just continued to provide overhead coverage for them and train them when we had downtime, so they would stay effective and sharp.

During our time working at OP Nevada, we had this horrible Navy commander that was over us. So, there are four squads in a platoon; one squad would do base support, one would be QRF[24], one would be in the training cycle, and the other would be up on OP Nevada for a week. Every so often, I would go up and do a rotation, spending time on the OP to be out there with the guys. We had some weights that you could do a little P.T. with just to pass the time. I remember my uniform was filthy, and I was washing it with water bottles. The guys told me that they found out that the Navy commander would have the TOC monitor the OP with a camera that was up there. He should have been watching the perimeter, not my guys. So, I put some weights on the bar and said we'll find out if he's watching us. I started doing thrusters, like a front squat and then a shoulder press. I had nothing on—remember I was washing my uniform. I did a couple of reps waiting to see if the Navy Commander would radio over to find

---

24   QRF stands for Quick Reaction Force

out what was going on. While there were no radio calls, and we figured they were watching the perimeter as they should, the Afghan soldiers who had been walking around now wanted to be my friend. We had some good times up there. Like every deployment, there are good times and bad times. Those silly things like that get you through the bad days.

However, when there were bad days, there were really bad days. And this is where all that training paid off.

Up on OP Nevada, it's uneven terrain, so some areas are really steep. At this point, I'm no longer on OP Nevada, but I am back at the FOB Sergeant Wood; one of the guys in my squad started getting information that someone was probing the perimeter. With those steep areas and hills, it was hard to see down sometimes. So, when they were penetrating the perimeter, the terrain made it difficult to keep eye on the situation.

Sergeant Wood had called down to me, asking me to switch to the platoon frequency. He advised that he would send out a patrol around the perimeter as there was a lot of radio traffic. Well, a short while later, Sergeant Wood called back down to me, saying they "got a guy." I asked him what he meant by that, and the guy they captured had been putting rocks on the concertina wire to flatten it and got inside the perimeter. Sergeant Wood went on to say the guy had a radio, so they (Sergeant Wood and the troops on OP Nevada) held him. A government agency staying in the main camp sent a helicopter to take the guy with the radio away.

Not much later, the team picked up more chatter on the radio. Come to find out, the guy the government agency had taken away was the local Taliban commander's uncle. The Taliban leader wanted his uncle back and told his fighters to go get him back from the Americans, telling them to fight to the death.

We were tracking all of this back at the FOB, telling Sergeant Wood to stand by and be prepared to react to this. Our higher-ups thought the guys at OP Nevada were "well protected" and that this would turn out to be "nothing." The Taliban doesn't make many big threats, so I had my doubts. It started to play out as if nothing was going to happen, but as soon as it got dark, that's when things started kicking off.

The troops on OP Nevada radioed down to us to let us know they were getting a lot of radio chatter. And soon after, they radioed again to tell us they were now taking fire. You could see the rounds going back and forth from across the valley, all the way at the FOB from OP Nevada. You could see the mortar rounds and the RPG rounds going off. I can only imagine the energy they were all feeling in the heat of it; your adrenaline was pumping. So, I like to think that they were in good spirits up there to want to win.

My soldiers and I were down in the valley watching; we were anxious and concerned about what might be happening. The guys with me were like, "Sergeant Melson, what do we do?" I told them to calm down and to get ready. I told the squad leaders to have everyone stage their stuff, be ready to respond, and get themselves into the right mindset.

As the night went on, things started to intensify on OP Nevada. The Taliban still believed that the uncle was being held there, not realizing he had already been taken away by helicopter. They would attack from one direction and then break contact, so you'd think they were gone. And then they'd start from another direction. They were probing, trying to penetrate the OP. They were going back and forth for a while. We were trying to call the guys on the OP for a SITREP[25], asking about their status and staying hopeful. All the soldiers down in the valley were worrying about their buddies on the OP. Everyone was mentally preparing themselves.

During all of this, I wouldn't let anyone, besides myself and the Lieutenant, go in the TOC. I told the soldiers to stay out and to keep their gear ready. We started selecting who we would send up to respond on QRF and who we would send if we needed to send a second QRF

We called over to FOB Joyce, another FOB nearby, and they were unaware that Americans were on OP Nevada. I couldn't be-

---

25   SITREP stands for Situation Report.

lieve it. How could you not know? My guys and I have been up there providing support this whole time to them, *to FOB Joyce*! They thought it was just Afghans on the OP and believed they would fight it out. We told them we have guys up there who may need assistance.

Next thing you know, Sergeant Wood calls me on the radio, asking me to switch to the platoon frequency again. So, I ran out of the TOC to our platoon room and changed frequencies. He said, "We've been going for a while, man. I don't have much ammo left. Is anybody coming? Are you guys sending help?" I didn't want him to know what I was dealing with, with this Navy commander, so I told him, "Look, man, we've been in this before. We've been through this. Those kids are counting on you." I don't know how I would get there at this point, but he said to me, "John, don't hate me, but I don't know if we're going to make it. We're getting really low on ammo. I just need to know if you're coming." I said, "I'm coming for you. I'm not leaving you up there. Control your shots. Pick your shots; stop spraying and praying. Conserve your ammo." I told Brian (Sergeant Wood—we're on a first-name basis at this point), "Tell those kids I'm coming. You tell them to fight with rocks if they have to." He said he'd do what he needed to, but I just repeated, "Control your rates of fire, Brian, conserve your ammo. Give me some time."

I fought back and forth with this Navy commander, telling him if they ran out of ammo, this wouldn't be good. The Navy commander commented, *in front of everyone*, "They get paid to die."

I walked out of the TOC right then and there, slamming the door as I left, ripping it off the hinges. There were some ODA folks in our camp and the civil affairs commander, a Major. They pulled me aside and said nothing would get better in the TOC if I'm in there really hot (angry) like this. I looked over and saw two blue dots on the Blue Force Tracker—there were two Blackhawks in our area. Desperate to help these guys, I tapped on their icon and sent a message to them that we had Troops in Contact, asking if they could land and pick up an element to insert us as close as they could to OP Nevada. They advised that they had a mission to support and could not assist. What am I going to do? I can't leave them up there.

A couple of the ODA guys pulled me outside. They told me they would call down to their folks at Jalalabad to see if they could get any aircraft pushed our way. Then, they told me to get back to the TOC because they thought they were able to get something done.

Miraculously, the lights on the landing strip went out at Nangarhar in Jalalabad. So, the Blackhawks had to reroute and come back. I don't know for sure, but I think the ODA guys had pulled some strings to make those lights go out. The ODA guys were appalled that we weren't getting the support we were looking for. The Blackhawk pilots from Nangarhar asked if we could provide them fuel since they were low, and we had a refill station. They said if we could give them fuel, they would insert us. While it was still left to the commander's decision, the Major had made some ground with the Navy commander, convincing him that my guys were capable. They had been looking down on us because we were National Guard. He was concerned that if he sent us up there, the helicopter might get shot down with all the guys and make the situation worse. So, he was thinking more risk-averse than the other direction. That Major got us a big win. The Navy commander conceded that he would let us go up there when there was a break in contact.

I grabbed a bunch of supplies, bagged up a whole bunch of ammo and water—I knew they would need water—and put them in body bags. We had like three or four body bags filled up with supplies. I took about 12 guys with me.

I told the Lieutenant, "Sir, I'll go up there. I'll assess the situation, and I need you on the ground here to keep control of this."

The Navy commander finally gave us the green light to go. The Blackhawks came in, and we filled them up. I don't think there was a single one of my soldiers who weren't out there helping us load up. Everyone wanted to win; They wanted a check in the win column.

We'd only been in the country about three weeks at this point. So, everyone was like, wow, we're being tested right now.

As soon as there was a break in contact, the pilots inserted us near the OP. The only place to land the Blackhawks ended up putting us closer to the Taliban because that was the flattest ground. So, one had to fly in, drop us off and then take off, and then the other Blackhawk had to come in right behind it. They both couldn't land at the same time.

As we got off the bird, we could see some tracer fire, not as concentrated as sporadic shots. I started yelling to my guys; this is where you're going, that's where you're going. We had to push out security for the LZ for the other bird to land. I was scared. And I could see it in their eyes too. Everybody was nervous. I just hope I didn't exude any of that nervousness because I wanted to be in a position of confidence for them to look at me and think, "All right, he's going to lead me to the win. He's going to tell me what I need to do."

When we offloaded the Blackhawks, if I felt someone wasn't getting off quickly enough, I was throwing them, saying, "Let's go. Get off the bird." We were almost on top of the Taliban where we landed, so I was out there yelling at them to pull security. When I say they weren't getting off quick enough, it wasn't because they were hesitant. They were going for it, and they wanted it. These were their buddies on the O.P. and were ready to kick ass.

We got down in the prone position, everyone's pulling positions, and there were more sporadic shots. As we lay in our positions, I saw the second bird about to land on top of us. I pulled the Private next to me, and we started running, trying to get beyond the size of the Blackhawk. As the bird comes down, I pull him to the ground, hoping the blades wouldn't hit us. After the Blackhawk picked up, we did accountability with our night vision goggles.

As we tried to come off the L.Z., there was only one opening in the triple-strand concertina wire. Private Woods was there pulling security for us as we all came running. I tapped him on the shoulder after ensuring everyone was off the L.Z., thinking he would peel off and run up the trail with us. We still had about 100 meters to run to be inside the OP. We got up inside the OP, dropped off all the ammo, and everyone was like, "You came!"

I get Sergeant Wood to get a headcount of his people and start doing a headcount of everyone I came with. Oh my God, we were missing someone. I told Brian all of my QRF people were accounted for and asked if he was sure he had everyone. He said no, someone was missing. Gunfire starts going off, my guys start manning the machine gun, and I'm like, "Who the fuck are we missing?" How are we missing someone?

And then someone points to the LZ we just came from. It's Private Woods. He starts running toward the Taliban, and I yell, "Ceasefire!" I start yelling for Woods, asking "Where the fuck are you going?" He responded that he was looking for me. So, I tell the OP to start laying down cover for Woods, and he starts running back. As we were holding off the Taliban, Private Woods came running back inside the OP. I was so mad. He's out of breath, and I grabbed him, slammed him down on the ammo can, and told him not to move.

The Taliban broke contact, so we got a little bit of a break. I grabbed Brian (Sergeant Wood) and told him he needs to keep better accountability of his guys. This is how we lose people. I was so worked up. I turned to Private Woods and asked what he was doing out there. He told me he didn't see me run past and thought the Taliban got me. You've got to be kidding me. This kid is amazing. I turned around and was like, "All you mother fuckers were going to let the Taliban capture me, and the only one who was going to come after me was Woods." Everyone started laughing. Private Woods is a good kid.

After this tour to Afghanistan, I took time to pursue an opportunity to contract for a little while, but that didn't pan out as the company ended up in a situation with the government. After about 70-something days back from Afghanistan as a contractor, I was offered an opportunity to teach at the Warrior Training Center in Fort Benning—which meant returning to Ranger school to get certified as an instructor. I worked this job for about two and a half years, and in April of 2015, I was picked up for another deployment back to Afghanistan with the Special Operation Command (SOC).

This time, I was at Camp Integrity in Afghanistan, just north of the Kabul airport. There were maybe 100-150 people; it was a two-star command. It consisted of the Special Operations for all countries' command elements.

We had about a squad and a half of 10th Mountain infantry soldiers that provided base support and security. In the J-sections, there was J-1 for admin, J-2 for intel, J-3 for special operations and training, and that's what department they put me in, the J-3 shop. That's where many of the E-8 Green Berets were working out, so I was able to be around these types of people again, just like I was with the 3rd Group.

In August 2015, Camp Integrity was attacked. An a&p vehicle drove up to the gate and detonated. It was a VBIED[26]. Three to four suicide bombers ensued, coming into the base. We lost a buddy of mine, Andrew McKenna. My buddy George had been injured. The Taliban had made it inside the camp, and we had to try to defend and hold the camp, fighting from inside the compound. George made it but, unfortunately, was paralyzed from the chest down. He's doing great now, participating in the Special Olympics. It's great to see him bounce back from a horrible situation. The McKenna family they're great people. It was terrible to see Drew lose his life over there and the other soldiers I've been with.

That was one of my worst memories over there. This was the headquarters for all the NATO countries with special operations footprint in Afghanistan. Here's how it all went down. It was about 2200 (10:00 p.m.) when I was in my room, Skyping with my daughter, and she was making fun of me for eating Cocoa Krispies. She said, "Dad, that's a kid cereal." As I talked to her, I was getting ready for bed when an explosion went off. My window blew, shards of glass covered me, and my daughter was like, "Dad, what's going on?" And then I heard gunshots. I said to her,

---

26   VBIED stands for Vehicle-borne Improvised Explosive Device.

"Dad's got to go." And I shut my computer. I was only wearing my silkies, the really short shorts, and I put my sneakers, helmet, and plate carrier on. I grabbed my weapon, and I went outside. My room was probably 100-150 feet from the ECP when the a&p truck drove up and detonated. A VBIED had blown the ECP open; two steel doors were gone.

Approximately three to four suicide bombers had come in, and each time one came in, they would detonate, and the next would come a little further in and detonate. When I came out, other people were coming out of the buildings, looking at me. I told them we needed to move, to get to the gate because we'd been breached. So, we start running to the gate, and I see my buddy, Andrew McKenna. He was the camp's First Sergeant. He ran up to the ECP, and we all started taking positions. We see the suicide bombers come in and start shooting at them. And then Drew went down. He was across from us; we didn't know at the time that there were Taliban fighters who had already penetrated the camp. As we were all looking to face down the ECP they were already behind us. They hit Drew with a shot to the head. Another buddy, Ray, went to get Drew and started dragging him, but started taking rounds. Guys were shooting in the wrong direction because we didn't know where the rounds were coming from. I ran over and grabbed Drew with Ray. We ran him into the administrative building and established a casualty collection point. And he was gone. Drew was gone.

We turned around and ran back up. Ray, George, and I, and a couple of others, stacked behind a jersey wall. We told the others our plan to clear the ECP, telling the 10th mountain kids to get an M-ATV and get ready to pull into the ECP once we clear it, so they could block the ECP because it was wide open.

As we came out, we dropped a couple of Taliban while clearing out the ECP to establish a foothold. They pull up the M-ATV, and now, it's blocking the ECP entrance. We look to assess the damage to the tower at the gate; the windows were blown out, and there's no one manning it. So, George told me to get a machine gunner up there, and I was like, "You got it."

Ray and I go to where the tower is, and we clear the little rooms in the buildings. I go up to take the tower, and Ray says he's going back to George. They link up at the tower's base. As they began making their way back inside Camp Integrity, there was a Taliban fighter hiding between the up-armored vehicles. As they walked by, the Taliban fighter shot George, severing his spine. It went on his side and came out on the other side. As George went down, I could hear Ray yelling. This was happening like 50 feet away from me, but I couldn't leave the tower since there was no one else to man it. So, they get George to the casualty collection point and start reviving him while we try to clear out the rest of the camp.

We spent the next few hours trying to figure out where the Taliban fighters were, to isolate them and kill them. Then, finally, three or four hours later, the Ranger Regiment flew in, helped us establish security, and confirmed that we had control of the base again.

Losing Drew was pretty bad. As the First Sergeant for the whole camp, Drew had a big impact on us all. He didn't care what rank you were; if you were messed up, he'd tell you so. He just had that way about him, and many people appreciated that. Drew and George were competitors at the gym. We were all big into fitness, so there was a lot of banter. They were all Green Berets, and I was just a National Guardsman who was Ranger and Sapper qualified. I was fortunate to be around these kinds of people.

Drew was from Rhode Island; I'm from Massachusetts, so I have family in Rhode Island, too. I remember when they were going to transport his body back to the states. They wanted to ensure his medal was complete, signed, and going with him. They wanted his parents to be presented with a Silver Star. So, they were like, who can we get to jump on a helicopter to headquarters and hand carry this, get this signed, and then get it to Bagram? I told them to give it to me. I said, "Let me put my uniform on, and I'll fly with his stuff and get it all taken care of." They were all waiting for me when I got there. I brought it to the General, who signed it and then flew to Bagram with it. That medal is going to go to his mom and dad. I wish I could have done more, but again,

I don't think I struggle with survivor's guilt because he was one of the best-trained guys I've known.

What we did right during the war in Afghanistan was showing commitment and affording the people of Afghanistan the opportunity to excel.

For me, I don't think we could have done anything better. I think the failure was more culturally driven. We can't change the culture. If they're not willing to stand up to the Taliban and fight for themselves, how much more can you learn from us?

I hope the United States' goal in Afghanistan was the same as mine; to win and beat them so they don't return to hurt anybody here. Did we accomplish that goal? I think, yes, while we were there, we kept them busy.

When I think about us leaving Afghanistan, my thoughts are that we had to do it at some point. Right? I think we could have done it, preferably, differently than how we actually did it, though. Having spent two years embedded with the Afghan Army there, you didn't have to spend a lot of time with them to know they probably weren't going to stand up and fight for themselves for very long. They were okay with us taking the brunt of the fight. It was like we were always forcing them to be out in the front and do the right thing.

I've listened to a lot of people that have served and those that haven't—the armchair quarterbacks—say it was disrespectful, the way we pulled out, for all of those who sacrificed so much. But I don't look at it that way. All of those soldiers I know that have lost limbs, or had issues, or given their life over there, it wasn't for nothing. I think that it's really insulting for fellow veterans to say it was all for nothing. No, it wasn't. It was for me. It was for you. We did what we did for those people to our left and right. We weren't the ones in charge of policy. We're not the ones who decide whether we're at war or not, but what we are there for is each other because we're there to be that frontline. We were there to be those links in the chain to keep Americans safe. My viewpoint is probably not shared by many.

I don't believe that just because President Biden said we're going to pull out and this is how we're going to do it detracted from any of our hard work. It was still committed work; there was still sacrifice. If we lost the war, that doesn't mean it's a waste. We still believed in our cause. To me, that's still an honorable thing. I think saying that *because* we pulled out our sacrifices meant nothing. That's more disrespectful than anything in that aspect.

As we talk about the cost of war, I've got to say this. It goes both ways for me. I would say I had to give up some things to benefit in other areas. I gave up opportunities to be an in-person, contributing father to my children to be a part of something bigger than just myself. So, I try to rationalize, "Was it worth the fact that my kids…I can't make that time up to them. I can't put it on my charge card and get more time back to go be more in their life." But I try to rationalize it, that it was all worth it because of all the lives that I've impacted in the bigger picture that I hope will one day be a payoff to my kids. I signed over my college benefits to my kids. My daughter will be the first to use it this fall. So, I'm excited, but that doesn't make up for it. When your daughter starts dating, she gets her heart broken and wants her dad. So, I struggle with the cost of it.

Is it selfish to say I'm not going to deploy so I can be home with my kids? I struggle with this a lot, especially with my peers. I'd looked on negatively for deploying so much—by my peers. I try to rationalize this by saying, "Well, I'm going because one of you isn't going. So, are your kids and your life worth more than mine? I'm not complaining about it. I'll go, raise my hand again, and know what I must give up in return. But I struggle with the regret part of it because I see other people with relationships with their kids, and I envy that. I try and get through that struggle by rationalizing it was for a good reason. And I just struggle with that. That is my biggest struggle, my darkest place. It makes me feel like I chose the Army over my kids.

I hope that through all of this, it can be something my kids can look on favorably one day. I do it so we can have a better life and help all these other people.

When people see me, they think I look hard and almost unapproachable. Actually, I'm extremely passionate and very caring. I have a love for life. Only people close to me know that I'm a big softy. If you saw me in front of a formation, in training, or on a combat deployment, you'd think, "no way." I look more like I'd eat your soul than that big softy I just mentioned, but it's not true. I would do everything in my power to preserve your soul. And I hope my kids can be proud of me.

We're all a team, and you're only as fast as your slowest guy. So, when my kids come into adulthood with that mentality, when they enter the employment world, the civilian sector, or perhaps join the military, they will understand that everything is a team effort.

PART III

THE BLOODY RESURGENCE

Chapter 6

THE GROWTH OF ANTI-AMERICAN SENTIMENT

Aptly named, 2006 was the year of the Taliban's "bloody re-surgence." As a result, 2006 through 2007 saw a dramatic uptick in the use of Improvised Explosive Devices (IEDs) and suicide bombers. Suicide attacks increased by 42 percent between 2006 and 2007, with July 2007 hitting a peak of 18 suicide bombings in one month.[27] [28]

It's essential to bear in mind that during the Soviet invasion, there wasn't a single known suicide bombing. It was not a tactic that insurgents in Afghanistan had deployed—until al-Qaeda, sanctioned by the Taliban, had used suicide bombers in the assassination of Ahmad Shah Massoud on September 9, 2001.

In 2006, the Taliban started regaining control over some regions of Afghanistan. But why were they making this resurgence? Well, as you'll see in the coming pages, the anti-American sentiment amongst the people of Afghanistan was rapidly growing.

In May of 2006, a U.S. convoy was the cause of a traffic accident that resulted in five Afghans' death and sparked large-scale

---

27   *The National Academy of Sciences defines an IED as "an explosive device that is placed or fabricated in an improvised manner."*

28   "Read 'Disrupting Improvised Explosive Device Terror Campaigns: Basic Research Opportunities: A Workshop Report' at Nap.edu," SUMMARY | Disrupting Improvised Explosive Device Terror Campaigns: Basic Research Opportunities: A Workshop Report |The National Academies Press, accessed July 12, 2022, https // nap.nationalacademies.org/read/12437/chapter/2.

anti-American riots throughout Kabul, the capital of Afghanistan. After the crash occurred, Afghans began throwing rocks at the humvees and soldiers of the convoy. Some witnesses to the events had said U.S. troops started firing on Afghans after they began throwing rocks. However, it would later come out that they had only fired warning shots into the air and had not fired on any civilians. Based on our Rules of Engagement (ROE) and Escalation of Force (EOF)29, it is likely this step was taken in response to the immediate threat.

The crowd would grow more unruly as rumors spread that the U.S. had rammed cars, causing the accident intentionally.

These riots went on for about six hours, with rioters rampaging through the streets of Kabul, looting and setting fire to random offices, buildings, cars, and even police posts. These riots would result in 14 people dying and countless others being wounded. During these riots, the Afghan police and the Afghan Army fired into the crowd, trying to get them to disperse.

As anti-American sentiment was growing, Afghans were becoming increasingly frustrated and angry. The people of Afghanistan were frustrated with the lack of progress in the reconstruction efforts. They were tired of watching civilians being killed by U.S. and coalition bombings. They were angry over allegations that Afghan prisoners were being abused at U.S. detention centers. And who could blame them? We were there to bring them peace and help them reconstruct their nation, yet we were the root cause of at least some of their hardships.

---

29   *Escalation of force is when troops would identify hostile intent or a hostile act and then begin implementing a series of actions: Shout (verbal warnings), Show (that you are armed by displaying your weapon), Shove (physically push the individual to restrain or detain), Shoot (fire warning shots), Shoot (to kill). If shouting works—or any along the escalation of force—the next step would not be necessary or taken. If shouting doesn't work, the troop would proceed to show their weapon in order to control the situation. If that doesn't work either, the troop would then move on to shove, in which they would physically engage the individual in an effort to detain or retrain the threat. If shove is not an option or fails to control the situation, troops would then fire warning shots. Warning shots were intended to warn and not to harm any individuals. Should the warning shots fail to contain the situation and the threat has continued to increase, troops would then shoot to kill.*

Here are a few more incidents in which our actions caused the anti-American sentiment to grow.

The U.S. conducted an airstrike in early 2006 in which a bomb was dropped over Kandahar, killing at least 35 civilians. Of note, various news outlets report varied numbers of casualties. On May 23, 2006, then-Afghan president Hamid Karzai ordered this incident to be investigated.[30]

A few weeks before that, in a separate incident, a U.S. airstrike had killed seven civilians in Kunar Province during an airstrike against insurgents.

As tensions and anti-American sentiment grew, the Taliban played this to their advantage. They used this as part of their propaganda and recruiting efforts—and it worked.

The Taliban's bloody resurgence would continue its path of death and destruction, but in its wake, it would also invoke a response from the U.S. and coalition forces. We would not stand by idly and watch.

These couple of airstrikes, however, wouldn't be the only things we had going against us. The collateral damage was mounting, and so too was the Taliban's bloody resurgence fueled in part by the growing anti-American sentiment.

"I would hope that by 2008 we will have made considerable progress with a _more stable political architecture in place,_ and with a strong interface between NATO and the civilian agencies and effective, trusted Afghan security forces gradually taking control."—NATO Secretary-General Jaap de Hoop Scheffer[31]

There will be collateral damage in all wars, including collateral killings/death. I don't say this to justify what happened or even say it's okay, but rather to bring some perspective to the table.

But when do we say enough is enough?

---

30   Carlotta Gall, "Karzai Orders Investigation of U.S. Attack," The New York Times (The New York Times, May 24, 2006), https://www.nytimes.com/2006/05/24/world/asia/karzai-orders-investigation-of-us-attack.html.

31   "Timeline: U.S. War in Afghanistan," Council on Foreign Relations (Council on Foreign Relations), accessed July 12, 2022, https://www.cfr.org/timeline/us-war-afghanistan.

When we think about the cost of war, we think about money, time, and casualties as the primary factors. But when we look at losses, are we looking at our casualties? For example, the U.S. and coalition force casualties? Or are we also taking into account those that died in a "collateral killing"? These Afghan civilians had simply been at the wrong place at the wrong time.

Up to this point, there had been a number of collateral killings; civilians had been killed while the U.S. and coalition forces had been conducting airstrikes against insurgents. The people of Afghanistan were getting sick of it, to say the least. They were sad and angry.

And these collateral killings provided the Taliban with more propaganda to boost their recruitment and fundraising efforts.

On July 6, 2008, an airstrike was carried out in Nuristan Province, Afghanistan, against a group of insurgents when one of the missiles fired went off course. The missile killed 47 civilians, including 39 women and children attending a wedding. The bride was amongst those who had been killed in the airstrike. What should have been a day of celebration turned into a day of mourning?

A few weeks later, on July 20, another U.S. airstrike killed nine Afghan National Police (ANP) officers in Farah Province.

Just a month after that, the U.S. carried out an operation against a Taliban commander, Mullah Sidiq, in Azizabad, which is located in Shindad District, Herat Province, Afghanistan. The Taliban commander had fled from where the operation began to a local village called Azizabad. Reportedly, U.S. Special Forces had called in air support to conduct an airstrike against the Taliban commander in the village.

The airstrike, intending to kill the Taliban commander, had killed between 33 to 90 civilians. Many organizations have investigated this incident, including the U.S., the U.N., the Afghan government, UNAMA, and more. The U.N. had reported the numbers on the higher end of that range, with the U.S. reporting it towards the lower end of that range. In addition to the civilians killed, several homes had been demolished due to the airstrike, displacing many Afghan families.

An Afghan human rights organization that visited the village to investigate believed there were 76 civilians killed, including 50 children.

The U.S. believed that the reports of higher numbers of casualties were a result of propaganda by insurgents.

The truth likely lies somewhere in between all of this.

Regardless of whether it was 33 or 90, the villagers of Azizabad were angry. The people of Afghanistan were angry.

ANA soldiers arrived at the village the next day to provide food and other supplies to the residents but were met with protests and anger. The villagers threw stones at the ANA soldiers to show their discontent with what happened. And in response, the ANA soldiers made the situation worse by firing into the air, which wounded several more civilians.

The Taliban would use this airstrike against the U.S. and coalition forces in their propaganda to fundraise, generally draw support, and recruit new members.

Villagers believed that their village (and homes) were targeted by a rival villager who had provided false information as a "tip" to the whereabouts of Mullah Sidiq to U.S. and coalition forces targeting Sidiq.

"We must avoid the trap of winning tactical victories, but suffering strategic defeats, by causing civilian casualties or excessive damage and thus alienating the people."—Gen Stanley McChrystal32

These were not the only instances of collateral killings. They were not the first and certainly would not be the last.

The high number of civilian casualties was of great concern for then President of Afghanistan Hamid Karzai, straining the relationship with the U.S. In 2019, Karzai was interviewed and

---

32   "The Strategic Benefits of Minimizing Civilian Harm in Counterterrorism Strikes," Human Rights First, accessed July 12, 2022, https://www.humanrightsfirst. org/resource/strategic-benefits-minimizing-civilian-harm-counterterrorism-strikes.

described an argument he had with U.S. officials: "I told them so many times, 'If you want to fight terrorism and bad people, I won't stop you, but please leave the Afghan people alone.'"33

With corruption shrouding his political career, one must wonder if those words had been spoken in 2007 as he said they were. However, whether they were or weren't spoken remains a moot point, as that sentiment was (and is) shared by the people of Afghanistan.

According to the Costs of War34 undertaken by Brown University, there were approximately 241,000 killed in Afghanistan and Pakistan since 2001. About 71,000 of those had been civilians whose only mistake was being in the wrong place at the wrong time.

When we think about wars, we think of war-torn nations, devastation, etc. However, something that runs rampant through every war throughout history is a form of propaganda.

For years following the First World War, the term propaganda has caught a bad rep. But unfortunately, its Orwellian image has not done it any favors, especially in light of the recent overtaking of Afghanistan by the Taliban.

Throughout this last section, I mentioned the word propaganda a number of times, but what is propaganda? Let's talk about what it is and how the Taliban (and other insurgents) use it to bolster their ranks.

Propaganda refers to a collection of methods intended to instill a perspective in people. This perspective is often in the form of a political, religious, or ethical ideology. The main goal of propaganda is to make people believe in a cause.

---

33   Pamela Constable, "Former Afghan Leader Hamid Karzai Grew Estranged from His American Allies during 10 Years in Power. Here's What He Says about the Afghanistan Papers," The Washington Post (WP Company, December 18, 2019), https://www.washingtonpost.com/world/former-afghan-leader-hamid-karzai-grew-estranged-from-his-american-allies-during-10-years-in-power-heres-what-he-says-about-the-afghanistan-papers/2019/12/18/ef4ccb32-20dc-11ea-b034-de7d-c2b5199b_story.html.
34   "Listen," The Costs of War, accessed July 12, 2022, https://watson.brown.edu/costsofwar/.

The interesting thing about propaganda is that it not only converts people to new ideologies. It also confirms and consolidates existing ones.

The Taliban invokes Islam as the foundation of its propaganda, citing passages from the Quran to justify its war. In addition, the Taliban quickly highlights how foreign forces from the United States have led to Afghanistan's deteriorating state. Collateral killings and damages have been a significant source of propaganda for the Taliban.

By presenting evidence across various media platforms, the Taliban can draw support at the village level. It is also from those villages where the Taliban recruits many soldiers.

However, propaganda isn't the Taliban's only way of recruiting new members; they also use fear to coerce villagers into joining their cause.

Fear and religion seem to be the cornerstones of the Taliban's propaganda. The group has used the two to fuel anti-American sentiment at the level of villages. Here are several examples of how the Taliban has achieved this: (1) The invoking of the Quran to brand Americans as infidels or non-believers who deserve death, (2) Montages featuring American and other foreign troops as invaders of Afghanistan, and (3) Videos depicting executions of Americans and other foreign nationals, to name a few.

While all this was happening, U.S. and coalition forces were still fighting the fight against terrorism.

The collateral killings and collateral damage were mounting, but there was also good occurring across Afghanistan simultaneously. We weren't just over there killing innocent civilians—indeed, those collateral killings had not intentionally targeted civilians. Throughout 2008 (and the entire war), U.S. and coalition forces continued to provide peace and security to the people of Afghanistan by keeping the insurgents at bay.

When the U.S. invaded in 2001, the Taliban had control of Afghanistan. The Taliban attempted to seize control of certain areas throughout the 20 years we were there (notably in 2006 during the "bloody resurgence"). Still, thanks to U.S. and coalition forces being willing to risk their lives continually, Afghanistan could overcome those threats and remain in the control of the people and their newly elected government.

The year 2008 was hailed as the most violent year since the U.S. invaded in 2001. In addition, one year brought an uptick in the number of Taliban attacks. It also increased the number of service members killed over there.

We were what stood between the Taliban and the people of Afghanistan. But, unfortunately, at this point, we were both unwanted and necessary, murderers and guardians—the yin and the yang.

The year 2012 would not start on the right foot for the U.S.—and it wouldn't get any better.

In January of 2012, a video surfaced of four U.S. Marines laughing and joking while urinating on three corpses, believed to be the bodies of insurgents. The video spread like wildfire across the world and across Afghanistan.

President Hamid Karzai condemned the acts, calling them "inhumane," and called for an investigation into what had occurred. U.S. officials and NATO commanders condemned the actions of the four Marines. They tried to work quickly to mitigate the fallout that was sure to come.

The U.S. and Taliban were in the process of brokering a peace deal when this video surfaced. However, the Taliban assured the U.S. that it would not impact negotiations.

Despite the ongoing peace negotiations, the Taliban had conducted several suicide bombings killing at least 20, most of those civilians.

"Everyone is now desperately trying to find U.S. soldiers to take revenge for the desecration of the bodies," said Babar, an insurgent quoted in a Reuters article.[35]

---

35   "Marine Tape Reaction Sets Taliban Fighters against Commanders," Reuters (Thomson Reuters, January 20, 2012), https://www.reuters.com/article/uk-afghanistan-pakistan-taliban/marine-tape-reaction-sets-taliban-fighters-against-commanders-idUKTRE80J0CZ20120120.

In that same article, Mullah Abdullah was quoted as saying, "From now on, hate against the foreign troops will grow in the hearts of every Muslim, especially in Afghanistan."

Tensions were rising, and with the benefit of hindsight knowledge, we know it wasn't about to get better anytime soon.

As I mentioned earlier in the book, Afghans are very devout in their faith. The Quran holds immense value to both Afghans and Muslims everywhere. Therefore, the Quran is a sacred text to Muslims, and the desecration of the Quran is considered a crime punishable by death.

On February 22, 2012, U.S. forces on Bagram Airfield (BAF) disposed of a number of Qurans by burning them. Afghan forces reported what had occurred, sparking violent protests that had resulted in 41 deaths, including 4 Americans, and at least 270 others being wounded.

You see, there was a detention center at BAF with several Taliban prisoners. Those Taliban prisoners had been writing messages to each other in the Qurans. So, the Qurans containing extremist inscriptions needed to be disposed of. However, what was sent to the incinerator was not only the Qurans. There were 1,652 damaged books, including Islamic texts and 48 Qurans, that were destroyed and/or had been used to communicate amongst prisoners that had been burned.

Afghan garbage collectors working on BAF had noticed some charred books amongst the trash and had found the burned Qurans. So, they hastily notified the Afghan forces' commander of their findings.

Protests broke out across Afghanistan. The anti-American sentiment was widespread, and at least some of the protestors were reportedly chanting "death to America, death to Obama, death to Karzai." The Muslims of Afghanistan was hurt and very angry.

Of course, President Obama and ISAF Commander John R. Allen issued public apologies to the people of Afghanistan and Muslims of the world. Still, those apologies did little to appease those demonstrating. On the contrary, the violence would only worsen as they began attacking French, Norwegian, and American bases throughout Afghanistan.

As a result of the riots, four Americans were killed. Two had been killed by individuals wearing Afghan National Security Force (ANSF) uniforms. The other two Americans were reportedly high-ranking military officials that had been working in the Afghan Interior Ministry in Kabul as advisors. The Taliban, not long after the protests, had claimed responsibility for the deaths of the four Americans killed. However, even with the death of the four U.S. personnel, the riots and protests were not at an end.

Protestors had tried to burn down the U.N. building, a car bomb had been detonated at the entrance to the Jalalabad airport, and other coalition bases were attacked. BAF, in particular, had been besieged with riots and attacks. Bombs, stones, and petrol were launched into the base.

It goes without saying that the Taliban and other groups had used this to incite anti-American sentiment and had essentially "poured oil on the fire for their own purposes." The desecration of the Qurans was internationally condemned and is an event that Afghans would not forget.

Less than a month after the Quran burning and the subsequent protests, the anti-American sentiment would yet grow even higher when a U.S. soldier walked off the base and committed a horrible crime.

On March 11, 2012, U.S. Army Staff Sergeant (SSG) Robert Bales walked off Camp Belamby, where he was stationed in Kandahar, Afghanistan, and murdered civilians in two different villages. Bales left the base under cover of night, walked to the village with his weapon, and then opened fire, killing a total of 16 civilians—four men, three women, and nine children. He had also wounded and/or shot at an additional six civilians—a man, a woman, and four children.

After shooting and killing some of the victims, Bales then set fire to their bodies. Under Islamic Law, setting fire to the bodies equated to desecrating the dead, adding further insult to an already horrific situation.

Bales' actions were deliberate and of his own volition. There was no operation in the area when this took place. Shortly after the killings, Bales turned himself into ISAF, saying, "I did it."

"I don't want any compensation. I don't want money; I don't want a trip to Mecca; I don't want a house. I want nothing. But what I absolutely want is the punishment of the Americans. This is my demand, my demand, my demand, and my demand." –a villager whose brother had been killed by SSG Robert Bales.[36]

More than 300 locals had gathered near Camp Belamby to protest what Bales had done; some had even brought with them burned blankets. Hundreds of students had gathered in Jalalabad to protest, chanting "Death to America, death to Obama." They were burning effigies of President Obama along with a Christian cross.

It was events like this that the Taliban and other terrorist organizations benefited from. They used this to fuel their recruitment and fundraising efforts. They used this in their propaganda.

Haji Muhammad Wazir, an Afghan citizen, had lost all immediate family members except his four-year-old son to Bales' massacre. In an interview (in 2021, after the U.S. left Afghanistan), he was interviewed by The Guardian to which he confessed to helping the Taliban after Bales killed his wife, eight children, and two other relatives, "I could not go and fight, because I was the only person left from my family to look after my son, but I was supporting them financially and in other ways."[37]

In the same article that featured the interview with Haji Muhammad Wazir, the Panjwai District Taliban commander remarked, "Although some people were supporting us before, after this incident, everyone joined or helped us in some way."

---

36   Mirwais Harooni and Laura Myers, "Karzai Slams Us over Afghan Massacre, Soldier Identified," Reuters (Thomson Reuters, March 17, 2012), https://www.reuters.com/article/afghanistan/karzai-slams-us-over-afghan-massacre-soldier-identified-idINDEE82E0JY20120317.
37   "How Mass Killings by US Forces after 9/11 Boosted Support for the Taliban," The Guardian (Guardian News and Media, September 10, 2021), https://www.theguardian.com/us-news/2021/sep/10/how-mass-killings-by-us-forces-after-911-boosted-support-for-the-taliban.

To compensate the families of those Bales had killed, the U.S. paid $10,000 for each person killed. Despite Afghans calling for Bales to be tried before an Afghan court in Afghanistan, he was sent back to Fort Leavenworth in the United States. "This [was] an assassination, an intentional killing of innocent civilians and cannot be forgiven."—Hamid Karzai38

As tensions weren't already strained, this event put even more pressure on a fragile relationship between the U.S. and Afghan governments. Following these murders, Karzai demanded that NATO leave Afghan villages and withdraw to significant bases within the country. Further, Karzai demanded that U.S. and coalition forces refrain from carrying out any more night raids—which were already highly controversial.

Just from the last portion of the text alone, you can see why Karzai was pushing for the U.S. and coalition forces to cease night raids and to withdraw at least partially. However, we do need to back up a little bit here as well. One major source of controversy between the U.S. and Afghan governments was the Parwan detention facility. And you'll see why momentarily.

The Parwan detention facility was a jail on Bagram Airfield (BAF). With rumors of torture and even deaths occurring at the hands of Americans, the Parwan detention facility was a constant source of tension between the U.S. and Afghan governments.

Let's get some context going here.

Under the Geneva Conventions, it is necessary to have a "competent tribunal" to classify prisoners of war. However, the Bush administration had gotten around these tribunals by not calling them prisoners of war but instead called them "unlawful enemy combatants." The Bush administration had even taken this farther by initially denying them access to the U.S. legal system, claiming they (the unlawful enemy combatants) could not access it.

However, in 2004 the U.S. Supreme Court ruled in the case of Rasul v. Bush that the detainees did have access to the U.S. legal

38   "Briefing," Time (Time Inc., March 26, 2012), https://content.time.com/time/subscriber/article/0,33009,2109142,00.html.

system and that the executive branch (i.e., the president) lacked the authority under our constitution to suspend detainees' writs of habeas corpus. During this case, the Supreme Court also established Combatant Status Review Tribunals, which would verify that the individuals being detained had, in fact, been rightfully detained and classified correctly.

Now, here's where it gets sticky—perhaps stickier is a better word here; the U.S. took that and applied it to prisoners being detained at Guantanamo Bay, NOT the Parwan detention facility.

Prisoners at the Parwan detention facility did not have access to lawyers or the U.S. legal system, and no tribunal convened for any of them to determine their prisoner of war status.

In 2009, President Obama announced that his administration would continue the policy in which detainees in Afghanistan could not challenge their detention. A few months after this, a District Court judge would rule that, in fact, detainees in Afghanistan should be able to submit a writ of *habeas corpus*. However, the Obama administration appealed this, and the ruling was overturned. *"There is a reason we have never allowed enemy prisoners detained overseas in an active war zone to sue in federal court for their release. It simply makes no sense and would be the ultimate act of turning the war into a crime."—Senator Lindsey Graham*[39]

So, the prisoners held at Parwan detention center had absolutely no rights, and rightly so as they were not merely prisoners—they were enemy combatants and prisoners of war.

Also, in 2009, Major General Douglas Stone, a general in the Marine Corps Reserves who had been sent to Afghanistan by General David Petraeus, reported that more than half of the 600 prisoners being held at the Parwan Detention facility did not belong there and they had posed no threat. He said many in the detention facility had been "swept up during raids" and had no ties to the insurgency. His concern was that by wrongfully detaining

---

39   James Vicini, "U.S. Court Rejects Appeal by Afghanistan Prisoners," Reuters (Thomson Reuters, May 21, 2010), https://www.reuters.com/article/us-usa-security-bagram/u-s-court-rejects-appeal-by-afghanistan-prisoners-idINTRE-64K4EI20100521.

and holding those that were innocent, we would be driving them to radicalism and, ultimately, to support the insurgency.

What prison isn't rife with allegations of those in power torturing and abusing prisoners?? Just like every other prison everywhere, the Parwan detention facility had no shortage of accusations—some of them justified, others mere rumors... or were they?

In March of 2003, the media began reporting on the deaths of two prisoners at this very detention center—one on December 4, the other on December 10, and both in 2002. There were ultimately 28 U.S. service members under investigation and facing charges ranging from involuntary manslaughter, maiming, and mistreatment to dereliction of duty and conspiracy.

As a constant source of tension between our two governments, a Memorandum of Understanding was signed in 2012 that the Parwan Detention facility would be turned over to the Afghan government. Control over the prison was handed over to the Afghans in September of 2012 in an official ceremony; however, as the U.S. began transferring detainees back to the Afghan government, some issues arose with the U.S. refusing to transfer at least several hundred of them.

Afghan President Hamid Karzai said, *"Now, the Bagram prison is converted to one of Afghanistan's regular prisons where the innocents will be freed, and the rest of the prisoners will be sentenced according to the laws of Afghanistan."*[40]

On November 18, 2012, Karzai accused the U.S. of violating the handover agreement as they still refused to turn over all detainees. The U.S. was concerned that if they had transferred those couple of hundred prisoners over to the Afghan government that they would be released almost immediately.

In January 2013, President Obama met with Karzai and agreed to hand over complete control of the prisoners and the prisons. The formal handover occurred in March of 2013 and was made

---

40   "Bagram Prison Handed over to Afghan Forces despite US Concerns over Future of Inmates," CBS News (CBS Interactive), accessed July 12, 2022, https://www.cbsnews.com/news/bagram-prison-handed-over-to-afghan-forces-despite-us-concerns-over-future-of-inmates/.

public. The U.S. maintained control over six prisoners, but there were no issues with this between our two governments as those six prisoners were not citizens of Afghanistan.

The turning over of the Parwan detention facility did not include the "black jail."

As most of the allegations of abuse and torture seemed to center around the Parwan detention facility on BAF, the "black jail" is not as well known. In fact, for many, many years, it was a government secret. Early reports of the black jail began to come about when prisoners had contacted the International Committee of the Red Cross (ICRC). Around August of 2009, it had been common practice for the U.S. to inform the Red Cross within 14 days when a new prisoner had been detained.

Prisoners referred to it as Tor Jail which roughly translates to the "black jail." The black jail was located in an old, abandoned brick factory in Kabul.

Some of the reports that the ICRC had received included prisoners being made to stay in cold prison cells where lights were on all day and all night and that U.S. military personnel were depriving them of sleep there. Vice Admiral Robert Harward denied the allegations that any prison outside the Parwan detention facility existed.

CIA "black sites" were a network of secret detention centers run by the CIA and had been authorized under the Bush administration in September of 2001 in a classified Presidential directive. Though the existence of these "black sites" weren't acknowledged by the Bush administration until five years later, in 2006. President Bush would not reveal the location of the sites but did go on record to say that the interrogation methods were "tough and they were safe, and lawful, and necessary."41

President Obama ordered the closure of all CIA black sites in 2009; however, that order did not include the black jail in Afghanistan. What he did put in place, though, was an order that

---

41   "President Bush's Speech on Terrorism," The New York Times (The New York Times, September 6, 2006), https://www.nytimes.com/2006/09/06/washington/06bush_transcript.html.

the prisoners were not to spend more than two weeks at the black jail before having to be moved on.

Some reports named the black jail the "salt pit," a.k.a. "cobalt," and the allegations of abuse are enormous, from forcing prisoners to live in the nude as a form of humiliation to loud music blaring non-stop. Reportedly, the walls and windows were all painted pitch black, and lights would be kept on in cells 24/7 to ensure that the prisoners could not determine whether it was night or day. In addition, some reports detail that the prisoners were barred from practicing their religion. Other prisoners said they were kept in total darkness—which isn't hard to believe with the walls and windows having been painted all black. A number even claim to have been deprived of food and water, while some say that they contained visible dirt and grime when they were served food and water.

In 2005, two of the detainees at the black jail died. An investigation conducted by the Department of Defense concluded that it was murder.

Much of the information known today was released in 2014 through the Senate Intelligence Committee Report.

The Bureau of Prisons had visited the Salt Pit (a.k.a. the black jail) after the CIA had brought them in to ensure that the conditions weren't so harsh that it would render any intelligence gathered unreliable.

The Senate Intelligence Committee report noted one interrogator saying that the detainees *"literally looked like (dogs) that had been kenneled."*[42] Another official had reportedly remarked on the facility being the closest thing he had seen to a dungeon after he visited the black jail.

Despite this, the Bureau of Prisons deemed the facility "not inhumane," so interrogations, torture, and abuse continued.

---

42   Ken Silverstein, "The Charmed Life of a CIA Torturer: How Fate Diverged for Matthew Zirbel, Aka CIA Officer 1, and Gul Rahman," The Intercept (The Intercept, December 15, 2014), https://theintercept.com/2014/12/15/charmed-life-cia-torturer/.

Chapter 7

COALITION SUCCESS

While the U.S. and coalition allies had come under fire for collateral killings and inhumane practices, we also achieved quite a bit of good. Let's cover some of the coalition's successes.

The Battle of Panjwai took place in July 2006 in two phases, ending after three months. A NATO-led group of Afghanistan and Canadian soldiers comprised most of the forces but was also teamed up with the Dutch, British, and Americans, the soldiers, to confront the Taliban. The coalition was victorious and had defeated over 3,000 Taliban soldiers, according to NATO estimations.

A month before the battle of Panjwai, there were many confrontations between Canadian forces and the Taliban. It resulted in the first female combat arms casualty from Canada. After this first round of fighting, Task Force Orion deployed to the district to engage.

The battles took place over several weeks, with 37 recorded firefights. The soldiers took on several Taliban groups with around 30 to 40 soldiers each. It was a running fight, and the Canadian forces seized control of Panjwai while other soldiers moved to Northern Kandahar. Following their control over the area, the soldiers began undertaking several operations.

Also known as Operation Zahara, Mountain Thrust was the first large-scale battle. More than 11,000 soldiers from Canada,

Afghanistan, the U.S., and the U.K. joined together to quell the insurgency in the area. Despite having an advantage, the Taliban was well-coordinated, making this operation a significant challenge.

One of the factors that turned the tide for the coalition was heavy air support. The aerial bombing led to the death of thousands of insurgents and the capture of nearly 400. But, even then, NATO lost around 150 soldiers, and some Afghan policemen in the area became hostages.

While the operation hoped to quell the insurgency, it did not succeed. On the contrary, the attacks were relentless and increased in intensity. Attacks happened in Panjwai and the surrounding regions. There were even cases of suicide bombings that killed civilians.

Three commanders of the Taliban died, and NATO uncovered plans to attack Kandahar city. The Taliban then attacked the Panjwai District Center, which the coalition defended.

Operation Medusa had many Canadian forces. Over 2,000 soldiers from the coalition participated. The goal was to establish a government in the Kandahar Province centered in Panjwai. NATO believed that the Taliban were hiding in numerous farming villages southwest. Soon enough, the Taliban was once more trying to take control of the area.

The first fights occurred south, where many Taliban died fighting back, leading to a few casualties in coalition forces. However, the resistance was strong, and the Taliban placed many traps to stop NATO from advancing. Soldiers redirected people away from the city as fights escalated in Panjwai.

Artillery and airstrikes continued with the Canadian forces providing support for ground operations. They killed over 40 Taliban fighters in each battle.

Battles continued for two weeks, though the superior tactics of NATO led to victory. Over 30 soldiers died in confrontations and bombings. Despite losing many, the Taliban remained in Kandahar, refusing to surrender. Operation Medusa is the largest in scale among land operations organized by NATO.

Because of the continued resistance of the Taliban, Operation Mountain Fury was a follow-up. The goal of the operation was to clear Taliban forces from eastern Afghanistan. It was also so that reconstruction projects could begin once more in retaken areas. There were 7,000 soldiers involved in the fighting, most from Afghanistan. Soldiers from Italy and Estonia also joined in support.

The Taliban resorted to guerilla tactics to try and stop the soldier's foothold. The use of improvised explosive devices (IEDs) became commonplace. Canada had a separate force that began taking control of former Taliban villages and towns. They brought their tanks and artillery to clear out pockets of resistance.

The U.S. soldiers also began clearing eastern provinces and establishing remote outposts. However, there were many attacks in their footholds. The British Royal Marines then attacked Garmsir but soon retreated because of strong resistance. Finally, NATO ordered an airstrike in Helmand, which killed the top commander of the Taliban, Mullah Dadullah.

Reconstruction efforts began after Operation Medusa in hopes of rekindling the economy. Attacks on some of the construction workers and engineers occurred, including traps. However, civilian casualties were light as Canadian and Afghanistan troops focused on moving people away.

Some civilians were victims in the crossfire, but most operations successfully targeted Taliban forces. With clear boundaries of control, the fighting lessened for the rest of the year.

Like many other Taliban members, Mullah Dadullah had been a part of the mujahideen during the fight against the Soviets. While fighting against the Soviets, he lost his leg. However, his fighting days would not be behind him after that.

As a close aide to Mullah Omar, the founder of the Taliban, he quickly rose through the ranks. From successful recruitment efforts to massacres of ethnic Hazaras and Shi'as, Dadullah was greatly feared.

In 2001, following the battle of Mazar-i-Sharif, Dadullah was said to have 8,000 fighters and was heading there to reclaim the territory. As a result, the U.S. reportedly airlifted 1,000 troops into the city to defend it from Dadullah.

His death was a major setback for the Taliban when he was killed in 2007.

As time progresses and changes, so does the U.S. government and its policies.

The year 2009 marked the beginning of a new era. From the terror attacks on September 11 until January of 2009, America was led by President Bush. However, January of 2009 would see a new President sworn into the White House—President Barack Obama.

About a month after his swearing-in as the 44th president of the United States, President Obama recommitted the U.S. to the war in Afghanistan. In recommitting the U.S. to this war, President Obama had also vowed to send an additional 17,000 troops to Afghanistan. For reference, there were approximately 37,000 troops in Afghanistan as of January 2009. Obama intended the additional troops to help stem the flow of foreign fighters coming into Afghanistan from Pakistan and curb the Taliban's resurgence.

Anyone who has served in the military knows that with new leadership comes changes, and a new President means precisely the same thing—change.

In March of 2009, President Obama announced a new Afghanistan war strategy. The new plan would ultimately be to "disrupt, dismantle, and defeat al-Qaeda and its safe havens in Pakistan, and to prevent their return to Pakistan or Afghanistan."43 In addition to the new strategy, Obama had committed to sending an additional 4,000 troops to Afghanistan to train the ANA and ANP. So no longer would we just be there on our mission, but we'd be

---

43   "Disrupt, Dismantle, and Defeat...", https://www.outlookindia.com/, February 3, 2022, https://www.outlookindia.com/website/story/disrupt-dismantle-and-defeat/240056/.

essentially training Afghanistan's forces, preparing them for our eventual departure.

Adjusting to the change in administration and its policy, in April of 2009, several senior military officials called on NATO to step up. After a two-day summit, NATO agreed to send 5,000 troops to Afghanistan to help train ANA and ANP forces.

It seemed as if each new calendar month would bring a recent significant change from the Obama administration to the war in Afghanistan; he replaced the top military commander in Afghanistan with General Stanley McChrystal, a former Special Forces commander. He believed General McChrystal's experience in the Special Forces could help counter insurgency tactics.

Come December of 2009, Obama committed to sending an additional 30,000 troops to Afghanistan, bringing the number of soldiers over there to a record high. However, Obama also proposed to begin withdrawing troops within the next 18 months.

With the Taliban advancing in Afghanistan, Obama would end his first year as president with approximately 71,000 troops in Afghanistan—a sharp contrast from the 34,000 at the start of the year.

One significant operation to occur during this time was Operation Khanjar.

Operation Khanjar, also known as Operation Strike of the Sword, was a US Marine Operation carried out to eliminate Taliban influence in Helmand province, Afghanistan, and to remove the terrorist organization from power in Taliban-dominant areas. This was the most significant Marine operation since Operation Phantom Fury in Iraq and the largest airlift operation since the Vietnam War.

Following President Obama's announcement confirming the troop surge in Afghanistan, 21,000 US marines poured into Afghanistan. Operation Khanjar began approximately 13 days after Operation Panther's Claw, led by the British Army. U.S. forces joined with the Afghan forces to eradicate terrorism ahead of the 2009 Afghan Presidential elections.

According to U.S. and Afghan forces, they were worried about the fairness of the elections because the Taliban influenced a majority of southern Afghanistan. As a result, troops were deployed between a 75-mile-long area between Lashkar Gah and the Helmand River Valley.

With the help of NATO planes, approximately 11,000 US Marines were taken to launch an attack against the extremist group. The operation began on July 2, 2009, and it took the terrorist organization by surprise. Moreover, this marked the beginning of U.S. troops entering territories they had never attempted to enter before.

While the Marines and other forces had tried to take control of Helmand Province, other troops began moving into remote areas to keep the organization distracted. The troops focused on taking control as quickly as possible without causing civilian casualties.

The battle began when the troops entered Lashkar Gah, and the enemy opened fire. At the same time, troops also started operations on the outskirts of the town of Sorkh-Duz. The next day, June 3, Marines entered the Garmsir district, where they fought for eight hours. Finally, the terrorists at Lashkar Gah's tree lines and those in the Garmsir district were defeated by airstrikes-killing approximately 30-50 of the Taliban members.

The Marines also began operations in the village of Nawa-I-Barakzayi, where instead of fighting head-on, the terrorist organization retreated to observe the Marines from a distance. After seizing a compound, U.S. forces discovered significant amounts of explosives, rifles, opium, poppy seeds, and hashish.

Simultaneously, troops were posted outside of Khanashin, the capital of the Khan Neshin district, on July 2. This was the first time that the forces had entered the heart of the Southern Helmand River Valley. There was no resistance by the groups here; instead, both parties indulged in negotiations.

Meanwhile, on August 12, 2009, the Taliban-dominant town of Dahaneh was also under attack by the forces. This town had been under insurgent control for approximately four years. The battle in Dahaneh began in Naw Zad, a town located north of Dahaneh. The U.S. soldiers seized and established a base at one of the enemy compounds- after arresting a total of five men.

On the first day of the war in Dahaneh, the troops captured about 66 pounds of opium. They killed about ten enemy soldiers after launching an airstrike. However, the first day was unsuccessful. The U.S. and Afghan forces suspected the enemy knew their attack plans and prepared accordingly.

By the second day, the U.S. soldiers and Afghan forces seized control of almost half of the town of Dahaneh. After that, however, the war continued as the Taliban forces attacked U.S. and coalition forces. Nevertheless, the soldiers saw success when they decided to launch a pre-dawn surprise attack on the third day.

After blowing up two towers and attacking the insurgents on the southern edge of the town, the U.S. and Afghan forces found roadside bomb materials and marijuana plants. By the end of August 14, the fourth day of the battle in Dahaneh, the Marines were able to take control of the whole town.

The U.S.' motives were not only fueled by the agenda to remove the Taliban organization from power but also gain public trust. For this reason, many service members rested in empty houses instead of setting a base camp during the night. However, it is debatable whether or not they successfully eliminated the terrorist organization's influence.

Some reports suggested that rather than removing the Taliban from power, U.S. and Afghan forces forced them to migrate to the northern Helmand and eastern Farah provinces, protected by the German and Italian troops, respectively. While the U.S. military could remove the enemies from the control of the targeted areas, they were unsuccessful in disbanding the terrorist organization. The problem of the extremist group was now a burden for the Italian and German forces, who were questioning the U.S. Marines' ability to take charge.

Many Taliban soldiers fled to Pakistan during Operation Khanjar (a.k.a. Operation Strike of the Sword). However, the Taliban was still recruiting soldiers from Baluchistan, Pakistan. During the operation, two Afghan Forces soldiers, 14 U.S. marines, and an interpreter were killed. The battle began on July 2, 2009, and ended on August 20, 2009. A minimum of approximately 49-62 terrorists were killed during this time.

Just as every four years, a new president is elected in the United States, so too must the president of Afghanistan.

The presidential elections in Afghanistan were held on August 20, 2009. The candidates were Hamid Karzai, who would be running for reelection since he was the standing president of Afghanistan at the time and Abdullah Abdullah. Remember that name from the Northern Alliance?

When called on earlier in 2009 by U.S. military officials, NATO had pledged additional troops to train the ANA and ANP but had also committed to assisting in ensuring the security of the Afghan presidential elections. Despite that, this election was shrouded in fraud claims and a lack of security- though the results would stand. Hamid Karzai won his second term as president.

Even with the additional 30k troops and having a few months to prepare for the elections, when the time came, 12 of the 34 provinces were deemed to be "high risk." As a result, they were left with limited to no government or military presence.

Due to security concerns, the locations of polling stations were only announced the day prior and of those 7,000 polling stations, only about 6,200 actually opened on election day.

Out of fear of low voter turnout, the Afghan government also imposed a media blackout, barring media outlets from showing violence during certain hours to not scare voters.

The threat was real. Attacks were becoming more frequent. The Taliban was threatening those that had planned to vote. And sure enough, on election day, there were 73 reports of violence throughout 15 different provinces, with at least 26 killed during the election day violence.

But that number was an initial estimate by the Afghan government. ISAF would later find that there had been over 400 attacks on election day, with a reported 31 civilians being killed as a result. This was declared one of the country's most violent days spanning the past 15 years.

Even after election day, the attacks and violence would continue throughout Afghanistan, with bombings taking center stage and causing many fatalities to the U.S., coalition forces, and the people of Afghanistan.

All in all, August 2009 was the bloodiest month since the U.S. invaded in 2001—which should tell you just how bad it was.

I'm sure this played a part in Obama's decision to send in more troops come December of 2009, as the election would continue to cause attacks and violence throughout Afghanistan well past August.

On September 12, 2009, a day when the first full primary results should have been announced to the public, a chain of attacks rocked Afghanistan. At least 66 were killed in these attacks.

From suicide bombers and car bombers to gunning people down in the streets, the Taliban caused more bloodshed and violence than Afghanistan had seen in a long time.

In the years leading up to the Kandahar offensive of 2010 and 2011, one operation was arguably the most heavily publicized during the Afghanistan campaign. Operation Moshtarak was more than a pacification campaign. It was an operation meant to break new ground in the war in Afghanistan.

Intended to be led by the Afghans and spearheaded by the Marines, Operation Moshtarak was a joint effort conducted by the U.S., coalition, and Afghan forces. The name "Moshtarak" means togetherness. The operation's goal was two-fold — to retake the city of Marjah and cut off the Taliban's funding. Operation Moshtarak was unique in its goals and approach to collaborative urban warfare.

When it comes to funding, the Taliban absolutely had their ways of securing money.

The city of Marjah in Helmand Province has been a stronghold of Taliban forces for many years. It had provided the Taliban with a strategic advantage over American and Afghan troops.

More than the city's urban environment, the city of Marjah was also the source of the Taliban's funding. Marjah was close to some of the largest poppy fields in Afghanistan. As we discussed earlier in the book, the Taliban capitalized on this as they produced and sold opium to fund their operations. I say this in the past tense as we're specifically talking about Operation Moshtarak, but the Taliban is still growing and selling opium to support their organization.

Marjah was one of the Taliban's last few strongholds before its seizure by NATO in 2013. Although the conflict was declared at an end just three years prior, 2013 was when fighting in the city stopped utterly.

Gaining control of Marjah was challenging due to the urban environment. This is why Operation Moshtarak consisted of 12 days of ground fighting. Taking part in the skirmish was a mix of US, British, Estonian, Afghan, and Canadian forces, to name a few.

The battle of Marjah marked the introduction of a new approach to the war in Afghanistan. At the end of the operation, NATO forces "installed" Afghan administrators in the city to return control to the country's government.

This approach was a far cry from various operations in the campaign that sought to control and hold locations for as long as possible.

Forty-five U.S. Service Members were killed in Operation Moshtarak, along with 13 British troops and 13 ANA members.

The operation resulted in 120 insurgents being killed and another 56 insurgents being captured.

The countries that were members of NATO rang in 2010 with talks of Afghanistan. But, recognizing that we could not stay in Afghanistan forever, the discussions began to form more of "when" we would leave.

In November of 2010, members of NATO agreed and declared that they would hand over the security of Afghanistan to the government of Afghanistan by the end of 2014.

The U.S., coalition forces, and NATO had sent additional troops to Afghanistan starting in 2009 with the specific goal of training Afghan forces, and this plan made total sense. That gave us three years to prepare the Afghan troops to maintain their own country's peace and security.

And with that, the year 2011 would see our mission become increasingly more focused on training Afghan forces and less on eradicating terrorists—though that was still one of our goals and was still an ongoing operation.

That is until we found Osama bin Laden.

It's the moment we've all been waiting since September 11, 2001—Operation Neptune Spear, whose mission was to kill or capture Osama bin Laden.

For the first time in years, the U.S. had actionable intelligence as to the whereabouts of Osama bin Laden. And better than that, we had a green light.

Osama bin Laden was elusive. Intelligence agencies had been unable to locate bin Laden for years, but that all changed in August of 2010 when they traced him to a compound in Abbottabad, Pakistan.

Now, you may be wondering, if we found him in August of 2010, why did we wait until May of 2011? There's a lot that goes into planning an operation like this. From preparing troops—in this case, SEAL Team 6—to get the green light legally to go in with a mission of kill/capture a high-profile target like bin Laden. And even one tiny intel leak on this operation or hint that we'd found him could have compromised the entire thing.

After just returning from their mission to Afghanistan, the Red Squadron of SEAL Team 6 was the perfect element to conduct the raid on bin Laden's compound as they were supposed to be on leave. For those unfamiliar with military terms, being "on leave" means they were taking paid time off to rest and recuperate with their families and friends. No one would suspect them to be preparing or even conducting the raid since they weren't meant to be working, giving the operation another layer of secrecy.

The date is now May 1, 2011. Twenty-three specially trained U.S. Navy SEALs, an interpreter, and a combat dog boarded a helicopter around 10:30 pm.

Have you ever seen any of the Army recruiting videos where they're rappelling from a helicopter and conducting specialized operations? "Down With the Sickness" by Disturbed plays in the background of the video I'm thinking of. When I picture how this particular operation went down, that recruiting video always comes to mind. Still, to this day, when that song comes on, all I can think of is that video.

At 10:30 pm, two Army helicopters loaded with SEALs ready to get revenge for the United States took off from Jalalabad, Afghanistan, with a destination of Osama bin Laden's compound in Abbottabad, Pakistan.

On bin Laden's compound, there was a guest house where his couriers resided with their families. The SEALs prepared to blow down the locked door of that guesthouse when shots were fired from the enemy through that door. A woman carrying a child emerged through the door as the SEALs returned fire. Behind that woman lay a dead male combatant. His name was Abu Ahmad al-Kuwaiti, and he was bin Laden's top courier.

The women on the compound, the wives, had been trying to martyr themselves to save their husbands. They knew exactly what their husbands had done and why the SEALs were there.

After clearing the first and second floors of the main house, they found Osama bin Laden on the third floor in a bedroom with his weapon nearby.

I keep saying revenge for America, but the truth is this wasn't only a revenge killing. Osama bin Laden was the mastermind behind many global attacks that killed too many people. And left alive, he would have continued his plan for global jihad, which would have likely ended in quite a few more deaths and widespread destruction—because that's what he's already done many times over.

The SEALs had collected various items from his compound, including documents, electronics, and other materials.

Bin Laden's body was brought back, where his DNA and biometrics confirmed that he was, in fact, Osama bin Laden.

His body was then transported to the USS Carl Vinson, where, after receiving religious funeral rites, he was buried at sea so that his gravesite would not become a shrine to his followers.

In a speech following Osama bin Laden's killing, President Obama announced his death.

"Justice has been done."—*President Barack Obama*[44]

With this news, Americans across the nation took to the streets to celebrate. Crowds had come together in New York, in front of the White House, and many other cities. It was over. The 10-year (ish) hunt for Osama bin Laden was finally at an end.

With this MAJOR victory behind us, President Obama addressed the nation a few months later, on June 22, 2011, announcing a troop drawdown in Afghanistan.

He planned to remove 10,000 troops from Afghanistan by the end of 2011 and an additional 33,000 by the end of 2012.

In President Obama's address to the nation, he said:

"When I announced this surge at West Point, we set clear objectives: to refocus on al-Qaeda, to reverse the Taliban's momentum, and train Afghan security forces to defend their own country. I also made it clear that our commitment would not be open-ended and that we would begin to draw down our forces this July.

Tonight, I can tell you that we are fulfilling that commitment. Thanks to our extraordinary men and women in uniform, our civilian personnel, and our many coalition partners, we are meeting our goals. As a result, starting next month, we will be able to remove 10,000 of our troops from Afghanistan by the end of this year, and we will bring home a total of 33,000 troops by next summer, fully recovering the surge I announced at West Point. After this initial reduction, our troops will continue com-

44   "Osama Bin Laden Dead," National Archives and Records Administration (National Archives and Records Administration), accessed July 12, 2022, https:// obamawhitehouse.archives.gov/blog/2011/05/02/osama-bin-laden-dead.

ing home at a steady pace as Afghan security forces move into the lead. Our mission will change from combat to support. By 2014, this process of transition will be complete, and the Afghan people will be responsible for their own security.

We're starting this drawdown from a position of strength.

In all that we do, we must remember that what sets America apart is not solely our power —*it is the principles upon which our union was founded. We're a nation that brings our enemies to justice while adhering to the rule of law and respecting the rights of all our citizens. We protect our own freedom and prosperity by extending it to others. We stand not for empire, but for self-determination. That is why we have a stake in the democratic aspirations that are now washing across the Arab world. We will support those revolutions with fidelity to our ideals, with the power of our example, and with an unwavering belief that all human beings deserve to live with freedom and dignity.*

Above all, we are a nation whose strength abroad has been anchored in opportunity for our citizens here at home. Over the last decade, we have spent a trillion dollars on war, at a time of rising debt and hard economic times. Now, we must invest in America's greatest resource –- our people. We must unleash innovation that creates new jobs and industries, while living within our means. We must rebuild our infrastructure and find new and clean sources of energy. And most of all, after a decade of passionate debate, we must recapture the common purpose that we shared at the beginning of this time of war. For our nation draws strength from our differences, and when our union is strong no hill is too steep, no horizon is beyond our reach.

America, it is time to focus on nation-building here at home."45

If only those words would ring true, but alas, it would still be another ten years before we leave Afghanistan.

David Stanton

---

45   "Remarks by the President on The Way Forward in Afghanistan," National Archives and Records Administration (National Archives and Records Administration), accessed July 12, 2022, https://obamawhitehouse.archives.gov/the-press-office/2011/06/22/remarks-president-way-forward-Afghanistan.

At the age of 21, I joined the Army. Why? Well, my reason for joining was simple; I was looking to get out of Kokomo, Indiana. So, that's what I did. I joined the Army, served on active duty, and ended up working in intelligence.

When 9/11 happened, I was 27. I had already finished my enlistment with the Army and was now working as a contractor in the United Kingdom.

It would be another ten years after 9/11 before I deployed to Afghanistan at the age of 37. I went to Afghanistan not as a military member but as a contractor. When I left for Afghanistan, I was married with one kid and served there from 2011 to 2013.

Remembering the trip to Afghanistan, I felt nervous but was happy that I could still support my family, who remained in the U.K. I spent my time there working out of Bagram Airfield (BAF) but went to MEZ and Kandahar.

Bagram was like "little America." In fact, it was commonly referred to as just that—little America—since it had been built up with little shops, USO shows, gyms, fast food places, and even a massage parlor. My living quarters there were pretty nice for a contractor, and overall, the morale there was good.

When I think about my happiest memories over there, I can recall talking to the locals who were working at the market. They told me they hoped the Americans would stay for generations to make the effort worth it; otherwise, the Taliban that they feared would come back.

My worst memories in Afghanistan were the frequent rocket attacks on the base.

When the news that Osama Bin Laden had been killed broke, it was May 2011, and I was still in Afghanistan. Even though I was in Afghanistan when it happened, I didn't actually learn about his death until watching CNN report on it. As news spread throughout the base, the overall feeling was more of an "about time" mixed with apathy.

I can't say that I'm sure of what our goal in Afghanistan was, but the locals had hoped we would fix their society from being overrun by the extremism of the Taliban. Unfortunately, the clear answer to whether we were able to accomplish that goal is a resounding no.

In my opinion, the U.S. pulling out of Afghanistan was a foolish mistake. I believe we still needed to be there until all of the extremists aged off. We should have stayed and continued educating the nationals for a few generations.

What was my cost of war? For me, the answer is clear and simple; None. I had a job and was able to take care of my family.

SSG Patterson

Even as a kid, I knew without a doubt that I was destined to join the military. I enlisted in the Army on active duty in 1997, when I was 20. I joined and served as an 11B Infantryman.

On September 11th, 2001, I was 20 years old, and when the news of the terrorist attacks came through, I was in a high-end furniture store just down the street from the Pentagon, wiring a light.

When I deployed to Afghanistan, I was 32 years old, married with a one-year-old child.

It was 2009 when I set boots on the ground in Afghanistan, and I was anxious on the plane ride over there. Like many others, I arrived in Bagram and transitioned to COP Xio Haq in Laghman province. The COP was newly built, and there was no running water. The only places that had electricity at the time were the TOC (tactical operations center) and the chow hall. My squad and I slept in a shed there. Despite those conditions, I believe the morale for my squad and me was good. I think that the morale being the way it was is because of the people we were there with and the camaraderie. My happiest memories were waking up at sunrise and calling my wife.

My worst memory? The loss of SSG Rivera during an attack on the COP (combat outpost). SSG Rivera was one of the best NCOs that I got to meet, and the members of the unit loved him. We all loved him. While I wasn't on BAF to witness his procession down Disney Drive, we did have a memorial service for him at the COP.

While on COP Xio Haq, I did leave the base. When we went outside the wire, I conducted KLEs, present patrols, raids, and served as QRF (quick reactionary force)—though I don't remember any of the village names we had toured.

Would I go back to Afghanistan if I had a chance? No.

I believe our goal in Afghanistan was initially retaliation for 9/11, but then to eliminate the Taliban. Did we succeed in meeting that goal? Absolutely not.

The good that I feel we accomplished while in Afghanistan is that we built schools and helped to hold off the Taliban. However, things we could have done better are having a better exit strategy and taking care of those that helped us while we were there.

How do I feel about the U.S. pulling out of Afghanistan? It made my deployment worthless.

What was my cost of war? I came home with PTSD. And when I got home, it took my daughter over a year to let me do anything for her.

PART IV

THE PATHWAY TO PEACE

Chapter 8

STRAINED RELATIONS

In the summer of 2011, Afghan President Karzai confirmed to the media that the U.S. government was engaged in secret peace talks with the Taliban. However, this round of peace talks fell apart in August of 2011. While efforts were made to resume the peace talks, the Taliban effectively canceled them completely in March of 2012.

When President Hamid Karzai took office as the interim president in 2001, he offered amnesty to the Taliban. Part of this amnesty offer was not provided or recognized by the United States as the U.S. was not all right with allowing Mullah Omar to "live in dignity" in Kandahar. In case you don't remember by this point, Mullah Omar was the founder of the Taliban.

From 2010 through 2011, when the U.S. was engaging the Taliban in peace talks, the Taliban had flat out refused to meet with the Afghan government calling them "America's puppets."

In October 2010, the Taliban were escorted from Pakistan by NATO forces to Kabul to carry out peace talks with the U.S. and NATO allies. This meeting was called the Quetta Shura. NATO had assured the Taliban leaders that they would not be apprehended while attending the conference. However, fearful that it may be a trap, Akhtar Monsour, the Taliban's second in command, had sent an imposter in his place and did not attend himself. This would only become known after the talks had concluded.

While I'm sure there were several factors influencing the Taliban's decision to cancel the peace talks, one reason cited was a disagreement between the Afghan government and the Taliban over the Taliban having a political office in Qatar, with president Karzai accusing the Taliban of trying to portray themselves as an exiled government.

The U.S. had been engaging in peace talks with the Taliban from 2010 through 2011. Initially, the Taliban refused to meet with the Afghan government calling them "America's puppets."

I'm sure there were a number of factors influencing the Taliban's decision to cancel the peace talks; one reason cited was a disagreement between the Afghan government and the Taliban over the Taliban having a political office in Qatar, with president Karzai accusing the Taliban of trying to portray themselves as an exiled government.

It may seem like the U.S. was the biggest wrong in Afghanistan in 2012. Still, the fact of the matter is that even though everything that occurred thus far, the U.S. and coalition forces were still constantly on the front lines, protecting the people of Afghanistan and working to eradicate terrorism. We may seem like monsters based on the actions of a few, but the majority of those who served in Afghanistan were not those monsters in question; they were the barrier keeping the wolves at bay.

And about halfway through 2012, the U.S. would join the U.K. on a rescue operation that was nothing short of daring.

On May 22, 2012, four female aid workers (a Brit, a Kenyan, and two Afghans) were kidnapped by individuals with close ties to the Taliban. They were believed to be in danger of being killed or handed over to vicious extremists.

Soon after the women had been captured, the kidnappers released a video demanding $9.5 million in ransom along with the release of one of their comrades from a detention center. Reportedly, a conversation between the kidnappers and the Taliban had been intercepted; the Taliban were telling the kidnappers to put on a "show of intent."46

Intelligence analysts determined that the women were held in separate caves in Badakhshan Province, Afghanistan.

With a team of around 70 special forces operators already positioned at a FOB in Badakhshan, a plan was put into place to rescue the aid workers. The SAS and Navy SEAL operators were loaded into Blackhawks and dropped at a rendezvous point approximately 3 kilometers from the caves in which the aid workers were being held captive. Once in position, U.S. and U.K. troops stormed the various caves, killing 11 kidnappers and rescuing the four hostages.

The careful planning and intelligence gathering coupled with the brilliant execution of this operation resulted in a successful rescue operation, which allowed all four women to be returned to their homes—alive.

To further the strained relations on both ends of the spectrum, 2012 brought about a rise in green-on-blue attacks, with ANSF and ANP/ALP turning against U.S. and coalition forces. It's roughly estimated that about half of those ANSF/ANP/ALP members that killed U.S. and coalition forces had either turned to the Taliban, with the other half noted to have had some grievances with the person(s) they killed. However, those numbers are not necessarily accurate as the U.S. has always been rather tight-lipped on this topic.

On August 10, 2012, a 15-year-old local named Aynoddin killed three unarmed U.S. Marines and wounded another—on base.

---

46   "Special Forces Rescue Aid Workers - Details Emerge," british special forces, accessed July 12, 2022, https://www.eliteukforces.info/uk-military-news/030612-british-special-forces-rescue-details.php.

He was the Afghan police commander Sarwar Jan's bacha ba-zi.47 Sarwar Jan said that Aynoddin had been "given to him" and claimed he believed the boy to be a police officer. This was a clear lie.

Aynoddin took one of the Afghan police officers AK-47's and went into the gym, where he met the four unarmed Marines and opened fire. After killing three and wounding the fourth, Aynod-din walked out of the gym, rifle in hand, and said to the Afghan police officers, "I just did jihad. Don't you want to do jihad, too? If not, I will kill you too."

The Afghan police disarmed Aynoddin, but it would become apparent not long after that he had, in fact, been working with insurgents.

Once U.S. forces discovered that the Afghan police had allowed him on base AND saw the police weapons strewn everywhere, they were furious. Changes would be coming down the pipeline, that's for sure.

This was not the only green-on-blue type of attack. In fact, from January through August of 2012 alone, 28 "insider" attacks had resulted in the deaths of 39 members of coalition forces, in-cluding the three U.S. Marines killed by Aynoddin.

There were two other green-on-blue attacks the very same week this had occurred. First, two Afghans wearing Afghan army uniforms had killed a U.S. soldier in another part of Afghanistan. Then, in a separate incident, U.S. troops had to kill an Afghan sol-dier after the Afghan soldier tried to gun them down in Laghman Province, Afghanistan.

The enemy doesn't always look the same or dress the same; sometimes, it can be the "ally" standing right in front of you. War

---

47   *Bacha bazi* is slang for child sex abuse between older men and younger boys. Other words for this term include "tea boys" and "dancing boys". Bacha bazi is still to this day practiced in Afghanistan and parts of Pakistan. However, during the Afghan Civil War from 1996 - 2001, the Taliban made bacha bazi an offense which was punishable by death. However, post-Taliban rule, even though bacha bazi was still illegal, police were complicit in enforcing this law as it was practiced by high-ranking officials—even within the police ranks—and well-armed warlords.

is hard. Understanding the enemy is brutal. It's no wonder that so many troops came home with PTSD.

While we haven't covered even a fraction of the suicide bombings that have occurred, they happen all the time. I mean ALL. THE. TIME. If you're curious, query Google for terms like "Afghanistan suicide bombing + 2013" or whatever year you're curious about. There is no shortage of results that will be returned—and not all events have been documented.

And when it comes to understanding the enemy, it's not so black and white. For example, when you hear of suicide bombings and attacks in Afghanistan, they are primarily attributed to the Taliban—or perhaps al-Qaeda. Still, the fact is that there are more terrorist organizations out there in Afghanistan than just the Taliban and al-Qaeda. Hezb-e-Islami is one of those groups.

Hezb-e-Islami, according to the National Counterterrorism Center, *"is a political and paramilitary organization in Afghanistan founded in 1976 by former Afghan prime minister Gulbuddin Hekmatyar, who has been prominent in various Afghan conflicts since the late 1970s."*

At 8:00 a.m. on May 16, 2013, a suicide bomber attacked two coalition convoys, resulting in 15 people being killed—including six Americans. An additional 37+ individuals were wounded. Kanishka Baktash, a spokesman for the Health Ministry, told the media that *"some of the dead civilians were badly burnt and cannot be recognized."*[48]

The blast from the bomb had done significant structural damage to a number of the buildings, including at least ten private residences, as it took place in a residential neighborhood of Kabul, Afghanistan.

Afghan officials said body parts were strewn all over the street, and windows were shattered several blocks away. They reported that there were 15 dead and another 70 wounded from the blast.

48   Miriam Arghandiwal, "Bomber in Afghanistan Kills 15, Including Six Americans," Reuters (Thomson Reuters, May 16, 2013), https://www.reuters.com/article/us-afghanistan-attack/bomber-in-afghanistan-kills-15-including-six-americans-idUSBRE94F0632013051.6.

The National Counterterrorism Center reveals that Hezb-e-Islami was *"responsible for a May 16, 2013 suicide VBIED attack in Kabul, which destroyed a U.S. armored SUV and killed two U.S. soldiers, four U.S. civilian contractors, eight Afghans—including two children—and wounded at least 37 others. The attack marked the deadliest incident against U.S. personnel in Kabul in 2013."*[49]

In a telephone interview with the press, Haroon Zarghoun, a spokesman for Hezb-e-Islami, revealed that they had carried out the attack **due to the insincerity of the United States in solving Afghanistan's problems**. During the interview, he said, *"We will step up jihad, and our first target will be American forces. We have a committee planning and choosing targets for more suicide attacks."* This interview was in the same article as the Health Minister mentioned above.

Bear in mind this section was on strained relations. And for the Hezb-e Islami spokesman to publicly blame the U.S.' insincerity in solving Afghanistan's problems for the attack they conducted, I'm sure it didn't help sway the people of Afghanistan's hearts and minds in our favor. While we did not commit the crime, our presence in Afghanistan could be seen as problematic since the insurgents were using us as an excuse to conduct attacks.

---

49   Nctc, "National Counterterrorism Center: Groups," National Counterterrorism Center | Groups, accessed July 12, 2022, https://www.dni.gov/nctc/groups/hezb_e_islami.html.

Chapter 9

AGREEMENTS

"Our Afghan partners can and will take the fight from here."
—General John F. Campbell, Commander of ISAF[50]

What aggravated the prevailing political fragmentation of Afghanistan was the lack of power on the part of the Afghan national government. In the years leading up to 2013, the national government, under the administration of Hamid Karzai, looked to NATO for the country's security.

The nation had remained dependent on NATO and coalition forces until 2013. However, 2013 was the year that marked yet another shift in power in Afghanistan's history. In that year, Afghan forces reclaimed responsibility for Afghanistan's security.

A United Nations mandate legitimized the presence of the International Security Assistance Force or ISAF. The ISAF consisted of more than 100,000 troops from 51 NATO countries, including the United States and the United Kingdom.

Tasked to protect the Afghan capital of Kabul, the ISAF took on expanding roles each year following 2003. By 2006, the ISAF had already established its military presence in many parts of Afghanistan.

---

50   "General John F. Campbell ISAF-Resolute Support Transition Ceremony Address," American Rhetoric: The Power of Oratory in the United States (American Rhetoric, December 28, 2014), https://www.americanrhetoric.com/speeches/john-campbellresolutesupportceremony.htm.

The growing presence of the ISAF quickly drew the attention of various militant groups, including Al-Qaeda and the Taliban. As a result, attacks grew rampant in Kabul and multiple parts of the country.

In the years following 2006, the ISAF constantly engaged many insurgent groups threatening Afghan security. The fighting would prove too much for even 140,000 NATO-backed troops in the country.

An additional 40,000 troops were deployed as reinforcements to the already-embattled ISAF. With the arrival of reinforcements came a new counter-insurgency strategy to aid Afghan forces in combating the insurgency.

The results of the collaboration paved the way for the handover of power to Afghan security forces. However, with insurgency still at its peak, the handover needed to be gradual and facilitated by training and support.

In 2009, the ISAF began providing support and training to Afghan troops. However, the support also bolstered the numbers in favor of security forces. As a result, the number of Afghan troops and police continued to surge until 2012.

By 2013, Afghan security forces had already broken past the 300,000-mark, enlisting 350,000 troops from the country's military and law enforcement. The numbers were enough to generate confidence in the country's ability to take on insurgents.

The ISAF remained in the country. However, the ISAF's agreement with the national government settled on the assistance force's decreasing presence rather than an abrupt exit.

NATO troops remained under the condition that they could not intervene in the Afghan government's security operations.

Hamid Karzai held power in Afghanistan as its chief executive for over a decade. Taking his place as the Afghan president on December 22, 2001, he stepped down from the presidency thirteen years later.

Before relinquishing office in 2014, a new round of presidential elections was held. Throughout the election, the proverbial tug-of-war for the presidency occurred between two particular candidates.

On one end of the proverbial rope was Abdullah Abdullah. Abdullah Abdullah was a man known at the time for his tenure as the secretary of the Massoud Foundation from 2006.

On the other was Ashraf Ghani — Afghanistan's former finance minister and former member of the United Nations and the World Bank.

The two men would compete for the highest position in the country, with Ashraf Ghani narrowly coming out the victor. However, like most other elections in Afghanistan, the election was shrouded with accusations of fraud. These widespread accusations resulted in the delay of the new president being announced and the necessity for a mediator. Then U.S. Secretary of State, John Kerry, served as the mediator between Ashraf Ghani and Abdullah Abdullah. Together, after several interactions, they had determined they would form the National Unity Government to share the power.

Ashraf Ghani's narrow win warranted the involvement of Abdullah Abdullah in the affairs of the country. The consideration resulted in the formation of Afghanistan's first National Unity Government.

The National Unity Government was the product of an agreement between Ghani and Abdullah. In the agreement, power would be shared. However, Ghani still retained authority as the president of Afghanistan.

A cabinet was formed in light of the new arrangement. In this arrangement, Abdullah Abdullah would assume the office of chief executive officer and appoint the chairmanship of the cabinet. He was able to select who filled the role similar to that of a prime minister in other countries.

The cabinet, chaired by Abdullah, would run the day-to-day affairs of the national government. However, President Ashraf Ghani would still be in charge of Afghanistan's strategic issues and undertakings.

In effect, the new National Unity Government operated with two branches — the executive under the presidency of Ashraf Ghani and the ministerial under the chairmanship of Abdullah Abdullah.

President Barack Obama announced in May 2014 that he planned to leave 9,800 troops in Afghanistan past the December 2014 deadline. Instead, he announced that troops would remain in Afghanistan until 2016.

"I am confident that if we carry out this approach, we can not only responsibly end our war in Afghanistan and achieve the objectives that took us to war in the first place, we'll also be able to begin a new chapter in the story of American leadership around the world."—President Obama in his speech from the Rose Garden.51

With that, however, he planned to end the combat mission in Afghanistan, except for eradicating those connected to al-Qaeda and focusing on training and advising Afghanistan's forces to prepare for our departure.

President Obama announced that by the end of 2016, the end of his presidency, only a small group would remain in Afghanistan to support the Embassy there, just as the U.S. had done with Iraq.

However, Obama's plan hinged on the Afghan government signing the Bilateral Security Agreement, which Afghan President Hamid Karzai had refused to endorse. The BSA ensured that U.S. troops maintained their legal protections in Afghanistan, which would have been detrimental to the mission had it not gone through.

With the new president of Afghanistan coming, though, there was room for new opportunities.

On September 14, 2014, Afghan National Security Advisor Hanif Atmar and U.S. Ambassador James Cunningham signed a Bilateral Security Agreement (BSA) between the two countries.

51　　Julie Pace, "President Obama Looks to Start 'New Chapter' in U.S. Foreign Policy," PBS (Public Broadcasting Service, May 28, 2014), https://www.pbs.org/newshour/politics/president-obama-looks-start-new-chapter-u-s-foreign-policy.

This momentous event was also witnessed by newly elected Afghan President Ashraf Ghani, who quickly accepted the agreement to strengthen the military relationship that began over a decade ago.

Before signing the agreement, U.S. Secretary of State John Kerry conducted frequent trips to Kabul to discuss matters with former president Karzai, who was never convinced despite the political pressure surrounding the process.

The terms of the Bilateral Security Agreement, which took three years to finalize, were an invitation from the Afghan government to the U.S. government to continue its presence in Afghanistan beyond 2014. Specifically, it provided the required legal protection to allow the entry of 9,800 US soldiers, which would aid the existing 2,000 NATO forces in the country. Their mission was to support the Afghan troops as they contained the Taliban fighters.

The increased U.S. military presence in the country aimed to train and advise the Afghan National Security Forces in their fight against the Al-Qaeda extremists and to conduct counter-terrorism missions to assist the Afghan government forces. Additional U.S. military personnel were also deployed to operate strategic bases, which ensured a more robust U.S. presence in the region.

The BSA was completed after the first Afghan election, a historic moment in the country's quest for peace and democracy. President Ghani's willingness to sign the agreement manifested his more open foreign policy. President Ghani prepared Afghanistan for democracy by welcoming foreign assistance and cooperation and stronger foreign relations with other countries.

The primary goal of the BSA was to strengthen security in Afghanistan and promote peace in the region. Accordingly, the U.S. military and government would provide training and support to its Afghan counterparts in defending itself against internal and external threats, precisely, those involving its security, territorial integrity, sovereignty, and constitutional order. Because the United States cannot participate in combat operations in Afghanistan unless mutually agreed upon, all its activities would be closely coordinated with the Afghan military and government.

The United States was to engage most in support activities that involved training, advising, supporting, and equipping the Afghan National Defense and Security Forces (ANDSF). In addition, the United States was to share its expertise in field engineering, countering improvised explosive devices, and explosive disposal.

They were also to participate in developing the Afghan Air Force, the ANDSF logistics and transportation systems, and intelligence operations. The mentioned activities may be improved following the matters discussed at the Afghan-United States Bilateral Security Consultative Forum.

The BSA ensured that the ANDSF would be responsible for national security, particularly for the Afghan population and territories. The role of the United States was to provide support and, when requested, determine the type of support it would provide to ANDSF to protect its country from threats.

Should the U.S. conduct military operations against Al-Qaeda, it will support the ANDSF, with the ANDSF leading the counter-terrorism operations. The U.S. was to respect Afghan sovereignty and the safety and property of its people.

Related to the terms of the agreement, the United States will perform activities that support their missions in Afghanistan, such as transport and other necessary activities to support themselves, as mutually agreed by the parties.

The BSA covered the U.S. military presence in Afghanistan and the presence of U.S. contractors and their employees in certain situations.

Through the BSA, the U.S. military and civilian entities agreed to respect the Constitution and the laws of Afghanistan. They were also to abstain from participating in any political activity in Afghanistan.

The U.S. forces were not permitted to conduct military operations in Afghan residences, arrest Afghan nationals, or operate detention facilities. In developing Afghanistan's defense and security capabilities, the U.S. could only assist as the Afghan government increased its responsibility for funding and sustaining the ANDSF.

The Afghan government should be fully committed to developing its military capabilities. It will ensure total contribution, as permitted by its resources, to sustain its security and defense forces.

The Afghan government and NATO signed the NATO Status of Forces Agreement on the same day. This gave the Allied forces and its partner's legal rights for continued presence to pursue its NATO Resolute Support missions in Afghanistan when the ISAF expires by the end of 2014.

In signing the US-Afghan Bilateral Security Agreement and the NATO Status of Forces Agreement, the Afghan government sent a strong message that it was ready to open the country to diplomatic relations with democratic nations.

During Obama's presidency, another major event that took place was the release of Bowe Bergdahl.

One of the most storied events of the American campaign in Afghanistan was the disappearance of Sergeant Bowe Bergdahl.

Bowe Bergdahl was a U.S. Army sergeant who the Taliban captured. The capture was reported to have occurred back in 2009 when the United States Army was deployed for counter-insurgency operations.

The Idaho-born Army Sergeant's disappearance, capture, and release have been the focal point of much media attention and controversy. Much of the attention has been on Bergdahl's act of desertion; an act frowned upon across all branches of the United States military.

In 2008, Bow Bergdahl was deployed in Afghanistan as part of the U.S. military's counter-insurgency operations in various regions. His unit, the 501st Infantry Regiment, was stationed in

Paktika Province. While there, Bergdahl was assigned observation duties at their outpost.

On the night of June 30, 2009, Bergdahl was nowhere to be found, according to military accounts. While his absence varied by source, the consensus was that he "walked away" from his post.

Some reports claim he was kidnapped, whereas other sources indicate that he left the base perimeter outside his duty hours. However, a series of emails to his father and his equipment being in order after his disappearance strengthened the idea of desertion.

A month after the disappearance of Bergdahl, the Taliban released a video of the soldier with his dog tags. Clothed in his combat uniform, Bergdahl provided the details of his deployment in the video.

Videos of Bergdahl would be shown for more than a year. In one of the videos released in 2010, Bergdahl delivered instructions to release Taliban prisoners held at Bagram Airfield and Guantanamo Bay under pressure from the Taliban.

The Obama administration eventually agreed to a "prisoner swap." As a result, on May 31, 2014, Bowe Bergdahl was released. On that day, a Special Forces unit made its way to retrieve and secure the U.S. Army Sergeant, bringing him to Bagram Airfield for medical attention.

The terms of the prisoner exchange between the United States and the Taliban had the condition of releasing five Taliban prisoners in exchange for Bergdahl. Agreeing to the terms, the Obama administration allowed the release of Taliban prisoners.

There were five Taliban prisoners exchanged for Bowe Bergdahl, and they would become known as the Taliban Five. The five prisoners had reportedly been held at Guantanamo Bay since 2002 yet had not been charged with anything. They were also confirmed high-ranking members of the Taliban. These men were deemed «high risk» to the United States, meaning they were definitely a security threat.

There were consequences for both the Obama administration and Bergdahl.

For Bergdahl, he was court-martialed three months after his release. The military trial followed a period of military investigation surrounding the circumstances of his disappearance.

With evidence, the military court charged Bergdahl with desertion, a charge to which the Sergeant pleaded "guilty." Despite the charges, Bowe Bergdahl returned to active duty as a military clerk in 2015.

The Obama administration drew criticism for setting the example of dealing with terrorists. More specifically, the House Intelligence Committee deemed the agreement to the prisoner exchange as a willingness to negotiate with terrorist and insurgency groups.

When Afghanistan fell to the Taliban during our departure in 2021 (jumping ahead just slightly, I know!), the Taliban Five that had been released in exchange for Bergdahl would become senior members of the new Taliban government.

As time went on, al-Qaeda faced another significant blow.

In October of 2014, in the Nazyan District of Nangarhar Province, near the border of Pakistan, the U.S. killed Abu Bara al-Kuwaiti in an airstrike (not to be confused with Abu Bakar al-Kuwaiti). Abu Bara al-Kuwaiti was a leader within the al-Qaeda ranks. Still, according to the NDS (the Afghan intelligence division), al-Kuwaiti had served as the Taliban's shadow governor for Achin District in Nangarhar. Al-Kuwaiti had been staying at the home of Abdul Samad Khanjari. The NDS reported that he had close ties to Ayman al-Zawahiri, the leader of al-Qaeda.

Following the airstrike, Afghan special forces, together with U.S. Special Forces, conducted a raid on Khanjari›s home. What they seized from that house would be a massive gain for the intelligence community and future operations in counterinsurgency. When I say «huge gain,» I mean incredibly significant. This raid was the most important since Operation Neptune Spear when bin Laden was killed.

Unlike many other high-profile operations, however, there isn›t much information available to the public besides what the NDS/Afghan government released, which fueled much of the U.S. media›s articles/info about this event.

U.S. and Afghan forces had seized weapons, a laptop, and a number of documents. The laptop reportedly contained a plethora of information about al-Qaeda operations on «both sides of the border» (reference to Afghanistan and Pakistan).

A few months later, by February of 2015, there had been a noticeable uptick in the number of raids and strikes conducted jointly by the Afghan forces and the U.S. What›s significant about this is that the media believed this uptick in the number of operations was a direct result of intelligence obtained from al-Kuwaiti›s seized laptop from the October raid.

A concern would later be raised regarding the number of raids we were participating in and whether we allowed the Afghans to lead the charge as we had agreed upon. To that, Rear Admiral John Kirby, the Pentagon press secretary, would have this to say in February of 2015:

"We've been clear that counterterrorism operations remain a part of our mission in Afghanistan. We've also been clear that we will conduct these operations in partnership with the Afghans to eliminate threats to our forces, our partners, and our interests." [52]

Beginning in 2011, the United Nations gradually shifted control back to the Afghan government, with ISAF›s mission ending in December 2014. The idea behind this was to ensure that Afghan forces (both their military and police forces) would be independent and sustainable forces capable of defending the people of Afghanistan.

At its peak, ISAF boasted more than 130,000 troops in Afghanistan, with more than 51 NATO and partner nations taking part in the mission.

---

52   Matthew Rosenberg and Eric Schmitt, "U.S. Is Escalating a Secretive War in Afghanistan," The New York Times (The New York Times, February 12, 2015), https://www.nytimes.com/2015/02/13/world/asia/data-from-seized-computer-fuels-a-surge-in-us-raids-on-al-Qaeda.html.

This did not mean that our mission in Afghanistan was over, however. Instead, ISAF›s combat mission was over, but we transitioned to a new mission: «Resolute Support.»

Resolute Support began on January 1, 2015, and its mission/purpose was to train, advise and assist Afghan security forces. When ISAF›s mission ended in December of 2014, the security of Afghanistan was handed over to the Afghan government and its forces. Members of ISAF would start redeploying home shortly after handing over the reins.

"Our Afghan partners can and will take the fight from here, " said General John F. Campbell, Commander of ISAF.

CPL Dom Mancuso

I lived in Northern California in a town just off the San Francisco Bay Area called Antioch on September 11th, 2001. Because of the time difference, I was still asleep when the first tower hit. I woke up to my mother screaming as the news started flowing that the first tower had been hit. I ran downstairs to see what was going on just in time to see the 2nd tower get hit; I then watched them both collapse.

When 9/11 happened, I was only 12 years old. Old enough to understand the importance of it but way too young to do anything about it. I had to wait years, stewing on it constantly, watching the news and seeing our guys get killed, while I had to carry on with my childhood like nothing was happening.

On my 17th birthday, I enlisted, joining as early as I possibly could have. I can honestly say that I would have probably still gone in even if 9/11 didn't happen, but how I went in might have been a bit different.

I enlisted in the Army National Guard as an 11B Infantryman. I chose the guard because in 2006, when I enlisted, the National Guard was the only service that allowed people to volunteer to fight overseas directly. So, since that was my goal, I joined and did precisely what I planned on doing. I volunteered to deploy three times.

My three deployments were to Iraq in 2008, Afghanistan in 2010, and Egypt from 2011-2012.

While serving in Afghanistan, I turned 21. Hell of an "I'm a legal beagle now" birthday... I honestly forgot and didn't realize my birthday had passed until a few days after.

As I got on the plane to Afghanistan, I felt excited. I had already been to combat in Iraq, so I had a pretty good idea of what to expect on the logistics side of things. What I didn't know was what Afghanistan would be like, especially in comparison to Iraq. As I found, there was little comparison. They were two very different conflicts. But I was proud because now I was truly going to be going after "the enemy." I had wanted to get a piece of the action since I was 12. I had an extreme feeling of self-actualization.

My taskforce flagpole was at Bagram Airfield (BAF), but we operated all over Regional Command East. My role over there was primarily a vehicle gunner.

Landing at BAF was a bit different than landing in Iraq. In Iraq, we had to do combat landings as planes still took sporadic gunfire from the ground. In Bagram, we landed as a typical plane does. We offloaded the Greyback and were immediately ushered into waiting tents, where we received our first brief that was very down and dirty. The brief went something like, "you will all be bussed over to the new Warrior side of Bagram on the other side of the airfield. From there, you will be put in transient housing, and your CoC (chain of command) will be briefed on what they will do. Oh, and if you hear "incoming," hop in a bunker... they like to shoot rockets at us all the time, but they hardly ever hit anything." And sure enough, about two minutes later, a rocket impacted the airfield. The guy said, "See, didn't hit anything." It was a bit surreal. Still, we all took on the speaker's nonchalant demeanor fairly quickly. Not sure if it was a survival mechanism or "monkey see, monkey do," but I never once had a fear of indirect fire, even though we were subjected to it all. The. Time. It was so bad that I actually looked down on the people who freaked out from it. Anyways, it felt good to be in Afghanistan. It felt good to be taking the fight to the bastards that helped the other bastards attack us.

We spent half our time at Bagram and half out at various Combat Outposts (COPs). Because of our mission, we were always out at different places and doing different things. It was nice because it kept things from becoming mundane or letting complacency slip in. We were our Task Force's PSD platoon (Personal Security Detachment), but because our principal didn't like going outside the wire very much, we got passed around like hookers as the "do everything" platoon. So, we did Quick Reaction Force, Aerial Reaction Force, Route Clearance, Short Range Patrolling, Long Range Patrolling, Raiding, and Force Protection.

While on Bagram, we lived in a wooden B-hut with makeshift interior walls and doors for a bit of privacy. On missions, if we had to sleep outside the wire, we usually did so in our trucks (MRAPS/M-ATVs), but sometimes on the ground. If we were near another FOB or COP, we would just RON (rest overnight) within their security perimeter. Sleep was a kind of "get it while you can" thing.

It blew my mind when I found out that some "fobbits" (service members who did not ever leave the Forward Operating Base a.k.a FOB), on deployment and in a combat zone, had a regular 8-hour working day rotation. Meanwhile, we are routinely being run into the ground with follow-on mission after follow-on mission after follow-on mission, going days without sleep — literally days. Then we go back on base and get yelled at because our uniforms smell, and all we want is some chow before we slip into a coma and before the inevitable spin-up for our next mission.

It was like two wars were going on: The one that consisted of us fighting the enemy and the other one, which seemed like a damned vacation for a good portion of those sent over there, but never stepped one foot outside the wire.

Morale for our platoon, for the most part, was pretty good. We were all individual volunteers, augmented to this task force to help fill billets. During our mobilization training at Camp Atterbury, the platoon was formed to do the PSD mission specifically. As we were all volunteers and not organic to that unit, it was apparently the thing to do. Since we were all in the same position, none of us knew any of the other soldiers or the unit's culture, and that became what brought us together. The Brigade we were going over with was the 86th Infantry Brigade Combat Team (Mountain), out of the Vermont National Guard. As such, and for a bit of platoon esprit de corps, we called ourselves the VFL (the Vermont Foreign Legion).

Thinking back, one of my happiest memories from over there was any time we went to the Parwan provincial capital of Charikar. This little boy and his friend would ALWAYS find us. No matter what part of the city we were in, they always knew it was us, even when we changed vehicles. They would come running up to us, excited to make some money. You see, they were our little errand boys. They would run into the local market and grab us anything we wanted. The local food was excellent, so we always had them run out and bring us back plate upon plate of food. I often wonder what came of those boys; They would be of fighting age by now. Unfortunately, like many things, I do not remember their names.

My worst experience was on May 19, 2010. A complex attack was launched on Bagram Airfield. The enemy breached the base defenses in multiple places, and our platoon was one of the only combat arms units on base at the time. The Special Forces (SF) guys on BAF had shut the gates on their compounds and, at first, wouldn't help clear the base, so we had to do it. We got to one of the breaches in the wire on the north side of Bagram and found it being held by a wounded Marine and an Airforce guy out on his morning run. We helped secure the breach and saw that the enemy was wearing U.S. Uniforms, down to the green socks in tan boots and unit patches of units currently stationed on Bagram.

We found guys with suicide vests, and one of my squad leaders, SSG Rhodes (who later passed away from cancer connected to his time in the Army), double-tapped (shot twice) a guy in the head who was going for the kill switch. After doing a quick Battle Damage Assessment (BDA), we got word from our higher headquarters that a bunch of enemy combatants was spotted just outside the wire in our area, so we were ordered to dismount and pursue. Not too long into the pursuit, my Lieutenant (LT), LT Bobby Withers, stepped on a landmine blowing his leg off and peppering a few others with shrapnel. The Taliban had moved all the red and white rocks, denoting it was a minefield. Getting out of that minefield sucked.

That same day a large IED created a MasCal (mass casualty) in Kabul, and Kandahar Airfield (KAF) was also hit. But, again, it was a well-coordinated attack. Hell, the guys we found with suicide vests had detailed maps of BAF and the location of every chow hall, TOC, and PX marked on it—anywhere troops would gather.

Going outside the wire was all I did over there. For the most part, I spent my Afghanistan war riding in the gun turret of a gun truck (MRAP/ M-ATV). This was just as the Crows system was coming out, and we didn't really get them. So, all our gunners were still up in their turret for the world to see and shoot at. Which happened often enough to make you respect that fact, but usually only pop-shots when not fully engaged. For the most part, gunners acted as another set of eyes for the driver while also pulling security.

I liked being outside the wire. I liked being on a mission. I felt like my presence alone was doing good. We were doing good, helping to provide stability and control to the region. For the most part, we had a lot of positive interactions with the local populace. Though more than a few times, older Afghans had no problem pulling their genitals out, waving them at us, and shouting obscenities. These were, however, the exception and not the rule.

An overwhelming majority of the local people were friendly, curious, and always willing to share a meal and conversation. It was like being in a different world. It's like what one imagines when they think of the stereotype that is presented when talking about biblical times. Mud brick huts, mud brick walls, damn near no electricity and throw a few A.K. 's and Toyota Corollas in there, and you've got 2010 Afghanistan.

Unfortunately, my Brigade and Task Force had their share of casualties. The three I would most like to mention are LT Bobby Withers, SSG Ed Matayka, and SPC Ryan Grady. LT Bobby Withers had his leg blown off from either an old Russian mine or an IED (unsure to this day). SSG Ed Matayka, a Combat Medic, had his legs blown off when his MRAP was ripped in two by an IED. Specialist Ryan Grady was KIA from the same IED blast that took Matayka's legs. In his honor, the chow hall on the Warrior side of Bagram was named Grady Hall. I was with Ed's wife, SSG Karen Matayka, a combat medic as well, on a different mission at the time of the incident. I'll never forget the emotions we all felt. The anger. The sorrow.

Honestly, I think our goal in Afghanistan was us realizing we dropped the ball back in 1989 when, at the conclusion of the Russian-Afghan war, a war in which we supported the Afghan Mujahideen in proxy against the Soviet Union when the Afghans begged us to stay and help them rebuild their country and re-form their government, we didn't. We didn't, and the country slipped into a three-way civil war with horrible atrocities on both sides until a little group called the Taliban came in and took over two-thirds of the country. It created a haven for other Islamic Terror Groups like Al-Qaeda, which opened the door for our attack on September 11th, 2001.

We went there under the guise of "We're going to hunt down Osama Bin laden." When that didn't even happen right away, and realizing how hard we dropped the ball on Afghanistan and how hard the situation can be put on us, we realized we had to do something to keep that situation from happening again. So, the mission changed to "Nation building," but we couldn't come out in the open and say, "we are fixing a mess-up of ours," because heaven forbid we look weak. *Insert eye roll*

Did we accomplish that goal? Nope. We have done the same thing to them all over again—dropped the ball and abandoned them. I foresee us getting attacked, with Afghanistan being at least a part of that attack, within the next ten years because of it. History keeps on repeating itself.

If we had stayed and really helped them form their government and uproot the corruption, then we could have done right over there.

What we could have done better in Afghanistan is to have actually fought the war we should have been fighting. You cannot win a guerilla war when the enemy has a safe haven. We didn't learn the lesson in Vietnam but instead repeated it in Afghanistan. We should have fought the enemy in Pakistan or wherever they went. Period. We shouldn't have fought it with big bases and places for us to "go back to" after the mission was over. Instead, we should have lived in and amongst the populace, shared in their suffering and their day-to-day life, to build a sense of communal care.

When the U.S. pulled out of Afghanistan, I hated it. I felt like the last thing I held onto, which gave me pride in my life, was pulled out from underneath me. Yet, I believed in what we were doing over there.

I have been fighting to find something good out of it, but how we left and what we did to that place haunts me.

Thinking about the cost of war, here's what I can say.

My cost is that my life no longer has the foundation of "I once did some good for people who needed it." It hasn't for some time, honestly. I have been diagnosed with severe PTSD. I cannot hold down a job to save my life because nothing seems worth my effort anymore.

I attempted suicide once because of it. I survived and learned that I didn't want to die (I was terrified of it), but I couldn't really find my reason for living. I feel like I'm just waiting around to die, and I don't care to improve that mindset anymore. Nothing is real. Nothing is sacred. I am alienated from my family, which is primarily liberal-leaning. I had an uncle call me a baby killer and a few cousins who openly tell people I committed war crimes just by being there. So that's fun.

What was my cost? I guess I could say my life... I don't have one.

Anonymous

After enlisting in the military, you seldom leave for basic training right away. You're in the limbo of no longer being a civilian, but also not quite a soldier, in the delayed entry program (DEP). When the terrorist attacks occurred on September 11th, I was 23 years old in DEP, waiting to ship out to basic training. For me, joining the military was a family tradition; it was just something I knew that I needed to do.

Watching the events unfold on 9/11 and knowing I'd be leaving for basic training soon, I was excited about it, thinking I would do great things for the US and the Afghans. I was looking forward to the adventure but also cautiously fearful of entering a warzone.

I left for basic training at 24 years old, joining active duty to become an intelligence analyst. In Basic Training, I don't think they quite caught up to the idea of being in war. Policy takes an average of 3 years to catch up and be written into doctrine. Aside from what I assume was the standard curriculum, we were still learning the new PRT exercises as we were the guinea pigs for that pilot program. We were also chosen to do roving guard with empty M16 mags, which I assume was a post-9/11 thing.

There was some Drill Sergeant (DS) talk about being in a warzone and maintaining situational awareness, but I don't know if they themselves had seen any combat. A few of them (the drill sergeants) were aggressively awkward enough to assume they were maybe in Bosnia or Somalia in the 90s.

While in the military, I served in Iraq and Afghanistan. I was 36 when I deployed to Afghanistan and was not married, nor did I have children.

As my plane was getting ready to land in Bagram, I could feel the adrenaline pumping, the excitement at being able to do my job and help the people of Afghanistan.

We were a small team who were primarily based out of Bagram but had traveled to Kabul and Kandahar as well. As a small team not attached to a larger unit, finding billeting, transportation, and other necessities was no small feat. Most everyone was helpful, though. My team was bringing in a new capability that got us a lot of scrutinies. But I at least kept the spot open for the next guy to do a better job.

Our gym and chow hall on the camp we stayed at while on Bagram were better than what they had on the central part of the base. We slept inside a small room inside a shipping container, and our closest bathroom was a port-a-potty.

In terms of morale, I was on my own from my team, so my morale was up and down. A lot of it was fighting the people in the section to prove the capability I brought was worthwhile.

Serving in Afghanistan allowed me to meet with people from different military disciplines and learn how they all contribute to the fight. That was probably one of my best memories of my time there.

On one of the days that I was there, I was with some contractors filming a rocket getting shot down (which you shouldn't do). We didn't realize that we were directly under the rocket, and parts started falling on us from the destroyed rocket. We all ran inside, which we thought was funny at the time.

While I was on a Special Forces compound, one thing I greatly appreciated was that they honored fallen Servicemen and women daily. The DFAC had a rotating slide deck of all the fallen in Afghanistan. Every shift change started with a story of a fallen Serviceman, so we all remembered who we were supporting. I was honored to get a glimpse of that side of the military.

One night, on a Muslim holiday, we were barraged by rockets the entire night. It scared the hell out of me. That was my worst memory from my time in Afghanistan.

Despite that, if I had the opportunity to go back, I would have.

Our goal in Afghanistan, to my understanding, was to eradicate the insurgent population so that the Afghan people were free to choose their way of life. And to show that America goes after those that attack us and does its best to restore the countries and territories it occupies.

Do I think we accomplished that goal? Not really. The Taliban, who supported Al-Qaeda, have since taken the country by force. Although we killed Bin Laden and showed our adversary our military might, they understood that a war like what we waged was ultimately unsustainable.

When we pulled out of Afghanistan, I was honestly relieved. Relieved that we were no longer sending our troops over there and that we could refocus our military. But I am also sad that we couldn't find a way for the Afghan people to choose their way of life outside of Taliban influence.

However, we showed the Afghans a more free way of life, if only for a short while. So, that's something. In a distantly supportive way, I feel I played a part in this.

In hindsight, while likely a relatively impossible task, trying to get a handle on the culture before going over there would have been beneficial. It's not like Afghan culture required reading in American schools. That, I think, was the biggest obstacle in understanding our adversary and the people we were trying to win over.

What was my cost of war?

I've been in the Army since 9/11, so I don't know about service life in a time of peace. That filled me with purpose, but so much that my mindset, even when not at work, is at war. This contributes to my disassociation from normal life. I've been in for almost 20 years and don't have a romantic life. Never married, no kids, rarely dated. I've also reverted at times to the rocket attack that scared the hell out of me and realized that I might have a slight PTSD.

PART V
WITHDRAWAL

Chapter 10

U.S. PREPARES TO WITHDRAW

"Fortresses cannot be built around countries and continents;
we live in a connected world and our security rests together."
- President of Afghanistan, Ashraf Ghani, in his address to the
American taxpayers.[53]

In mid-January of 2015, a counterterrorism operation was conducted in Afghanistan targeting members of al-Qaeda and an al-Qaeda compound along the Afghanistan-Pakistan border. But here's where it gets sticky.

The al-Qaeda commanders that the operation targeted were U.S. citizens, and both were killed during the mission. Also killed during this operation were two hostages: Warren Warrenstein, an American, and Giovanni Lo Porto, an Italian aid worker.

When the operation had been conducted, there was reportedly no intelligence to indicate that the hostages were present at that location.

During a press conference addressing the strike, President Obama remarked, *"As president and as commander in chief, I take full responsibility for all our counterterrorism operations in-*

53   "Obama Pushes Back Troop Drawdown in Afghanistan until after 2015," The Guardian (Guardian News and Media, March 24, 2015), https://www.theguardian.com/us-news/2015/mar/24/us-troop-levels-afghanistan-2015.

cluding the one that inadvertently took the lives of Warren and Giovanni."

White House press secretary John Earnest later remarked that President Obama did not «specifically approve the operations» but that the strikes had been lawfully carried out under the policy guidance.

Let's look at two other Americans that were targeted around the same time frame. Ahmed Farooq and Adam Gadahn were both U.S. citizens and members of al-Qaeda.

Ahmed Farooq was an al-Qaeda leader and the deputy emir of al-Qaeda in the Indian Subcontinent (AQIS). Farooq was killed in the same operation that had killed the two hostages. AQIS54 members confirmed his death. He quickly rose through the ranks with significant ties to senior al-Qaeda members. He was a Shura council member for al-Qaeda when he was killed.

There is not as much information about Farooq publicly available as Adam Gadahn, which is why this portion was a bit shorter and not as informative.

Born in Oregon, United States, Adam Pearlman converted to Islam in California in 1995. Soon after, he would take the name Adam Gadahn. Gadahn was killed the same week as Farooq, though likely in a different counterterrorism operation along the Afghanistan-Pakistan border. Gadahn, known as Azzam the American, served al-Qaeda as a senior operator, spokesman, «cultural interpreter,» and media advisor. In 2005, he appeared in a video threatening to conduct an attack in Los Angeles.

As tempting as it is to want to apply any sympathy to the fact that they were both American citizens, they were, in fact, traitors who had committed not only acts of treason but also, both either directly or indirectly, voluntarily participated in acts of terrorism, including executions. They were two very bad individuals who warrant absolutely no sympathy. They willingly chose their paths, knowing full well the consequences.

---

54   *For reference, Ayman al-Zawahiri, leader of al-Qaeda, announced the formation of AQIS in September of 2014.*

Warren Warrenstein, a U.S. citizen, had been working as a consultant for USAID in Lahore, Pakistan, when terrorists kidnaped him in August of 2011. His capture came just days before he was set to return home to Maryland.

As with almost all kidnappings, his captors had demanded that he be released. In addition, the terrorists wanted the U.S. to end all drone strikes—something the U.S. could not and would not do.

About four years after he was taken hostage, Warrenstein was killed in January of 2015—though not at the hands of his captors. A U.S. drone strike that had targeted an al-Qaeda compound rife with members of al-Qaeda killed Wallenstein. There was reportedly no intelligence to indicate that Warrenstein or Lo Porto were being held at that compound before the strike.

This was a devastating blow to his family, who had been still hoping for his release. He left behind his parents, wife, and children. The U.S. government financially compensated Warren Warrenstein›s family and Giovanni Lo Porto›s family.

Giovanni Lo Porto was an Italian aid worker. He had been taken hostage in Multan, Pakistan, along with his German colleague Bernd Muehlenbeck in January of 2012. Muehlenbeck had reportedly been held by the Taliban but was set free in Afghanistan in October of 2014—leaving the Lo Porto family and friends hope that he would be freed soon as well.

The Italian foreign ministry claimed they had worked tirelessly for three years to find Lo Porto and return him to his family.

«The conclusion unfortunately was different because of the tragic and fatal error of our American allies, which *was acknowledged by President Obama. The responsibility of his death and the death of Warren Weinstein ... rests entirely with the terrorists.*" [55]

When asked for a comment by the Asna news agency, Lo Porto's mother responded, *"Leave me along with my pain."*

---

55   "Giovanni Lo Porto, Killed in US Drone Strike, Was 'Incredibly Loyal' Friend," The Guardian (Guardian News and Media, April 23, 2015), https://www.theguardian. com/world/2015/apr/23/giovanni-lo-porto-killed-us-drone-strike-incredibly-loyal-friend?CMP=gu_com.

A notable attack in 2014 was one that would be remembered forever.

In December 2014, the Tehrik-i-Taliban Pakistan (TTP) conducted an attack at the Army Public School in Peshawar, Pakistan. Six shooters walked into the school and opened fire on both children and their teachers. This attack had killed 149 in total, with 132 of those being children with ages ranging between eight and 18. It was the world's fourth deadliest school massacre.

While Pakistani forces killed all six gunmen, the real masterminds behind these attacks remained at large.

In February of 2015, Afghan forces arrested five men in an «eastern province» of Afghanistan who were believed to have a hand in the Peshawar School Massacre. The Taliban said that this attack was in response to a government offensive in North Waziristan. A video released not long after this by TTP leader Mullah Fazlullah showed him vowing to conduct more attacks on children.

North Waziristan has played host to several militant groups. But, of these groups, the most dangerous is the Tehrik-i-Taliban Pakistan or TTP. The mountains of North Waziristan have served as the Tehrik-i-Taliban Pakistan›s stronghold since 2007. And from this part of Pakistan, the TTP has struck nearby parts of the country and parts of Afghanistan along the border.

In a press conference, the Tehrik-i-Taliban Pakistan spokesperson expressed the militant group›s intentions. Not only was the group seeking dominance within the region they controlled but all throughout Pakistan and parts of Afghanistan.

The Tehrik-i-Taliban Pakistan (or TTP) was formed in 2007 under the "leadership" of Baitullah Mehsud. The TTP was established under the umbrella of the Pakistani Taliban. They began as a collection of 30 radical Islamist groups seeking retribution against the Pakistani government for working with the United States in the War on Terror.

The TTP›s ranks grew to an accumulation of at least 40 militant groups. These new additions comprised other Taliban subsets and Pashtun groups. Since its founding in 2007, the group has claimed responsibility for many notable terrorist attacks, particularly in Islamabad.

The Tehrik-i-Taliban Pakistan's first recorded attack occurred in Mingora on December 23, 2007. When a military convoy was passing through the streets of the Pakistani city, a suicide bomber triggered an IED. The suicide attack led to the deaths of 13 people, injuring at least 20 people.

Perhaps the most well-documented attack of the Tehrik-i-Taliban Pakistan was the Peshawar School Massacre, which we just covered.

Afghan President Ashraf Ghani and his counterpart Abdullah Abdullah visited the U.S. in March 2015. During their visit, President Obama went on record to announce that he would not be reducing troops from 9,800 to 5,000 by the end of the year as he had previously planned.

A part of the reason why Ghani visited was to request more assistance in dealing with the increase in insurgent attacks in Afghanistan—and Obama obliged. During Obama's press conference with Ghani, Ghani had shared a few words of his own. After thanking the American taxpayers[53], Ghani said, *"Fortresses cannot be built around countries and continents; we live in a connected world, and our security rests together."*

Ghani's request came with good reason. With an increase in threats and conflicts ongoing throughout Afghanistan, they still needed coalition support.

What happens next lead to the successful destruction of two large al-Qaeda training camps—if not *the* largest. Let's take a closer look at the events that led to this success.

This was one of the largest, if not the most prominent, ground assault operations the U.S. had taken part in, in Afghanistan.

Jointly conducted with Afghan forces, the operation targeted two large al-Qaeda training camps in Shorabak district, Kandahar province. There were approximately 200 Afghan and U.S. troops that participated in this operation.

A U.S. military strike force conducted the operation spanning four days to clear these al-Qaeda training camps. Reportedly, one of the two training camps covered 30 square miles and was home to large caches of weapons, ammunition, foreign passports, thumb drives, laptops, anti-aircraft weapons, and other supplies, such as those to make IEDs. Sixty-three airstrikes supported the operation. While the exact number was kept under wraps, one Afghan source had reported the operation resulted in the death of over 100 insurgents and another 50 insurgents being wounded.

Brigadier General Wilson Shoffner was quoted in a press release saying that the raids were "one of the largest joint ground-assault operations we have ever conducted in Afghanistan. We struck a major al-Qaeda sanctuary in the center of the Taliban's historic heartland." 56

While the mission was a resounding success, questions raised concerns about how the al-Qaeda training camps had gone unknown for so long. For a training camp to be 30 square miles and that significant, how had it gone unknown at all? These questions led to the general sentiment that the U.S. had underestimated al-Qaeda's presence in Afghanistan.

Throughout Obama›s presidency, our mission changed to a «train, advise, assist» mission. Then-President Obama said: «It›s in our national interest—*after all the blood and treasure we have invested*—*that we give our Afghan partners the support to succeed.*" 57

In our continued preparation for our eventual withdrawal, the Afghan National Security Forces (ANSF) and the Afghan National Police (ANP) continued to be the forces responsible for the

56   "US Military Strikes Large Al-Qaeda Training Camps in Southern Afghanistan," FDD's Long War Journal, accessed July 12, 2022, https://www.longwarjournal.org/archives/2015/10/us-military-strikes-large-al-Qaeda-training-camps-in-southern-afghanistan.php.

57   "Obama: 8,400 U.S. Troops to Remain in Afghanistan through January," U.S. Department of Defense, accessed July 12, 2022, https://www.defense.gov/News/News-Stories/Article/Article/827640/obama-8400-us-troops-to-remain-in-afghanistan-through-january/.

security of Afghanistan. Their forces continued to work towards becoming an independent and sustainable force.

There were two notable raids the Afghan forces conducted in 2016—all against Taliban prisons that had been holding citizens of Afghanistan hostage. However, I would be remiss if I did not also mention that ANSF had raided a few other Taliban prisons in December 2015.

We›ve covered some of the main events in this book, but at this stage, coalition forces had left Helmand province entirely. So now, Helmand was in a deteriorating situation where the Taliban were going head-to-head with ANSF, who were losing ground. The very presence of these Taliban prisons was a clear indication of that.

The first of those raids occurred on January 2, 2016, when Afghan forces conducted a raid on a Taliban prison located in Helmand Province. The prisoners at this jail primarily consisted of Afghan military members and police. Afghan forces had reportedly freed 59 prisoners during this raid.

In February, Afghan forces, believed to be Afghan Special Forces, conducted a raid «in an area between Nad Ali and Marjah districts.» The results of this raid led to them being able to free 35 individuals from that Taliban prison. Reportedly, they rescued five men, five women, and 25 children.

A few months later, in May, Afghan forces were able to liberate another 60 Afghan citizens from a Taliban prison in Nowzad district, Helmand province. In addition to freeing those 60 individuals, Afghan forces had killed two insurgents and reportedly detained several other prisoners.

The Afghan forces were finding success in raiding these Taliban prisons, but with threats stemming from not just the Taliban but other extremist groups as well, there would always be more conflicts and more prisons. Let's talk about ISIL for a bit.

When the Islamic State of Iraq and the Levant (ISIL) formed in January 2015, the eastern part of Afghanistan quickly fell under the group›s control. Within months, Nangarhar Province witnessed how a militant force of 1,000 grew to 3,000.

As more Islamist fighters joined the ranks of ISIL, Nangarhar became recognized as a stronghold for the militant group. With the looming threat of ISIL taking over the adjacent parts of Afghanistan and Pakistan, Afghan National Security Forces needed help—even if it came from foreign powers.

For many years, the United States had maintained its military presence in the country. Hence, it was only a matter of time before the United States military would intervene in a skirmish involving ISIL.

In early 2016, the intervention came in the form of a three-week offensive aimed at eradicating the ISIL presence in the region. This three-week period beginning on February 14, 2016, and ending on March 6, 2016, was the "Nangarhar Offensive."

After the Pentagon approved U.S. military action in the province of Nangarhar, Afghan military assets were mobilized. The U.S. military rendered support in the form of Predator and Reaper drones deployed on the day of the assault.

Drone strikes were invaluable in the retaking of the Nangarhar districts of Bati Kot and Achin. The drone strikes led to the deaths of dozens of ISIL fighters, with two documented civilian casualties.

The drone strikes killed a significant number of ISIL forces in the Bati Kot and Achin districts. Indeed, the strikes were sufficient to thin ISIL's ranks in the region. However, the Afghan military continued its operations, cornering the remaining ISIL fighters in Achin and killing them.

As more casualties mounted on the ISIL front, Afghan security forces moved into Achin District. The presence of the security forces solidified control of the district. Meanwhile, drone strikes in nearby ISIL strongholds killed more militants, also destroying an ISIL weapons cache.

Concerns mounted over the security of nearby villages. For this reason, civilians established checkpoints to guard against any remaining ISIL fighters.

Then-president Ashraf Ghani announced control of all previously ISIL-held territory. As the fighting moved to the Shinwar District, more ISIL fighters were killed. Government sources report hundreds of ISIL casualties in the offensive, with most occurring during the final day.

Days later, reports about a small concentration of ISIL fighters moving into Kunduz Province surfaced.

The Nangarhar offensive was a joint operation between the United States military and Afghan National Security Forces. While success resulted from the collaboration between the two forces, few will deny the role airstrikes played during the offensive.

Drone strikes were responsible for the most ISIL casualties. With this in mind, it is hard to imagine the same outcome had U.S. air support been withdrawn or denied to the Afghan Security Forces.

October 31, 2016, marked the Kunduz-Takhar highway hostage crisis. Taliban militants disguised as government officials kidnapped about 220 civilians while driving along a major highway in northern Kunduz province. This seemed to be the first incident wherein the political movement, and the military group had taken a city since losing its power in Afghanistan in 2001.

At around 2 A.M. in October of 2016, Taliban militants set up a fake checkpoint. They abducted civilian passengers of three cars, four buses, and three vans. Local government officials reported that 12 people were killed in the ambush, including soldiers, police officers, and national agency officials. According to the militant group, Afghan security officials were their primary target.

While most passengers were released after the Taliban militants' interrogation, 17 people were reported dead. The other 18 passengers were held hostage. Some civilians were shot on-site, while others were killed in Omarkhel in Char Dara. Residents were forced to witness the killings.

Several months before the incident, Taliban militants had been trying to take control of the northern provinces. In fact, they successfully took over Kunduz in 2015. However, the security forces were able to reclaim the city quickly.

After the Kunduz-Takhar Highway Hostage Crisis, nine people were killed, and 13 were injured after four suicide bombers' courthouse attacked in Ghazni. Before that incident, which was after Mullah Akhtar Mansour's death, 11 people were killed in another attack.

In 2016, a year after the Nangarhar Offensive, several countries amassed an effort to rid the world of the Islamic State (IS) terrorist group residing in Afghanistan. They were responsible for many acts of violence and death in different parts of the world. We talked about the ISIL earlier; ISIL is a faction of IS.

Many of these militants were trying to establish a foothold in Afghanistan. However, a coalition of U.S. forces and Afghan soldiers retaliated to prevent them from advancing. Terrorists began attacking police checkpoints and residences a month earlier, leading to clashes. In a week, the media reported around 225 loyalists of the different I.S. groups died in various operations.

A week later, a U.S. drone strike targeted a location near the Pakistan border. The goal was to target high-profile ISIL-K members. The strike was successful, and among the dead was Umar Khalifa, who had organized a Pakistani school attack just two years earlier. He was responsible for the deaths of over 150 people, most of whom were children.

Troops continued operations targeting the mountainous region in Nangarhar. In addition, they held three counterterrorism operations in the Achin district. The U.S. began shifting much of its military might to the east of Afghanistan.

A day later, another drone strike hit the east, targeting a radio station. I.S. militants used the station to coordinate efforts. The insurgents were spreading propaganda to try and recruit people to their cause.

The drone strike would help delay their recruitment for months. Past successful operations against communication centers also provided the same result. Over a week later, two bombs exploded around Deh Mazang Square in Kabul. The target was Hazara protestors who were supporting an enlightenment movement. They were fighting against plans for large-scale power development. The Hazaras are minorities that were under oppression from Taliban rule.

When the dust settled, nearly a hundred people were found dead, while the injured numbered 260. Following the bombing, the ISIL claimed responsibility. However, they later retracted their statements. Even so, the U.S. pushed its efforts toward clearing more militants in the area.

Near the end of the month, another drone strike in the Achin district occurred. Again, it was successful, thanks to the collaborative effort of the Afghan special forces and the U.S. It led to the death of ISIS-K top leader Hafiz Sayed Khan.

For months, militants remained quiet while many withdrew from Afghanistan. Finally, it wasn't until October that a casualty occurred from U.S. forces due to a roadside bomb. The soldier was on patrol to hunt down ISIL-K militants when the explosion occurred. It would mark the first time a U.S. soldier died during these operations.

As 2016 came to a close, President Obama promised to draw troops down to 8,400 by the end of December 2016—the end of his administration.

Chapter 11

TALIBAN PREPARES FOR TAKEOVER

"[The attack was] a message for all the enemy soldiers, police, intelligence operatives, and relevant (Afghan) institutions that this year's operations will be more brutal and painful for them."—Zabihullah Mujahid, Taliban spokesman[58]

By 2017, the Taliban and other militant groups under its umbrella had gained a strong foothold over Northern Pakistan and many parts of rural Afghanistan. Many of the areas U.S. intelligence reports deemed strongholds were often either tribal villages or areas near the wilderness of a province or region.

Helmand Province is one of the areas the Taliban used as a stronghold. Despite a constant military presence, conflict in the area continued to ensue, seemingly out of nowhere. The coalition›s presence in the area did little to stave off the attacks launched by the Taliban.

Asymmetric warfare has always been a tactic of Taliban forces. Given the terrain surrounding the Sangin District of Helmand Province, tunnels proved pivotal to the Taliban's guerilla strategy.

---

58   Ayaz Gul, "At Least 140 Killed in Taliban Assault on Afghan Army Base," VCA (At Least 140 Killed in Taliban Assault on Afghan Army Base, April 22, 2017), https://www.voanews.com/a/more-than-100-killed-in-taliban-assault-on-afghan-army-base/3821184.html.

Since 2010, the Taliban has been using tunnels for various purposes. For example, tunnels were used to evacuate Taliban fighters from battlefields and areas besieged by coalition or U.S. forces. In 2011, the Taliban even used a tunnel to help prisoners escape from a Kandahar prison.

The terrain of the Eastern and Southern parts of Afghanistan was conducive to the strategy. These areas also already contained a network of caves from which the Taliban established its underground network.

Tunneling, or digging networks of tunnels, took on a more offensive role in the years leading up to 2017. For example, in 2017, the tunneling strategy was used to detonate an IED underneath an Afghan army post in the Sangin District of Helmand Province.

According to various sources on the ground after the attack, Taliban fighters dug tunnels in and around the Afghan military post. Following this, another tunnel from one of the tunnels surrounding the base was dug until the foundations of the post were reached.

The Taliban concentrated a large volume of IEDs and other explosives underneath the army post. The detonation of these explosives resulted in mass casualties. Sources indicate that the explosion claimed the lives of at least 20 soldiers.

Before this, the Taliban also tunneled near government checkpoints to attack local police in Helmand Province. The attack on checkpoints killed more than 100 Afghan national police.

The United States launched a retaliatory strike against the Taliban in response to these attacks. Aware of the Taliban's network of tunnels in Helmand Province, the U.S. military carried out airstrikes all over the region, including Sangin.

According to Brigadier General Charles H. Cleveland, the airstrike campaign had been planned to last for two days. Brigadier General Cleveland also stated that the strikes would be carried out precisely, minimizing the risk of civilian casualties.

As announced, the airstrikes lasted for 48 hours. According to various military sources, more than 13 airstrikes were performed. Of this number, about six airstrikes were around the Sangin District, where the Taliban established its presence. Afghan sources tallied the resulting Taliban casualties to 20. In addition, at least 40 were injured or wounded following the air raids.

While there were numerous bases and outposts throughout Helmand Province, Camp Bastion and Camp Leatherneck were perhaps the most well-known and most prominent. British forces had maintained Camp Bastion in Helmand Province, the most extensive base in that province, but had left the area in 2014. Camp Leatherneck was a smaller U.S. base conjoined to Camp Bastion in Helmand Province, but when Bastion closed down in 2014, so did Camp Leatherneck.

Between 2012 through 2014, all posts and bases were closed down with the exception of Bost Airfield. The airfield was where U.S. military advisors continued to work side by side with their Afghan counterparts as part of the Train, Advise, Assist mission. With coalition presence being almost non-existent for the last few years, the area was rife with Taliban.

On April 17, 2017, Qari Tayib, the Taliban's "shadow governor" for Takhar province, was killed in an airstrike in Kunduz province's Archi district (a.k.a. Dasht-e Archi) in Afghanistan. Tayib had long been a target of interest for the U.S.

According to U.S. officials, the airstrike was carried out to restrict the freedom of movement of the Taliban in the area. Tayib's compound was among the targets of the attack that also claimed the lives of eight other Taliban members.

A U.S. military official remarked, *"Tayib had been a target-of-interest since 2001 and was directly responsible for the deaths of U.S. service members in Afghanistan."*[59]

---

59   Ayaz Gul, "At Least 140 Killed in Taliban Assault on Afghan Army Base," VOA (At Least 140 Killed in Taliban Assault on Afghan Army Base, April 22, 2017), https://www.voanews.com/a/more-than-100-killed-in-taliban-assault-on-afghan-army-base/3821184.html.

In retaliation for Tayib's death, the Taliban carried out an attack on an army headquarters in Mazar-i-Sharif, as confirmed by Taliban spokesman Zabihullah Mujahid. He went on to say that the attack was "a message for all the enemy soldiers, police, intelligence operatives and relevant (Afghan) institutions that this year's operations will be more brutal and painful for them."[59]

Taliban insurgents posing as soldiers attacked a base in a northern region and opened fire, killing around 140 Afghan soldiers and injuring 80 more. According to an official, suicide bombers disguised their explosives in false casts and medical devices. Other attackers were carrying automatic weapons.

The assailants, who arrived in two military vehicles, convinced guards at the entrance that they were bringing injured soldiers and had to enter the base immediately. Some of those "soldiers" claimed to be injured, wearing leg splints and drips down their arms to get past the first checkpoint without being caught. Then, when the guards at the next checkpoint grew suspicious, a suicide bomber detonated his device.

At least two suicide bombers carried out their attacks within the base, one in the dining hall and the other near the mosque. The remaining assailants then proceeded to go on a shooting rampage, according to officials. This was the bloodiest attack in Afghanistan since two ISIS insurgents killed 80 Hazara demonstrators in July 2016. Zabihullah Mujahid, a spokesman for the Taliban, is a name you will continue to see throughout current events.

"Shadow governors," like Tayib, were in charge of Taliban insurgents all over the country's 34 provinces. They have more power in places where the Afghan government lacks control, such as the south, where the Taliban cultivate and trade opium.

A shadow government, which the Taliban had in place for many years during the war, was their version of the country's government. Each province and district throughout Afghanistan had a Provincial Governor and District Governor, respective to each location. Districts, of course, were lower than the Provincial Governor. And for each province and district, there was an official governor—established by the government—and a shadow governor—established by the Taliban. Since we already covered this early in the book, I'll leave it at that.

In May 2017, the Taliban carried out another deadly ambush, this time in Afghanistan›s Shah Joi district, Zabul province. Occurring in the Chino and Ghulam Tabat areas, the attack had targeted and killed 20 Afghan police officers, leaving another ten wounded.

Admitting they were responsible for the attacks, the Taliban claimed that the ambush was part of Operation Mansouri, a spring offensive recently announced in April. At the time of the Shah Joi ambush, it had already been 16 years since the Taliban insurgency arose, intending to topple the Western-supported government in Kabul.

Despite staging the attacks in the Shah Joi district, the Taliban themselves did not come out of it unharmed. Dozens of fighters from the militant group had also been wounded and killed.

On the same day, an international guest house in Kabul was also stormed by unidentified gunmen, which resulted in the death of a German aid worker and an Afghan soldier. The guest house was run by Operation Mercy, a Swedish relief organization.

A Finnish woman in the guest house had been abducted. She was later identified as another aid worker for Operation Mercy. Her kidnapping was, at the time, the latest in a series of attacks against aid workers in Afghanistan. Incidents like these were a severe problem in the conflict-hit country as aid workers were often the target of kidnappings, some of which were for ransom.

While no group had admitted to assaulting the guest house, it was believed that the Taliban may have been responsible considering they had attacked the Shah Joi district that same day.

After four months in captivity, the Finnish aid worker was finally released on September 14, 2017. Out of respect for her privacy, Finland's foreign ministry withheld details regarding her identity. It gave no further information about how she was released. The Finnish aid worker did not provide any public statements about her captivity or captors. Instead, the foreign ministry stated that the freed Finnish aid worker was "safe."

But, even after four months since the assault on the international guest house, no group came forward to claim responsibility for either the attack or the kidnapping of the Finnish aid worker. While it was possible that the Taliban may have conducted the attack and/or the abduction, the militant group did not release any statement about the incident, leaving everything else to conjecture.

The abduction and release of the Finnish aid worker were not the first, nor would it be the last. Weeks before she was released, two Red Cross workers who had been kidnapped in Jowzjan province in February were also freed. Similar to the Finnish aid worker, no details were provided regarding the abduction and release of the two Red Cross workers.

I briefly mentioned Operation Mansour moments ago, so let's come back to that now.

Operation Mansouri, named after the group's former leader (Mullah Akhtar Muhammad Mansour), who was killed in a U.S. drone strike in 2016, was the name of the Taliban's "spring offensive" in 2017. A statement from the insurgent group said that they will target foreign forces and Afghan forces with "conventional attacks, guerrilla warfare, complex martyrdom attacks, insider attacks" and continued to say, "The enemy will be targeted, harassed, killed or captured until they abandon their last posts." 60

Considered to be propaganda, the statement detailed Operation Mansouri as the following: *"The main focus of Operation Mansouri will be on foreign forces, their military, and intelligence infrastructure and in eliminating their internal mercenary apparatus."* 61

---

60   "Afghan Taliban Launch Spring Offensive as U.S. Reviews Strategy," Reuters (Thomson Reuters, April 28, 2017), https://www.reuters.com/article/us-afghanistan-taliban/afghan-taliban-launch-spring-offensive-as-u-s-reviews-strategy-idUSKBN17U0E9.
61   "Taliban Announces Start of 'Operation Mansouri,'" FDD's Long War Journal, April 28, 2017, https://www.longwarjournal.org/archives/2017/04/taliban-announce-start-of-operation-mansouri.php.

The "spring offensive" marks the start of fighting season each year. That's right...every year. The Taliban claimed they had control over (or contests) 211 of Afghanistan's 421 districts as of March 2017. However, according to U.S. estimates, it was believed that Afghan Security Forces had control of less than 60 percent of the country.

A group of Shia mosques was attacked by the Taliban in 2017 throughout Afghanistan. The initial suspicion is that the attack was motivated by sectarianism. Regardless of motive, this heinous act has violated the sanctity of houses of worship and has brought pain and suffering to the Shia community. Remember that the Taliban is a Sunni group that is divided from Shia. Think back to the Sunni-Shia divide.

With no regard for anything that doesn't fit in their "box," the Taliban has always been ruthless. For example, the Herat Mosque attack occurred on August 1, 2017. During prayers, two suicide bombers attacked the Jadwadia Mosque in Herat, Afghanistan. According to the New York Times, the attack resulted in 29 deaths and 64 injuries.

The building suffered terrible damage, including windows blown out. Shrapnel was embedded into its walls from bullets shot by extremist gunmen inside the mosque. Some victims died instantly or sustained severe injuries, while other survivors had taken cover behind rubble and walls. The Taliban, in an official statement, denied responsibility for this attack.

In a separate incident, on September 29, 2017, a suicide bomber detonated his suicide vest near a Shia Mosque, killing six people. The attack occurred where Ashura was being observed. For Shia Muslims, Ashura is a holy day where they mourn the death of Hussein, their third imam.

As the mosque attacks continued, a suicide bomber killed at least 39 people and wounded dozens more in attacks on mosques in Kabul and Ghor on October 20, 2017. First, a suicide bomber targeted worshippers in a Shia Mosque in Kabul, killing 39. The second attack occurred at a Sunni Mosque in Ghor, killing as many as 30 people.

ISIL, an increasingly relevant extremist group with members in Afghanistan, had claimed responsibility for the many attacks in Kabul. However, the Afghanistan government has accused Pakistan of being behind the attacks in Ghor province.

ISIL carried out the attack on a Shia cultural center in Kabul, which resulted in the death of 50 people and injured more than 80 others, many of whom suffered severe burns. The attack occurred on December 28, 2017, when a media outlet says four bombs were used in the assault.

President Ashraf Ghani calls the attack a crime against humanity and, therefore, an unforgivable act. The attacks on Shia mosques in Afghanistan by the Taliban were, and still are, an unfortunate reminder that religious persecution is still prevalent. These attacks were not only tragic but they were also used to fuel religious tensions and escalate violence between followers of different religions.

"[The plan was to] attack our adversaries, annihilate the Islamic State of Iraq and the Levant (ISIL), crush al-Qaeda, prevent the Taliban from taking control of the country, and prevent mass terror attacks against Americans before they occur."—President Donald Trump62

In recent years, the Taliban has been showing photos of the Red Unit, an equipped fighting force that has taken part in many attacks against local and foreign troops. Before the Taliban took power, few knew of their existence. This clearly indicates that the Taliban was growing in strength and becoming more organized and sophisticated. Perhaps it even shows a bit about our effectiveness up to this point.

For some reason, though, the Red Unit is rarely talked about in the news. Don't get me wrong; there are some articles out there—in fact, this section was stitched together using various news articles that were corroborated by multiple sources.

---

62   The New York Times, "Full Transcript and Video: Trump's Speech on Afghanistan," The New York Times (The New York Times, August 22, 2017), https://www.nytimes.com/2017/08/21/world/asia/trump-speech-afghanistan.html.

The Taliban began deploying elite soldiers in 2016 for specific operations, reflecting divisions within the top leadership over dealing with battlefield setbacks, such as the loss of Kunduz Province, when U.S. airstrikes helped Afghan forces to recapture it.

They are better trained than typical insurgent fighters, who lack rudimentary military skills and equipment such as night-vision goggles or GPS devices. So, who exactly are they?

The Red Unit, a.k.a. the Taliban's special force unit, is tasked with executing critical and dangerous operations. That's right; even the Taliban has a special forces unit. This fighting force has been deployed for specific missions. The Red Unit consists primarily of ethnic Pashtuns, and they are trained much better than the typical insurgent fighters.

While deployed in different parts of Afghanistan, they were often sent to Helmand, Kunduz, and other provinces to fight against government forces.

In 2016 the Red Unit had 300 members, reportedly swelling to around 3,000. Whether those numbers are still accurate, this author does not currently know.

For many years the Taliban suffered heavy casualties while fighting government forces. So, this "special force" was formed to address this problem.

The creation of the Red Unit signified that divisions were emerging from within the top leadership over how to deal with battlefield setbacks, such as losing control of Kunduz after the Afghan government recaptured it with help from the U.S.

After the Taliban rose to power, the Red Unit took up the role of protecting senior Taliban officials and leading offensives against rebels and terror groups. They took over the military bases and equipment left behind by the coalition forces and intend to use similar techniques to fight against ISIL. The Red Unit is meant to eliminate the ISIL target.

This "elite" fighting force originated after the fall of Kunduz in 2015, leading to a rift within the Taliban's top leadership over how to respond to losing such a key territory (as well as pressure from Pakistan).

The birth of "The Red Unit" is linked with Mullah Haibatullah Akhundzada's rise in the leadership of the Taliban. Red Unit members are considered very loyal, even more than the typical Pashtun fighters who make up most of the Taliban's ranks.

The Red Unit's primary function was to conduct military-style offensive operations against high-value targets, such as Afghan army checkpoints along the Kunduz-Khanabad highway near Takhar or between Farah and Helmand provinces. They also conducted raids on government compounds in Afghanistan to capture key officials, such as district governors or provincial council members.

Other roles include training suicide bombers as well as planting IEDs. They have more advanced weaponry as a fighting force than some regional groups within the Taliban.

The leadership of the Red Unit is unknown. Still, experts believe it to be under the command of Mullah Shah Wali, also known as Haji Nasir, who is believed to have been appointed by Taliban leader Akhtar Mohammad Mansour in early 2015.

Red Unit fighters carried out dozens of attacks against soldiers and civilians during this period. After insurgents captured Kunduz in September 2015, many other cities fell under Taliban control primarily due to poor coordination between security forces.

The fall of Kunduz was one of the main factors leading to the resignation of Defense Minister Bismillah Mohammadi and Army Chief of Staff General Sher Mohammad Karimi the following month.

The Red Unit played a crucial role in that attack. It was directly involved in coordinating the offensive and relocating forces from other provinces into Kunduz for this mission. The Red Unit is funded by drug trafficking and contributions from wealthy sympathizers worldwide — mostly Arabs and sympathizers living in countries like Iran and Pakistan—as is the Taliban, not just the Taliban special forces. The Taliban also raise funds by taxing the local population.

The Taliban is believed to raise between 700-800 million USD annually from drug trafficking alone.

It's easy to fall into the mindset of believing that because it's a third-world country and because they're insurgents that they don't have much in the way of funds or equipment. To think this would be positively naïve. Not only are they well-funded (thanks to drugs and donations), but they are also expansive (in many parts of the world) AND are more than competent in the latest technologies. They have members that are more than willing to lay down their lives in the name of jihad, and they have members that can write their own code and develop their own technologies. And now, they have their own special forces unit as well.

The Taliban, growing larger and steadier, still had their conflicts between not just coalition forces and the Afghan government but also other extremist organizations.

We must remember that this isn't their first rodeo when we consider current events with the Taliban once again being in control of Afghanistan. From seizing portions of Afghanistan—such as the Battle of Darzab in 2018—to seize complete control of the country back in 1996, the Taliban is no stranger to fighting for control.

In the Battle of Darzab, the Taliban and the Islamic State's Khorasan Province (ISIL-KP) had been fighting to control Darzab District in Jowzjan Province, Afghanistan. However, after several extreme encounters, ISIL-KP lost the battle, with many ISIL-KP fighters killed by the Taliban during the skirmish. We'll talk more about the Battle of Darzab shortly.

Since 2015, the Taliban and ISIL have had an intense rivalry. The Afghan branch of ISIL, known as Khorasan Province or ISIL-KP, tried to recruit dissatisfied Taliban members. This challenged the reputation that the Taliban was trying to build — the sole legitimate opposition in the country.

As you can imagine, this led to the two groups clashing several times, primarily when they competed for control over the provinces of Sar-e Pol, Faryab, and Jowzjan. Taliban defectors, a large group of mujahideen, and militants from the Islamic Movement of Uzbekistan (IMU—yet another insurgent group that we'll talk more about soon) strengthened the ISIL-KP forces. Mujahideen are those who participate in jihad or fight for their God and the Muslim community.

Qari Hekmat (a.k.a. Qari Hekmatullah), the Uzbek Islamic commander for the ISIL, then led the operation of recruiting fighters from Central Asia and taking them to Jowzjan Province. Thus, in 2017, the Islamic State gained control of most parts of the Darzab District in Jowzjan.

The Taliban attempted to defeat ISIL-KP and take over Darzab District, but they failed to do so. The latter's forces weakened, however, when Hekmat was killed in April 2018 during a U.S. airstrike.

Born in Uzbekistan, Qari Hekmatullah (a.k.a. Qari Hekmat) is said to be the son of Tohir Yo'Idosh—the founder of the Islamic Movement of Uzbekistan. Hekmatullah had been a member of the Taliban for some years. While serving as a member of the Taliban, he was the Taliban commander of Jowzjan Province and the Shadow Governor of Darzab District.

He did not leave the Taliban by choice. Instead, he was expelled by the Taliban for "cruel activities" when he planned to stone a woman to death after hearing allegations of her adultery. It would not be long after this that Hekmatullah would join the ISIL-KP.

A mere two years after joining the ISIL-KP, he was killed in a U.S. drone strike in Faryab Province, Afghanistan. His death was confirmed by both the U.S. and by General Faqir Muhammad Jawzjani, the Provincial Chief of Police for Faryab Province.

The Islamic Movement of Uzbekistan (IMU) is yet another Islamic militant group. IMU was formed in 1998 by Tohir Yo'Idosh and Juma Namangani. Namangani was a former Soviet paratrooper. Both founding members were ethnic Uzbeks.

The original goal of the militant group was to overthrow the president of Uzbekistan—Islam Karimov—and to create an "Islamic group under Sharia." A few years later, though, the group had reinvented itself as an ally of al-Qaeda. While the group had maintained a good relationship with the Taliban in the '90s, the relationship would soon see a steady decline.

IMU co-founder Juma Namangani was reportedly killed in a U.S. airstrike in November of 2001 when the U.S. invaded Afghanistan. Meanwhile, his counterpart, Yo'ldosh, along with the remaining IMU fighters, managed to escape with members of the Taliban to Waziristan, Pakistan. *Waziristan is located in the Federally Administered Tribal Areas of Pakistan.*

Reports surfaced around September 30, 2009, from his alleged bodyguard that Tohir Yo'ldosh had been killed in a U.S. drone strike. However, it would be almost a year after his death that his successor would be named.

The IMU publicly pledged its allegiance to the ISIL-KP in mid-2015.

The Battle of Darzab occurred from July 12 to August 1, 2018. It officially began when ISIL-KP seized a Taliban-dominated village in Darzab District. Approximately 10 Taliban members had been beheaded. Following this attack, the Taliban started urging its members to attack ISIL-KP bases on July 12. These include Darzab and Qush Tepa in Jowzjan. The attacks also extended to other provinces, such as Sar-e Pol and Faryab.

Four days after the attack, four Islamic State members and six Taliban fighters were killed during an encounter in Darzab. Then, another 15 jihadists were found dead in Sar-e Pol, Sayyad District.

The conflict between the two militant groups worsened when the Islamic State forces captured Taliban commander Mullah Burjan. Three days later, he (Mullah Burjan) was beheaded. This led to more attacks between the two groups in Darzab District. According to the reports, about 250 were killed during the battle.

Aiming to oust ISIL-KP from Jowzjan, the Taliban carried out major attacks by the middle of July. Around 2,000 fighters took part in the operation, with others coming from Helmand Province. Using their special forces, the Taliban defeated ISIL-KP in Darzab by attacking their strongest forces there. About 700 fighters from the Islamic State were said to be based in Darzab at the time.

The Taliban then defeated ISIL-KP, particularly at Mughal and Sardara, killing Haji Murad, who served as the group's deputy commander for Jowzjan. This also resulted in the displacement of up to 7,000 civilians because of the series of attacks.

With only two villages left, ISIL-KP, led by Mufti Nemat, sought protection from the Taliban and eventually surrendered to the government. In turn, the Afghan Air Force prevented the Taliban from seizing the rest of the Islamic State forces. As a result, on August 1, 2018, around 245 fighters surrendered. Meanwhile, others suddenly disappeared and were thought to have joined the Taliban.

ISIL-KP fighters who had surrendered were brought to Sheberghan, the center of Jowzjan Province. While they were reasonably well-accommodated, the civilians and other soldiers urged the Jowzjan governor to force the group to pay for their crimes. Meanwhile, the government was questioned for giving these militants refuge and protection, causing tension.

Several claims were made after the battle, namely that ISIL-KP had been ultimately defeated. However, this was false, as ISIL-KP still held a few districts. The U.S. military and Afghan government claimed they were responsible for ISIL-KP's surrender, even though the Taliban was primarily responsible.

Going backward in time to before the Battle of Darzab, we're going to be looking at ISIL's use of tunnels this time. Just a short time ago, I talked about the Taliban's use of the tunnels, but they were not the only extremist organization to make use of them.

On April 26, 2017, a joint U.S.-Afghan operation was conducted in Achin District, Nangarhar Province, which targeted the headquarters of Abdul Hasib, the emir of ISIL-KP. As a result, 50 Army Rangers from the 3rd Battalion, 75th Ranger Regiment, and 40 Afghan commandos were flown into Mohmand Valley. An intense, close-quarter firefight ensued for close to three hours.

During the encounter, AC-130 gunships, Apache helicopters, F-16 fighters, and drones were called to support the U.S.-Afghan troops fighting against the ISIL-KP militants. Achin District, where the operation occurred, has been the site of a long-running battle between the ISIL-KP fighters and Afghan National Defense Security Forces. In early April, a U.S. Army Special Forces soldier was killed while engaged in combat with the terror group. Moreover, the Pentagon deployed in the same district one of the U.S. military's most powerful non-nuclear bombs two weeks prior. The bomb, which garnered the nickname "mother of all bombs," targeted Islamic State fighters hiding in caves and a tunnel complex.

As a result of the deadly raid, Abdul Hasib, along with 18 to 35 ISIL-KP militants and an unspecified number of ISIL-KP leaders, were killed, thus rendering the operation a success. However, the area was yet to be cleared entirely of ISIL-KP militants With support from the U.S. Defense Department, Afghan security forces continued to fight with the remaining ISIL-KP fighters in Achin District.

Despite the operation's success, two Army Rangers were killed, Sgt. Joshua Rodgers of Bloomington, Illinois, and Sgt. Cameron Thomas of Kettering, Ohio. Both servicemen were deployed from Fort Benning, Georgia. The two American soldiers were medevac'd from the site but eventually succumbed to their injuries. The Pentagon looked at the possibility that the two soldiers may have been slain by friendly fire, either from the American forces or Afghan commandos jointly conducting the raid. A third Army Ranger was also wounded during the operation, though his injuries were not life-threatening.

Casualties from the U.S. and coalition sides have been dramatically reduced in Afghanistan since 2014. This was when the Afghan government took responsibility for heading combat operations. By 2016, at the behest of U.S. military advisers, the Afghan National Defense Security Forces began to launch a major offensive against ISIL-KP fighters. This is a separate endeavor from NATO's effort to train, assist, and advise the Afghan army and police force in their fight against the Taliban, another terror group.

Since the major offensive against Islamic State fighters, the group had lost about half of its fighters. In addition, it had been driven away from two-thirds of its territory. That is until about a year later, when ISIL and the Taliban would clash at the Battle of Darzab.

Chapter 12

PRESIDENT TRUMP'S STRATEGY IN AFGHANISTAN

On August 21, 2017, U.S. congressional officials were told that 4,000 more troops would be deployed to Afghanistan. This was in addition to the 8,500 already there. The plan, as President Trump declared[62], was to *"attack our adversaries, annihilate the Islamic State of Iraq and the Levant (ISIL), crush al-Qaeda, prevent the Taliban from taking control of the country, and prevent mass terror attacks against Americans before they occur."*

Let's take a closer look at President Trump's strategy and what happened with the war in Afghanistan from 2017 to 2018.

In August 2017, around 5,800 Afghans were killed in the war against the Taliban, while 18 American soldiers were killed in action. Sharing the Americans' frustration, President Trump revealed his new strategy for Afghanistan in a speech to the Nation on August 21, 2017.

The new strategy also engaged India to increase diplomatic and economic assistance, pressuring Pakistan to cooperate with the U.S. in its fight against terrorism.

In September 2017, the Trump administration increased U.S. troops by adding about 4,000 soldiers to fight against terrorism, leaving a total of more than 12,000 American soldiers in the country. But, according to President Trump, his new strategy differed from its predecessors because it did not have a fixed timeline or conditions for troops to leave. Joint Chief of Staff Joseph Dunford also recommended that the U.S. not withdraw its troops from Afghanistan. **The reason for this was that this would create instability in South Asia and allow terrorist groups to plan and carry out acts of terrorism against the American people.**

Read that last sentence again. If you're wondering why the U.S. was still in Afghanistan at this point, that right there is your answer.

The Afghan Institute for Strategic Studies Executive Director, Davood Moradian, said they were uplifted and reassured by President Trump's speech. This demonstrated confidence and resolution to the Afghans' besieged population and strained security forces.

On the other side, Kabul was now facing an internal subdivision. The Afghan government had been trying to gain the support of President Ashraf Ghani, who was now opposed to foreign troops being deployed in Afghanistan.

Trump declared shortly after taking office that he would delegate authority to the Pentagon to set military levels. Foreign policy analysts feared that this rapid increase of military troops might trigger a war similar to Pearl Harbor, the war that caused the death of 2,403 Americans.

Vice President Pence reassured everyone that the U.S. would not be dragged into another war. Instead, they would follow President Trump's "fight and win policy." He then began to brief the members of Congress on their new strategy in Afghanistan, where the Republicans praised the President's approach. But, at the same time, Democrats criticized the President and the lack of details.

Trump reiterated that the U.S. would not supply "unlimited" support and resources to calm the supporters› concerns. He continued that Afghanistan's government must carry the primary responsibility of their security and their share of the burden. The U.S. military would continue to be a part of it, but they also needed support from other countries, especially in economic assistance.

This new approach by President Trump to send more troops to Afghanistan was the outcome of a lengthy policy assessment conducted by his administration. After finalizing the plan with the top presidential advisers, President Trump supported a Pentagon plan to increase troop levels.

This decision reflected growing concern among military leaders that battlefield setbacks for Afghan government forces against the Taliban, al-Qaeda, and the Islamic State (and their affiliates) had led to a rapidly expanding territory in which these groups operated. This included pressuring the Pakistani border to prevent the Taliban from using safe havens there.

In a briefing, Mattis said that this number of troops would allow Afghan forces to more effectively target the Taliban and other extremist groups and carry out operations to reduce the threat in Afghanistan.

He stated that he would prioritize American security over any other interests. Further he said that the U.S. would no longer engage in nation-building but would focus on supporting Afghan forces to build their own country and fight terrorism.

President Trump's strategy for the war in Afghanistan was based on a three-pillar approach; to pressure Pakistan, bolster Afghan forces, and create conditions where terrorists could not find a safe haven.

The goal of this strategy was to reduce the number of civilian casualties and increase pressure on terrorist groups. Trump said he wanted to get the job done and would not pull out of Afghanistan.

In Afghanistan, President Trump was willing to follow his generals' advice, even if it meant reversing an earlier position of fighting against sending more troops into war zones.

On September 28, 2019, the Afghan presidential elections were held. There was a total of 18 presidential candidates, which included some ex-spies, former warlords, as well as members of the country's past communist government. However, five of those men (not a single woman ran for president) dropped out as time passed. The most notable of the remaining candidates were Ashraf Ghani, the country's incumbent President; Abdullah Abdullah, the incumbent Chief Executive of the National Coalition of Afghanistan; Gulbuddin Hekmatyar, a former Prime Minister, former warlord, and then leader of Hezb-e Islami, and Rahmatullah Nabil, a former Head of the National Directorate of Security.

Despite the deadly bomb attacks by militants and the heavy security placed across the country, people voted in Afghanistan's presidential poll. However, the turnout was historically low, with only 1.6 million people showing up out of the 9.7 million registered voters. To try and protect these voters, over 70,000 members of security forces were deployed.

Even with such security measures, at least four people were killed, and another 80 were wounded due to bomb and mortar attacks on voting centers. As a result, voter turnout was under 20%, with the low number being attributed to voters being concerned about threats from the Taliban.

Preliminary results showed that the incumbent president, Ashraf Ghani, had been re-elected. Due to disputes over the votes, delays occurred with the official results. Ghani was eventually declared the winner on February 18, 2020, holding 50.64% (923,592) of the votes. Runner-up Abdullah Abdullah rejected the results, commencing with his own inauguration and parallel government.

The announcement of these results led to a political crisis, as Abdullah Abdullah rejected the results and formed his government in northern Afghanistan. While Zalmay Khalilzad, an

American diplomat, tried to mediate between Abdullah and Ghani, they were unsuccessful in reaching an agreement. As a result, both ultimately took separate inaugurations on March 9, 2020.

The political turmoil between the two parties did not subside until May 16, 2020, when Ghani and Abdullah agreed to sign a power-sharing deal. It specified that while Ghani would remain the president and Abdullah was to lead the peace talks with the Taliban.

By March 23, 2020, the U.S. stated it would reduce its aid to Afghanistan by $1 billion or more if the two parties didn't agree. Finally, on May 17, 2020, Ghani and Abdullah signed a power-sharing deal that ended the political turmoil. However, Ashraf Ghani's presidency ended abruptly on August 15, 2021, when Taliban forces entered Kabul during the 2021 Taliban offensive.

As a result, Ghani fled the country, while Vice President Amrullah Saleh declared himself to be the transitional president in Bazarak, the capital of Panjshir Province. It was the last region still under the control of the government, but Saleh eventually had to leave. Then, on September 8, 2021, Panjshir was captured by the Taliban, who took complete control of the country.

Illegal drug cultivation and the drug trade have run rampant throughout Afghanistan for many years. Surprised? Don't be. While many in Afghanistan do not partake in illegal drugs, they have no qualms about selling them to non-Muslim communities across the globe.

Targeting Taliban drug labs and networks in Afghanistan, Operation Iron Tempest was a U.S. military campaign launched in 2017 and ended in late 2018.

Opium syrup that was produced from the crop of poppy fields in Afghanistan has been smuggled into different countries for many years. This syrup was used to create illicit substances such as heroin and morphine. You read that correctly. How do you think the insurgents (and portions of the government) are/were funding themselves? That's right, the drug trade.

Currently, a good portion of the refinement process happens in facilities across Afghanistan. While the Taliban previously banned poppy cultivation in the past, it has taken over the drug trade after it lost political power after being defeated by the U.S. military in 2001. According to the New York Post, approximately 65% of the current income of the Taliban is derived from opium trafficking.

Opium production under the Taliban is widespread in the south, particularly in Helmand Province. The group reportedly collects 10% taxes from poppy farmers. It also handles the trafficking of raw opium and heroin outside the country.

The U.S. military established Operation Iron Tempest in November of 2017. The campaign was part of the Trump administration's Afghanistan war strategy.

The Taliban was believed to operate around 500 drug laboratories. These facilities made it possible for the Taliban to earn an estimated $200 million a year, based on Stripes63 information. Using the revenue earned from these illegal operations, the Taliban was able to fund a significant portion of their operations.

The operation aimed to prevent the Taliban from gaining further profit from opium production and trafficking. The U.S. military launched hundreds of airstrikes targeting opium labs in Afghanistan.

However, Operation Iron Tempest failed in significantly decreasing the group's capacity to earn income from the illegal drug trade. As a result, the Defense of Department (DOD) Inspector General Operation announced that the campaign had ended officially as of the final quarter of 2018. The cessation of the operation took place as Trump administration officials held peace talks with Taliban leaders.

The campaign is just one of the costly failures in minimizing poppy cultivation and opium trafficking in Afghanistan. According to TIME, the U.S. has invested $8.9 billion in counternarcot-

---

63   "Stripes," Stars and Stripes, accessed July 12, 2022, https://www.stripes.com/.

ics activities since 2001. However, Afghanistan is still the source of approximately 85% of illicit opium all over the globe.

The airstrikes targeting the drug laboratories were numerous throughout the years against the illegal drug trade in Afghanistan. Troops stationed throughout Afghanistan had taken part over the many years in burning poppy fields, marijuana fields, and more.

After the failure of Operation Tempest, the U.S. government planned to establish other programs to curtail the drug trade in cooperation with the Afghanistan government. Nevertheless, the future of these programs was unclear because of various factors. Afghan President Ashraf Ghani has chosen to disband the Ministry of Counter Narcotics and consolidate it with different ministries.

In the Taliban's eyes, drugs are most definitely illegal. When they first seized control of Afghanistan in the 90s, from 1994 to 1996, they had completely banned anything and everything to do with everything related to illegal substances.

However, their stance would change come 1996 after they issued a new edict reading, "The cultivation of, and trading in chers (cannabis, used for hashish) is forbidden absolutely. The consumption of opiates is forbidden, as is the manufacture of heroin, but the production and trading in opium is not forbidden."64 And with that, they began taxing the farmers and the traffickers, generating a significant sum of money for the Taliban.

During an interview in 1997, an elderly farmer near Kandahar named Wali Jan expressed his gratitude to the Taliban, saying, *"We cannot be more grateful to the Taliban. The Taliban have brought us security so we can grow our poppy in peace. I need to grow poppy crop to support my 14 family members."*[65]

---

64   &58 Vanda Felbab-Brown, "Pipe Dreams: The Taliban and Drugs from the 1990s into Its New Regime," Brookings (Brookings, March 9, 2022), https://www.brookings.edu/articles/pipe-dreams-the-taliban-and-drugs-from-the-1990s-into-its-new-regime/.
65

Like a yo-yo effect, the Taliban would once again ban poppy cultivation in 1999. While their funding was severely impacted, the political cost to the Taliban was even greater.

During the Trump administration's tenure, the long-planned US-Taliban Peace Talks would finally come to fruition. To former President Donald Trump, the peace talks would set the wheels in motion toward what was to be a peaceful and self-governing Afghanistan.

The peace talks came to a close in February 2020. The outcome included a cease-fire that was observed by the negotiating parties — the U.S., the national government, and the Taliban.

Another resolved point was the withdrawal of U.S. and NATO forces from the region. The exit was agreed to be gradual, taking place over 135 days. Should the Taliban comply with all conditions, U.S. and NATO troops would completely withdraw from Afghanistan after 14 months.

The condition the Taliban needed to meet was for counterterrorism. But, given the history of Taliban insurgencies in the region, the United States and NATO saw it fit to opt for a prolonged exit.

The negotiations also pushed for Intra-Afghan negotiations — that is to say, peace talks between the Taliban and the Afghan government. As the Taliban branded the Afghan government as "in the pockets of Uncle Sam," the talks between the two parties proved challenging.

The peace talks were an opportunity to negotiate several pivotal goals for the prosperity and self-governance of Afghanistan. Among these goals was the gradual withdrawal of U.S. and NATO troops from the country. Others included reassurance from the Afghan government that Afghanistan would no longer be a haven for insurgent groups.

The peace talks of 2019 were meant to be between the Taliban and the U.S. However, with Afghanistan's national security concerns at the heart of the discussion, the Afghan government became the third interlocutor in the much-awaited discussion.

Afghanistan's national government desired the above-mentioned. Pursuant to the national security of the country, the Afghan government welcomed, albeit tacitly, a modicum of American and NATO intervention. The interventions were to be in the form of training and other forms of assistance, not involving direct military action.

The Taliban pushed for the swift withdrawal of U.S. forces and their NATO counterparts. Needless to say, the abrupt exit of the U.S. and NATO military presence in the country ran counter to America's and the Afghan government's aims.

This resulted in an obstacle on the discussion front. More specifically, the results became irreconcilable demands between the Taliban and the Afghan government. As a result, the challenge of negotiating peace talks between the Taliban and the Afghan national government grew more salient.

Though most Afghans supported the peace process, there were still many issues to be solved regarding intra-Afghan negotiations.

The war in Afghanistan led to mass casualties on every possible side—from U.S. service members to allies and to a significant number of citizens of Afghanistan. Plunging Afghanistan into two decades of geopolitical unrest, the war has created a clamor for peace within the region.

The calls and moves for a peaceful Afghanistan came to fruition as the United States and the Taliban engaged in dialogue on February 29, 2020.

The United States and the Taliban signed the Doha Agreement on this day. The Doha Agreement was envisioned as a pivotal step to bringing peace to the region after decades of war.

The Doha Agreement was meant to be a milestone in developing a self-governing Afghanistan. The agreement consisted of four pages visible to view on the U.S. State Department's website. The contents of the agreement involved the reduction of NATO's military presence and the ending of economic sanctions imposed on the country.

On the part of the Taliban, the agreement stipulated the protection of Taliban-controlled territories from insurgencies by Al-Qaeda and the release of prisoners.

The Agreement required the international community's backing to add legitimacy to its binding power. Among the handful of international bodies that oversaw the agreement was the United Nations Security Council.

The United Nations Security Council called for the full cooperation of the Taliban in severing its connections with international militant groups. Support for the agreement came from many nations, including Afghanistan's neighbor, Pakistan. India and Russia also voiced their support for the February 2020 agreement, with China following suit.

All countries expressing support for the agreement were unanimous in their sentiment. For Russia, China, Pakistan, and India, Afghanistan's sovereignty can only be asserted further through self-governance — the desired outcome of the agreement alongside regional peace.

The Doha Agreement contained stipulations on reducing military forces within the region and regional peace. More specifically, the agreement included a gradual reduction in NATO's military presence in Afghanistan. The withdrawal of military forces was to occur within a 14-month window, set to culminate around May of the following year.

Part of the withdrawal provisions were the closings of U.S. bases to take place within the projected 14-month time frame. The United States also pledged to ease and remove economic sanctions imposed on Afghanistan in exchange for compliance with the terms.

The complete and swift withdrawal of NATO forces was contingent upon the Taliban's ability to live up to the end of the agreement. On the part of the Taliban, it needed to ensure peace in the region in tandem with the Afghan government. This part of the agreement involved close coordination with the Afghan National Government and its security forces. In addition, the Taliban was expected to aid the national government in its mission to ward off insurgents, namely Al-Qaeda.

Another part of the agreement's terms was prisoner exchanges. In exchange for 5,000 prisoners held by Afghanistan's national government for insurgency-related charges, the Taliban had to set free 1,000 Afghan Security prisoners. The terms of prisoner exchange were agreed upon in the Intra-Afghan peace talks that took place in Oslo, Norway, weeks after the agreement's signing.

The United Nations Security Council ordered a region-wide cease-fire to facilitate the peace process. The cease-fire was set to be effective starting March 10, 2020, and was deemed necessary to the aims and objectives of the agreement.

Surprisingly, the Afghan government was not one of the parties involved in the Doha Agreement. However, since the goals and objectives involved the country, representatives from the Afghan government needed to be present in the Intra-Afghan Talks.

President Ghani traveled to Oslo alongside a negotiation team from his administration. In Oslo, the dialogue between the Afghan National Government and the Taliban took place. The talks were focused on furthering national interests. Along with other technical matters surrounding the agreement, one topic was of specific interest and dispute — the prisoner release agreement.

Early on, the Afghan president made it clear that he did not consent to nor agree with these terms. Nonetheless, on March 10, President Ghani signed a decree authorizing the release of 1,500 Taliban prisoners. However, a condition for the release was the non-reinstatement of the prisoners as Taliban fighters.

Taliban spokesperson, Suhail Shaheen, rejected the offer, adamantly pressing for the release of 3,500 more Taliban prisoners held in bases like Bagram. Discussions on the release of prisoners continued beyond Oslo until April 7, 2020.

April 7, 2020, marked the tensest moment of the prisoner exchange talks. During this time, Suhail Shaheen — alongside other members of the Taliban delegation — physically abandoned the location of the talks. According to the Taliban spokesperson, the negotiations have reached a "fruitless" point where the Afghan side refused to recognize its terms.

Eventually, under a new power-sharing regime, the Afghan government accommodated the Taliban's wishes, releasing 5,100 prisoners. Despite disagreements over specific prisoners who need to be released, the Taliban lived up to its end of the bargain. In August 2020, the Taliban released 1,000 prisoners, per the original terms of the prisoner swap agreement.

Despite the signing of the Doha Agreement, fighting in Afghanistan occurred concurrently to its effectiveness. Since the agreement's signing, there have been skirmishes in various parts of the country, including Helmand, a Taliban stronghold.

Withdrawing at a gradual pace as per the agreement, U.S. and Coalition forces remained in a limited capacity, only performing consultative roles. However, U.S. and Coalition forces continued to provide defensive support to Afghan Security Forces in many areas.

Fighting in the country prompted military action from the United States. Weeks before the planned complete withdrawal of NATO forces, the United States launched airstrikes on known Taliban strongholds. Pentagon spokesperson, Jonathan Hoffman, justified the actions by invoking the United States' role in safeguarding peace in the region.

June 22, 2020, saw numerous casualties on both sides. Afghan Security Forces suffered at the hands of numerous Taliban raids. The raids led to the deaths and injuries of more than 1,000 Afghan Security Force personnel. The Taliban also experienced its share of casualties, losing bases and hundreds of fighters across 18 provinces.

During the same week, reports surfaced about more than 40 civilians kidnapping. The kidnappings for which the Taliban claimed responsibility occurred mainly in Daykundi, a province in the central part of Afghanistan.

U.S. and Coalition forces had been withdrawing gradually since July 2020. The president at the time, Donald Trump, authorized the further withdrawal of U.S. forces until May 1, 2021 — the deadline of the Doha Agreement.

Concurrent to Trump's authorization, NATO Secretary-General followed suit, vowing the timely exit of more than 12,000 troops from the region. Initially, 12,000 troops would withdraw, with an additional 16,000 following the agreement's final date.

By July 1, 2020, more than 8,000 U.S. troops had already left Afghanistan. Trump originally wanted a drastic exit but was prevented by the U.S. Armed Services Committee. The Committee amended the National Defense Authorization Act by vote to prevent Trump from ordering the withdrawal of more troops.

The beginning of 2021 saw a changing of the guard in the U.S. presidency. First, President Joe Biden revisited the Doha Agreement›s terms pertaining to reducing military forces in Afghanistan. President Biden was under the guidance of his national security adviser, Jack Sullivan. The re-examination led to the total U.S. military withdrawal decision by August 31, 2021.

Elsewhere, other countries had already made their exits from Afghanistan. Germany and Italy were among the first Coalition countries to leave, fully withdrawing as early as July 2, 2021. Not long after, Australian military forces left the country on July 15, 2021.

Before August 31, 2021, only a few thousand troops were present in the country, and most were members of the U.S. military. The Taliban took control of the country shortly after, prompting a complete U.S. exit only one day before the planned date.

Chapter 13

PULLING OUT

"I made a commitment to the American people when I ran for President that I would bring America's military involvement in Afghanistan to an end. And while it's been hard and messy — and yes, far from perfect — I've honored that commitment.

More importantly, I made a commitment to the brave men and women who serve this nation that I wasn't going to ask them to continue to risk their lives in a military action that should have ended long ago. So, thank you. May God protect our troops, our diplomats, and all of the brave Americans serving in harm's way."
—President Joe Biden, August 2021.[66]

After years of justification against extending the U.S. military presence in Afghanistan, President Joe Biden decided on a total withdrawal by the anniversary of the 9/11 terrorist attacks, declaring an end to the country's longest war. Despite military officials' concerns that the departure could spark a revival of the same terrorist threats that have taken thousands of troops into battle over the previous two decades, Biden had already decided.

On April 14, 2021, President Biden made the final decision to withdraw the United States forces completely by 9/11, regard-

---

66   "Remarks by President Biden on Afghanistan," The White House (The United States Government, August 16, 2021), https://www.whitehouse.gov/briefing-room/speeches-remarks/2021/08/16/remarks-by-president-biden-on-afghanistan/.

less of the progress and result of the intra-Afghan peace talks. Whether the Taliban continued or ceased their attacks on Afghan National Security Forces and residents, the remaining U.S. troops in Afghanistan would be withdrawn. This came after his administration reviewed the US-Taliban peace deal, ensuring the Taliban followed through on their commitments.

However, Biden announced that the United States would continue to support Afghan forces and the peace process, even during the complete withdrawal of the troops.

On August 15, 2021, Taliban insurgents invaded Kabul and seized the presidential palace while forcing their way to establish an Islamic government. As President Ghani himself fled the nation, the invading Taliban forces encountered little to no resistance from Afghan forces.

Taliban commanders have said that they will meet with Afghan officials to construct an open, inclusive Islamic administration and that former Afghan President Hamid Karzai and Abdullah, who served as Ghani's top executive, will form a committee to promote a peaceful transfer of power to a Taliban government.

The world watched in horror as Kabul, the capital of Afghanistan, was handed over to the Taliban. Armed fighters seized the presidential palace — leaving Ashraf Ghani, the president of Afghanistan, no choice but to flee.

Taliban fighters spread across the capital, entering the deserted presidential palace. Kabul had been the last major Afghan city to hold out but succumbed to the Taliban's large numbers and formidable weaponry. Onlookers were surprised by how the city was almost effortlessly conquered.

The citizens of Kabul were crippled by panic and fear as soon as they heard the news. Civilians ran to the airport on foot, thinking it was the only way out of the impending chaos. People were rushing to banks, withdrawing all the money they had. Others barricaded themselves in their homes. Some citizens remained in parks and public areas, hoping for rescue.

Gunfire had been heard at the Kabul Airport, commercial flights were suspended, and military flights continued evacuating.

The U.S. had reportedly relocated its embassy to the airport, with troops trying to protect the area. However, Americans and their allied personnel continued their evacuations as the chaos ensued.

Although U.S. forces were still remaining in Afghanistan when the Taliban invaded Kabul, Biden maintained his decision to withdraw all the remaining U.S. forces completely. With the Taliban's takeover of Kabul, President Biden insisted that he made the correct decision by stopping U.S. military engagement in Afghanistan, claiming that the U.S. counterterrorism mission in Afghanistan was complete.

The Taliban claimed Kabul after President Ghani fled. Al Jazeera67 reported that President Ghani transferred to Tashkent, a neighbor of Afghanistan.

Before the sun set over Afghanistan's capital on August 15, the Taliban continued to attack city by city on motorbikes, terrorizing innocent citizens and gunning down anyone they considered "disobedient." Then, district by district, province by province collapsed, and the Afghan forces were either killed or had fled, surrendered, or denied their allegiance by stripping off their uniforms.

The President justified why American troops were withdrawn from the country by saying that American presence during another country's conflict was detrimental rather than beneficial. To remove this detriment, he implemented the evacuation order.

Meanwhile, Great Britain deployed 600 troops to evacuate their nationals. Boris Johnson, the U.K. Prime Minister, expressed that they prioritized those who have helped with their initiatives for over 20 years. This was done as safely and quickly as they could.

---

67   Al Jazeera, "Afghan President Ghani Flees Country as Taliban Enters Kabul," Ashraf Ghani News | Al Jazeera (Al Jazeera, August 16, 2021), https://www.aljazeera.com/news/2021/8/15/afghan-president-ghani-flees-country-as-taliban-surrounds-kabul.

In addition to the U.S. and U.K., other countries did their best to evacuate their nationals and close their embassies for protection. Russia expressed its intention to discuss the situation in Afghanistan through a U.N. Security Council emergency meeting. The country did not close its embassy because the Taliban reassured them that the fighters would not attack them.

Despite the Taliban's promise not to interfere with Kabul's business establishments and not trespass on people's homes, there were reported casualties, brutal acts, and revenge killings. Violence spread over the capital as the Taliban continued to impose their power over the civilians of Kabul.

The August 26 attack on Afghanistan's Hamid Karzai International Airport led to the deaths of 13 U.S. service members. The deceased service members were part of Operation Freedom Sentinel.

The military operation was a mission to facilitate the evacuation of U.S. civilians and personnel as Afghanistan transitioned to Taliban Control. Besides the 13 casualties the U.S. military sustained that day, the attacks also left 170 Afghans dead during the evacuation procedures.

According to General McKenzie Jr., U.S. CENTCOM commander, the August 26 attacks occurred mainly at the Abbey Gate of the Hamid Karzai International Airport in Kabul. The attacks happened at around 17:05 on Thursday, and explosions around the airport preceded them.

The explosion within the Abbey Gate resulted from a detonated explosive vest. Sources on the ground attributed the detonation to a suicide bomber. The suicide bomber detonated the vest along a canal near US-manned document processing posts, where many evacuees and U.S. service members happened to be.

Following the explosion, there were reports of gunfire. According to the Pentagon, militant fighters were seen firing on crowds at the airport's Abbey Gate during and shortly after the explosions.

The gunfire and explosions resulted in the deaths of the 13 service members identified earlier and at least 100 Afghans. The attacks also severely injured 100 other Afghans and 60 Taliban fighters.

Eleven marines, one navy corpsman, and a U.S. Army staff sergeant had been by the attack›s end. Following the incident, the respective military branches of the 13 service members notified family members and loved ones of their deaths in the line of duty.

Shortly after their families were notified, the deceased service members were identified publicly: Sergeant Johanny Rosaria Pichardo, Sergeant Nicole L. Gee, Staff Sergeant Darin T. Hoover, Corporal Hunter Lopez, Corporal Daegan W. Page, Corporal Humberto A. Sanchez, Lance Corporal David L. Espinoza, Lance Corporal Jared M. Schmitz, Lance Corporal Rylee L. McCollum, Lance Corporal Dylan R. Merola, Lance Corporal Kareem M. Nikoui, Navy Corpsman Maxton W. Soviak, and Army Staff Sergeant Ryan C. Knauss.

Twenty-four hours after the attacks, ISIL Khorasan (ISIL-K) went public, claiming full responsibility for the August 26 attack on Hamid Karzai International Airport. Pentagon sources have confirmed the suicide bombers' affiliations with the militant group with intelligence reports on the ground.

According to Reuters, the perpetrators had planned the attack days in advance. Reuters spoke to a Taliban official who interrogated a captured ISIL-K member seen at the airport days before the attack.

The ISIL-K member was seen going about the airport premises before being detained by the Taliban. Following the interrogation, the Taliban banned public gatherings on the 26th. The Taliban also advised its leaders to avoid public places due to the imminent attack.

While the motives behind the attacks were unclear, there have been speculations. The most prevalent, according to Reuters, was that the ISIL attacks were meant to destabilize the Western-backed leadership of Afghanistan.

The deaths of the 13 service members and at least 100 Afghans in the Abbey Gate attack reached Washington, prompting a response from President Joe Biden. Addressing the nation on the same day of the attack, President Biden expressed his condolences to the families and loved ones of the deceased.

During his speech, he made it clear that attacks similar to the one in Hamid Karzai International Airport would do little to deter or halt further US-led evacuation missions. In his address, he pledged retaliatory action against ISIS for their attacks on U.S. service members and civilians.

President Biden clarified that whatever form retaliation takes, the military would be precise in its approach. President Joe Biden said:

"With regard to finding, tracking down the ISIS leaders who ordered the attacks, we have reason to believe that we know who they are. We are not certain. We will find ways of choosing, without large-scale military operation, to get them — wherever they are."68

The president also recognized the heroic efforts of the service members who gave their lives for the values central to the United States. President Biden said that the brave service members were heroes for defending the country's values with their lives.

Certain Afghans, who aided U.S. and NATO forces in the decades-long war, were given a special immigrant visa (SIV), allowing them to take residence in the U.S. or other allied partner countries for their loyal service. However, there was a lack of progress in relocating members who participated in helping the country.

With the Taliban forces running rampant in their homeland, some Afghans were forced to keep their heads low and remain in hiding. With no major forces to stop the Taliban from raiding

---

68   "Remarks by President Biden on the Terror Attack at Hamid Karzai International Airport," The White House (The United States Government, August 27, 2021), https://www.whitehouse.gov/briefing-room/speeches-remarks/2021/08/26/re-marks-by-president-biden-on-the-terror-attack-at-hamid-karzai-international-airport/.

one town after another, the extremist group had become brazen in its attacks.

On August 30, 2021, the last and final American troops left Afghanistan, leaving the country under Taliban governance. The withdrawal came after a tumultuous two-week period in which the Taliban ruled Kabul.

Those who risked their lives fighting alongside U.S. troops or aiding them in other ways had been left to fend for themselves against the enemy they've long been fighting against.

As their hope teetered on a seeming tightrope, the abandoned Afghans tried to stay one step ahead of the rampaging extremist group. The surviving soldiers communicated via encrypted messaging tools.

Despite the efforts of the United States to relocate them, the process was painfully slow. The government was mainly focused on retrieving natural U.S. citizens and permanent residents during the evacuation.

Staying in one location for a long time was the equivalent of death for the surviving Afghan aids left behind. They felt utterly abandoned and hopeless without any communication from the United States.

According to Senior State Department officials, the U.S. government had done its best to retrieve these Afghans and provide them with a safe place to stay without specifying the government's action plan. Democratic Senator Richard Blumenthal shared in a senate hearing that he experienced difficulties in trying to reach out to the person or officer in charge of the rescue operation. This lack of clear communication caused a rift between Congress and the current administration.

Despite the government's lack of transparency and progress with the situation, several non-profit organizations took the matter into their own hands.

Independent U.S. veteran groups and former members of the U.S. Special Forces sent charter flights to help those we abandoned. The State Department didn't seem to support the veterans' voluntary rescue operative.

Digital Dunkirk, Pineapple Express, Project Dynamo, and No One Left Behind are some non-profit organizations that worked tirelessly to save those left behind.

No One Left Behind co-founder Matt Zeller expressed his frustration at the lack of progress from the U.S. government. Zeller is one of the many citizens that sounded the alarm and pushed the government to hasten its efforts to rescue the abandoned allies.

A ray of hope existed amidst this darkness as more and more people united to save the lives of the forgotten Afghan allies. The U.S. government may have abandoned them, but the citizens did not let them down.

Anonymous

Like everyone else, I can recall precisely where I was on September 11, 2001. It was my birthday, and I was on the phone with my mom. She would call me every year on my birthday to wish me a happy birthday. I had just turned 32 that day.

When I left for Afghanistan, I wasn't in the military—I went over as a civilian contractor. You could say I fell backward into the job after I had moved away from my job in home automation. The career switch resulted from feeling under-appreciated and under-utilized—not to mention drastically underpaid. In fact, I was never in the military at all.

I volunteered for a six-month deployment in 2009 and ended up staying in Afghanistan for ten almost consecutive years, returning home in 2019.

My role there was to provide IT support for a DoD (Department of Defense) contract that assisted with medical treatments. When I arrived in the country, I was 39 and married with no kids.

I recall how I felt boarding the plane to depart for my tour in Afghanistan. I was excited. I had worked hard to be considered for the position and was looking forward to finally feeling like I would be doing something important. But, until then, it felt like I had been coasting since 9/11.

During my ten years in Afghanistan, I spent time on quite a few different FOBs: Bagram, Kandahar, Bastion, Fenty, Salerno, Ghazni, Lagman, Qalat, Shank, Sharana, Khilegai, MEZ, Dwyer, Qal e Naw, Bala Murghab, Phoenix, Kabul Embassy, Shindand, Asadabad, Bostick, Herat, Farah, Pasab, Walton, Tarin Kowt, Scorpion, Orgun-e, Meymenah, a CIA base I can't name, and several other remote locations I can't recall. Despite having spent a few months in Iraq before this tour, I was stunned by the sheer size of Bagram Airfield. Whereas Bagram was almost like a little city, some of the other FOBs I mentioned were small in size and consisted of little more than camo covers and Hesco barriers. My living quarters were also vastly different. I sometimes stayed in private quarters with my own shower in a 400-person circus tent.

Morale amongst myself and those I worked with varied. As I had been working with the medical personnel, traumas and massacres brought the morale down amongst everyone. However, we found a way to create our positives.

After spending that long in theater, it's hard to leave without any good or bad memories.

I remember trying to throw a BBQ for the medical, CCAT, and dust-off crews every six months to provide everyone with at least one good day over there.

While there, I also started a branch of the Talibanned Cigar Aficionado Club at Bagram and went so far as to help others start up their branches at other locations in Afghanistan. Cigar nights were always a good time.

Holidays over there was always a good time as well.

Birthdays after 9/11 were always strange for me, beginning in 2001 when I lost my friend, Eric Eisenberg. I stopped celebrating my birthday after that. It was always a bad day in theater, especially for me. However, despite my best efforts to avoid celebrating my birthday, someone would inevitably find out it was my birthday. Next thing you know, cookies, cupcakes, and a collection of other goodies would be presented. My favorite birthday was when I turned 40 in Iraq. A great friend used the office fail/win of the day board to award me both; fail for being old and win for finally making it over the hill.

The little things on a deployment meant more than you could imagine.

There were more bad memories, though, than I care to remember. However, I'll share a few.

One day, a group of Afghan children had come in with trauma. The older brother had found an RPG, and while they were playing with it, they accidentally fired it. Traumas involving children and working dogs were always the worst there, and those kids were all in bad shape.

In a different incident, we had a young Marine who had spent a ton of time at the hospital as a patient guard. The entire staff at the hospital knew him well. A few weeks after he rotated to a different job, he was back in the hospital as a patient. I remember going to the trauma czar and informing him that every staff member knew this kid. Based on the severity of his injuries, we knew there was a good chance he wouldn't survive. But, after spending the night anxiously awaiting updates, he survived. That young Marine was a husband with his first child.

Another day out there, it was right before Thanksgiving in 2016; a massive explosion awakened me. A suicide bomber had waited until the base had decided to do a marathon-style run and had planned to attack. However, his efforts were somewhat foiled when a member of the 1st Cavalry Division spotted someone looking out of place and approached him. The suicide bomber panicked and detonated. Within seconds of the blast, I was standing outside our ER as I lived in the Conex behind the hospital. That morning, the hospital was short-handed as a large portion of the staff had joined in on the morning run.

There was a long pause between the suicide bomber detonating and the first wave of patients. Our thoughts were on our co-workers and whether they had been injured (or worse) in the detonation, so we were very stressed out. There had been hundreds of people participating in the run that morning, but luckily there had only been four killed as a result of that blast instead of mass casualties. It could have been much worse. Thanks to that member of the 1st Cavalry Division, there weren't more casualties. And fortunately, with the majority of the medical personnel there at the run, they could give aid on-site to those in dire need. I don't care to imagine what that day would have looked like if the suicide bomber hadn't been spotted early on. The number of mass casualties, including medics, nurses, doctors, and surgeons, would have been catastrophic if he had detonated in the dense crowd of people at the beginning of the race.

On a happier note, I can tell you that many patients who came through Bagram heard me tell them that every time they saw my ugly face, their day was getting a little bit better. I knew I would end up seeing them as they went further along through the trauma process. Sometimes I would ask them crazy questions like, "Have you been drinking and driving?" But, again, it's the little things that make a difference.

As an unarmed civilian, I was afforded the opportunity to go outside the wire (leave the base). I was always a passenger, the guy who always learned the hard way. I visited all those FOBs I mentioned earlier, traveling approximately every three to four days. Convoys were fun until they weren't.

Depending on the location, the towns and villages all varied drastically. Areas around Kabul were more modernized, reminding me of places I'd visited in Thailand, Indonesia, and Honduras. However, some of those villages we'd traveled through were farming villages. They had mud-walled compounds with mud brick buildings and dirt floors.

The locals were generous and sincere people. They were farmers who wanted to return to their lives, raising their families and maintaining their animals and crops. Afghans are proud people who couldn't take a gift without returning one and would share the last of their food. In addition, they were extremely grateful for advanced medical care and solutions to medical issues such as infections, rashes, scurvy, etc.

I worked with a number of Afghans on the bases. Many locals worked on the bases as interpreters or helped with maintenance and cleaning facilities. They have a fantastic sense of humor. And when there were only men around, the jokes and humor grew more inappropriate or dirty, if you will. However, inappropriate conversations never happened while women were present. The locals quickly adapted to new situations, technologies, and experiences.

From the early days of my arrival in Iraq to my last day leaving Afghanistan, I met the most amazing people. I celebrated birthdays, anniversaries, births, or even engagements with those folks. I was there to witness the first blossoms of love and to see them now married with their own kids. I made lifelong friends that I could never be separated from. And I adopted hundreds of those I worked with as my own kids.

I did know people who had been killed in Afghanistan, but I am not sure it's my place to recount what happened. But, I'll say, I lost far too many people both over there and when they came home—enough to last me ten lifetimes.

While on Bagram, there were processions for honorable departures and angel flights. It was heartbreaking and insanely mentally draining. It's nauseating to think of how little time they had, what they lost, and what they will never see or do.

If I had been given the opportunity to go back over there, I would have taken it.

I believe that our goal in Afghanistan was to stand up to the oppressive insanity of terrorism. Looking back, I don't think we accomplished that. We left them in worse shape than we found them. We abandoned the Afghans that risked their lives to help us. We left them to be hunted down by animals with no value for human life. I have stacks of photos of ID cards and personal information of people I worked with over there that our government abandoned.

While we were over there fighting the war, I think we did everything we could to make a better life for the amazing people of Afghanistan. However, we could have focused more on keeping terrorists out of the country. Instead, we abandoned the people of Afghanistan to the very terrorists we were over there fighting.

Looking back, the good we accomplished was in trying to build a desperately needed infrastructure so that the people of Afghanistan could become self-sufficient by selling their resources. I feel like I played a part in the good that we accomplished. I helped save lives, improve medical treatment, and deliver desperately needed medical equipment.

In pulling out of Afghanistan, what more is there to say other than we failed.

As hard as I tried to distance myself to ensure I wouldn't have to feel the horrendous pain of losing people or the emotional instability of having them as patients, they managed to push their way in. They refused to allow me to isolate myself. These friends, my kids, check in on me as often as I check in on them. I learned so much from them, even to this day. I've never felt more heartbreak than when I witnessed one of them losing someone or losing one of them myself. Yet, I've never felt more valued, supported, or loved than I have with them.

We can never support them enough for my liking. Those that served over there can never be compensated enough for what they went through together. I will *never* accept that there isn't more we could be doing for them. These are my kids, and I would protect them with my life if needed.

When I consider my war cost, here's what I can say.

It cost me ten years of missed Christmas, Thanksgiving, birthdays, weddings, funerals, and births.

It cost me my marriage and several relationships.

It cost me friends that I've lost to war, to PTSD, to illnesses they deny are connected to burn pits, sarin gas exposure, living next to "poo ponds," TBIs, to more than we can account for.

It cost me my sleep.

It cost me my sense of humor.

It cost me ten years of damage from untreated rheumatoid arthritis.

It cost me friends who we left behind to be murdered by terrorists.

It left me with scars, both mental and physical.

It left me with PTSD.

It left me with the graves of young men and women.

And yet, it also gave me a new family, people I chose to be my brothers and sisters, my kids—for life.

CONCLUSION

"And the truth is that all veterans pay with their lives. Some pay all at once, while others pay over a lifetime."—J.M. Storm.

The U.S. Invasion of Afghanistan began on October 7, 2001, less than a month after 9/11.

What followed was a lengthy and costly conflict with no clear victory in sight. The U.S. poured billions of dollars into the war effort, with the total cost estimated to be over $2.313 trillion—that's roughly $300 million per day. This includes increases to the Pentagon's base military budget, the reconstruction and democratizing of Afghanistan and training of its military, and spending on veterans in the Veteran Affairs system.

The Defense Department Overseas Contingency Operations (OCO) budget for Afghanistan in 2021 was $1.055 billion. This is followed by the estimated interest of $532 billion accrued on the debt from fighting the war.

Of course, the monetary cost is only one part of the equation. 2,448 US soldiers were killed in the war, with many more wounded. The human cost is immeasurable and something that we must never forget.

This does not include the cost of caring for the thousands of veterans who have returned home with physical and mental injuries. Through fiscal 2022, the U.S. Government spent $465 billion on disability and medical care for military personnel and veterans.

This figure does not yet include the future costs associated with future health care and disability for veterans of the Afghanistan war. When these are factored in, the total cost could exceed $2 trillion, according to a Harvard University scholar.

Allied service members, including NATO member states, have also paid a heavy price. One thousand one hundred forty-four died between 2001 and 2021, making it the deadliest war in NATO history.

Afghan civilians have also been caught in the crossfire. It's estimated that over 47,000 have been killed since 2001, with many more being wounded or displaced. The war has also taken a toll on the country's infrastructure, with much of it being destroyed.

The Afghan national military and police also suffer from high casualty rates. Sixty-six thousand have been killed. Since aid workers and journalists were also targeted, it made it more difficult to provide humanitarian assistance and information to reach those who need it most. More than 500 media and aid workers have been killed since 2001.

The combat veteran suicide rate is also alarmingly high.

According to a study published by Brown University, over 30,000 active-duty military personnel and veterans have committed suicide. The statistic is not just Afghanistan War veterans but all post-9/11 veterans. The study shows how traumatic brain injuries, post-traumatic stress disorder, military sexual trauma, and abuse have driven many to suicide. It also cited how the military's lack of mental health resources and the stigma surrounding seeking help have contributed to the problem. Experts agree that the veteran suicide rate is alarmingly high and are an issue that needs to be addressed.

While the war in Afghanistan may be over, the cost will continue to be paid for years. We must never forget the sacrifices made.

It is clear that the war has taken a heavy toll on all involved, and it's something that we must never forget.

All of this begs the question—was the war in Afghanistan worth it? Did we achieve our goals and complete the mission?

After all this time and all these lives lost, what have we achieved? Unfortunately, it's a question that doesn't have an easy answer.

Dubbed the longest war in U.S. history, the war in Afghanistan has come at a high cost. Not just in terms of money but also in lives lost. This clearly shows how wars are not just fought on the battlefield but also have long-lasting effects that are felt by many long after the fighting has stopped. Therefore, we must never forget this when sending our men and women into combat.

Want to hear more about what life was like for troops that served in Afghanistan? You can read more of their stories—including my own—in my forthcoming book *At What Cost: Voices From the Battlefields of Afghanistan,* set to be released in January 2023.

The Final Roll Call

The final roll call is a military tradition to honor those who have fallen. It is conducted as part of a unit's memorial ceremony. The final roll call's purpose is to honor the fallen and allow their comrades to pay their final respects. Performed at the conclusion of the unit's memorial service, the final roll call reminds us that the unit's formation is incomplete.

Below is an example of the final roll call, a military tradition to honor those who have fallen.

First Sergeant[69]: "Sergeant Smith"

Sergeant Smith: "Here, First Sergeant."

First Sergeant: "Specialist Jones"

Specialist Jones: "Here, First Sergeant."

First Sergeant: "Private First Class Lee"

Private First Class Lee: "Here, First Sergeant."

First Sergeant: "Private First Class Doe"

(silence)

First Sergeant: "Private First Class John Doe"

---

69   *The commander of the fallen troop(s) designates three soldiers to be present at the ceremony to participate in the final roll call. For the sake of this book, they are named Smith, Jones, and Lee. The deceased is Private First Class John A. Doe.*

(silence)

First Sergeant: "Private First Class John A. Doe"

(silence)

The seven members of the honor guard team, located just outside the chapel, would then fire three-volley shots for a 21-gun salute.

As the last shot rings out, the rifle team brings their weapons to present arms.[70]

The bugler now begins to play Taps.

From October 7, 2001, to September 11, 2021, 2,448 brave men and women were killed in action while serving in Afghanistan. We will never forget the sacrifice they made. Nor will we forget the sacrifice their loved ones made.

As a tribute to those we've lost, below you'll find a list of every service member who gave their life during this conflict in Afghanistan.

SPC	AAMOT, AARON SETH
SPC	ABAD, SERGIO SAGONI
SGT	ABBATE, MATTHEW THOMAS
SGT	ABEYTA, CHRISTOPHER PAUL
SSG	ACEVES, OMAR
SPC	ACOSTA, EDWARD JOSEPH
SPC	ACOSTA, RUDY ALEXANDER
CPT	ADAMKAVICIUS, CLAYTON LEE
SPC	ADAMS, CHRISTIAN MICHAEL
MSG	ADAMS, DANIAL RONALD
SGT	ADAMS, RYAN CHRISTOPHER
SSG	ADAMSKI, FRANK EDWARD III
SFC	ADKINS, CHARLES LEWIS
SPC	ADKINS, TREVOR BRANDON
SSG	ADKINSON, VINSON BRYON III
SGT	AGUILA, FRANCISCO XAVIER

---

70   *Present arms is a salute for service members holding a weapon.*

SGT	AGUILAR, AMARU
SGT	AGUON, EUGENE MICHAEL
SPC	AHMED, SHANE HASAN
SSG	AINSWORTH, JESSE WAYNE
SGT	AKINS, KEVIN DONUDELL
SGM	ALBERT, PHILLIP ROBERT
SGT	ALCARAZ, RAYMOND CHAVEZ JR
SRA	ALDEN, NICHOLAS JEROME
SPC	ALECKSEN, ERICA PAIGE
SGT	ALEMAN, NICHOLAS JOSE
SSG	ALEXANDER, LEROY EDWARD
2LT	ALEXANDER, TOBIAS CHRISTOPH
1LT	ALLBAUGH, JOSEPH TRENT
SGT	ALLEN, JUSTIN BRADLEY
SSG	ALLEN, NEKL BRUCE
PFC	ALLERS, THOMAS CRAIG
CW3	ALLGAIER, CHRISTOPHER MICHAEL
SGT	ALLISON, THOMAS FERRELL
SPC	ALT, EMBER MARIE
SSG	ALTMANN, JOSEPH JAMES
SPC	ALVAREZ, KENNETH CLIFFORD
MAJ	AMBARD, PHILIP DAVE
SSG	AMMERMAN, MATTHEW RYAN
LT	AMMON, JEFFREY ALAN
SGT	AMORES, JASON GIL
SSG	AMPER, NICANOR IV
CPL	AMUNDSON, WILLIAM MADDEN JR
SPC	ANDERS, MABRY JAMES
PV2	ANDERSON, BILLY GENE
SPC	ANDERSON, BRIAN MICHAEL
SPC	ANDERSON, MARC ANTHONY
LCPL	ANDERSON, NICHOLAS ROBERT
CPT	ANDERSON, TIMOTHY SHAUN
PFC	ANDRADE, JOHN EDWARD SR

2LT	ANDREWS, DARRYN DEEN
MSGT	ANDREWS, EVANDER EARL
SPC	ANDREWS, SCOTT ANTHONY
SGT	ANGUS, DANIEL MCKINNON
SSGT	ANTONIK, CHRISTOPHER JOHN
PFC	APARICIO, CARLOS ARTURO
SFC	APOLINAR, MARTIN RAMON
LCPL	ARAGON, CARLOS ALBERTO
CPT	ARCHULETA, TAMARA LEE
SFC	ARD, DUSTIN BRUCE
LCPL	ARGENTINE, JAMES DAVID
SGT	ARGONISH, JAN MICHAEL
SSG	ARIZMENDEZ, MARC A
SFC	ARRECHAGA, OFREN
CPL	ARRUDA, RAPHAEL RODRIGUES
SPC	ARSENAULT, BRIAN K
SGT	ASHLEY, JOSHUA RYAN
SSG	ASHLOCK, VINCENT WAYNE
SGT	ATIM, PAUL JED
SGT	ATWELL, BRADLEY WAYNE
MAJ	AUSBORN, JEFFREY ONIAL
PFC	AUSTIN, ALAN JEROME
PFC	AUSTIN, BARRETT LYLE
PO2	AXELSON, MATTHEW GENE
CW2	AYALA, DAVID
CPL	AYERS, JONATHAN RYAN
SGT	AYUBE, JAMES ANTHONY II
LCPL	BABINE, TRAVIS THORNTON
PFC	BACKUS, BRIAN JOHN
SPC	BADIE, DAVID JOHN
SSG	BAGWELL, CHARLIE LANE
CPL	BAILEY, MICHAEL CHAD
PV2	BAILEY, MICHAEL VINCENT
PFC	BAKER, CODY GLEN

LCPL	BAKER, DAVID RAYMOND
SFC	BAKER, JEFFREY CHRISTOPHER
SGT	BALDRIDGE, DILLON CHRISTOPHER
SGT	BALDUF, KEVIN BRIAN
LTC	BALDWIN, ROBERT FRANCIS
MSG	BALL, SCOTT ROWEN
CW2	BALLI, EDWARD
LCPL	BALTAZAR, CHRISTOPHER SHAWN JR
SGT	BALTHASER, JESSE MICHAEL
CAPT	BANCROFT, MATTHEW WILLIAM
SGM	BANKS, BARBARALIEN
MSG	BANNAR, GEORGE ALLEN JR
LCPL	BARBOZAFLORES, PEDRO ANTONIO
LCPL	BARFIELD, JASON NICHOLAS
SSG	BARNARD, SHANE STANLEY
MAJ	BARNES, ROCCO MARTIN
CSM	BARRERAS, MARTIN RAY
SFC	BARRETO ORTIZ, ELIS ANGEL
CAPT	BARRETT, BRANDON AARON
SGT	BARRETT, ROBERT JOHN
SGT	BARRY, MICHAEL CHRISTOPHER
SSGT	BARTELT, JUSTUS STEVEN JOE
CAPT	BARTLE, DANIEL BENJAMIN
SPC	BARTON, CHRISTOPHER RYAN
1SG	BARTON, ROBERT NICHOLAS II
LTC	BARTZ, PAUL ROBERT
LCPL	BASTEAN, JORDAN STEPHEN
CPL	BATEMAN, JON-LUKE
PFC	BATES, BRIAN RUSSELL JR
SPC	BATISTA, JONATHAN
SSG	BATTLE, RAYVON JR
SPC	BAUER, JOSEPH ANDREW
MAJ	BAUGUESS, LARRY JOHN JR
SSG	BAUM, TANE TRAVIS

SGT	BAUMANN, RYAN PATRICK
CPL	BAUNE, TAYLOR JOHN
SGT	BAYS, WILLIAM MARSHALL
SSG	BAYSORE, THOMAS ALLEN JR
SGT	BEACHNAW, LUCAS TYLER
SFC	BEALE, JOHN CURTIS
SFC	BEALE, JOSHUA ZACHARY
SSG	BEAR, JORDAN LOGAN
SGT	BEASLEY, BOBBY EDWARD
PO2	BEAUCHAMP, CLAYTON ROSS
SGT	BECKERMAN, MICHAEL JOE
SPC	BEDOY, GENARO
LTC	BELKOFER, THOMAS PATRICK
SRA	BELL, BRYAN RICHARD
SGT	BELL, CHRISTOPHER ROGER
SGT	BELL, JEROME CHARLES JR
1SG	BELL, RUSSELL RYAN
SSGT	BELL, VINCENT JAMES
PFC	BELMONTES, JOSE OSCAR
SSG	BENITEZ, CARLOS ALONZO
MSGT	BENJAMIN, ADAM FRANK
1LT	BENNEDSEN, ROBERT N
SGT	BENNETT, ALEXANDER JAMES
LCPL	BENNETT, DANIEL RYAN
SSG	BENNETT, KENNETH WADE
CPO	BENSON, DARRIK CARLYLE
SPC	BENSON, KEITH DAVID
SPC	BERISFORD, JULIAN LEE
SSGT	BERKY, BRYAN DAVID
LCPL	BERNARD, JOSHUA MATTHEW
SPC	BERNIER, NICHOLAS PAUL WILFRED
LTC	BERRETTINI, RICHARD JOSEPH
SSG	BERRY, RICHARD LIAM
PFC	BERTOLINO, MATTHEW LEE

LCPL	BERTRAND, BRYAN PAHL
SPC	BERTRAND, CORY JOSEPH
SSG	BESSA, JEREMY EUGENE
SGT	BIGAI BAEZ, RAFAEL ENRIQUE
CPO	BILL, BRIAN ROBERT
CW2	BILLINGS, RANDY LEE
SGT	BILLINGS, ROBERT JOHN
PFC	BILLINGSLEY, TRAMAINE JAMAL
LCPL	BIRCHFIELD, JOSHUA HAROLD
SSG	BIRDWELL, CHRISTOPHER JAMES
CPL	BISHOP, JOHN CHRISTIAN
SSG	BISHOP, KEITH ROBERT
MSG	BITNER, BENJAMIN FRANKLIN
1SG	BLAIR, JOHN DAVID
PV2	BLAKE, JOSEPH ROBERT
SGT	BLAMIRES, JESSE ALLEN
CPT	BLANCHARD, AARON ROY
SGT	BLANEY, JOSHUA CHARLES
SGT	BLASJO, AARON JOSEPH
SFC	BLASKOWSKI, MATTHEW DEAN
SSG	BLASS, STEVEN PATRICK
SGT	BLESSING, JAY ANTHONY
SPC	BLEVINS, WILLIAM SETH
PFC	BOARD, CODY ALLEN
SFC	BOATWRIGHT, ALVIN ALGERNON
SSGT	BOCK, MICHAEL ANDREW
SGT	BOCKS, PHILLIP ALLEN
LCPL	BOELK, JAMES DAVID
CPL	BOGAR, JASON MICHAEL
SGT	BOHALL, THOMAS ANDREW
SFC	BOHLE, BRADLEY SCOTT
SGT	BOHLER, PETER CHRISTOPHER
SGT	BOLEN, EDWARD HUBALEK
CSM	BOLYARD, TIMOTHY ALLEN

SSGT	BONACASA, LOUIS MICHAEL
SFC	BONIFACE, ROBERT RODRIGO
SSG	BORDER, JEREMIE SHANE
CPO	BORDER, RAYMOND JAMES
CPL	BORDONI, CHRISTOPHER DAVID
CPT	BORIS, DAVID ALBIN
SGT	BORJAS, FEDERICO GUERRA
SGT	BORN, JOSHUA ALAN
MAJ	BOSTICK, THOMAS GORDON JR
HMC	BOURGEOIS, MATTHEW JOSEPH
SGT	BOVIA, JOSEPH ANTHONY
SSG	BOWDEN, JOSHUA JAMES
SSG	BOWEN, CLAYTON PATRICK
SFC	BOWEN, COLLIN J
MSG	BOWERS, JAMAL HASAN
SSGT	BOWLES, TIMOTHY LOUIS
SPC	BOWMAN, BRIAN ROBERT
1LT	BOWMAN, TREVARIUS RAVON
CPL	BOYD, CHRISTOPHER JOHN
SSG	BRABANDER, DAVID THOMAS
PFC	BRADBURY, BRIAN JAY
CPT	BRADEN, MICHAEL CEAN
SGT	BRADLEY, MARK ANDREW
1LT	BRADSHAW, BRIAN N
SPC	BRAGG, MIKAYLA ANNE
LCPL	BRAGGS, RANDY RASHAD
CPT	BRAINARD, JOHN R III
PO2	BRAZAS, SEAN EDWARD
SGT	BRENNAN, JOSHUA CHARLES
LCPL	BRENNAN, JULIAN THOMAS
SGT	BREWSTER, BRYAN ALLEN
SPC	BRISENO ALVAREZ, FRANCISCO JAVIER JR
SSG	BRITTON-MIHALO, ANDREW TREVOR
LCPL	BRIXEY, BILLY DON JR

PFC	BROCHU, JORDAN MYKLE
MAJ	BRODEUR, DAVID LAWRENCE
PO1	BRODSKY, MICHAEL JOHN
LCPL	BROEHM, MATTHEW JAMES
1LT	BROSTROM, JONATHAN PAUL
CPO	BROWN, ADAM LEE MR
SFC	BROWN, ALLAN ERIC
SSG	BROWN, CHRISTOPHER LAWRANCE
SSG	BROWN, DANIEL JOSEPH
LCPL	BROWN, JARED WILLIAM
SPC	BROWN, JEREMY LYNN
TSGT	BROWN, JOHN WILLIAM
PV2	BROWN, MATTHEW WARREN
PO1	BROWN, MILTON W
SPC	BROWN, SETERIA LAFAYE
MSGT	BROWN, TARA RENIECE
SGT	BROWN, WILLIAM DEWITT III
SFC	BROWN, WILLIAM RUSSELL
SSG	BROWNING, CHARLES ROBERT
LCPL	BRUMMUND, GAVIN RODERICK
MSG	BRUNER, THOMAS LEE
SSG	BRUNKHORST, SCOTT WILLIAM
LTCOL	BRYANT, FRANK DIEHL JR
GYSGT	BRYSON, STEPHEN LAMON
SSGT	BUBACZ, ANDREW STEPHEN
LCPL	BUCKLEY, GREGORY THOMAS
LCPL	BUENAGUA, ARDENJOSEPH AYUSON
CPL	BUFFALO, LOREN MILES
SGT	BULL, DOUGLAS JOHN
SSG	BULLARD, JAMES DAVID
TSGT	BUNN, LARRY DOLAN
CPT	BUNTING, BRIAN MATTHEW
SRA	BURAS, MICHAEL JOHN
SSG	BURGESS, BRYAN ALLAN

SSG	BURGESS, SCOTT HAMILTON
SSG	BURKHOLDER, JASON EVAN
SPC	BURLEY, NICHOLAS BRIAN
HN	BURNETT, DUSTIN KELBY
SPC	BURNETT, JAMES ROLAND JR
CPL	BURNSIDE, ANTONIO CARLOS
LCPL	BURROW, DENNIS JAMES
SGT	BURY, BRANDON COLE
SPC	BUTCHER, SARINA NICOLE
SSG	BUTLER, AARON RHETT
SGT	BUTLER, THOMAS JEFFERSON IV
PFC	BUTTRY, BRANDON LUCAS
SPC	BUTZ, JAMES ARLAN
SPC	BUXBAUM, JUSTIN LEE
CPL	BUYES, ADAM JOSEPH
SGT	BUZINSKI, KEITH THOMAS
MAJ	BYERS, ANDREW DAVID
PFC	BYRD, JORDAN MATTHEW
LTJG	BYUS, STEPHEN FRANKLIN
SSG	CABACOY, CHRISTOPHER FRANCIS
SSG	CABAN, ERIC
SGT	CABLE, MICHAEL CHRISTOPHER
LTC	CABRERA, DAVID ELLIOT
SGT	CAHIR, WILLIAM JOHN
CPL	CAIN, JUSTIN JAMES
SPC	CAIN, NORMAN LEWIS III
MAJ	CALERO, JEFFREY RAY
SGT	CALHOUN, MARVIN RAY JR
SGT	CALLAHAN, SEAN TIMOTHY
CPL	CALLOWAY, ISAIAH
SGT	CALO, JASON DEAN
LCPL	CAMERO, CHRISTOPHER LABIANO
TSGT	CAMPBELL, ANTHONY CHARLES JR
CPO	CAMPBELL, CHRISTOPHER GEORGE

SSG	CAMPBELL, DAMION GARLAND
SPC	CAMPBELL, JOSHUA ROSS
SGT	CAMPBELL, KARL ANDREW
SPC	CAMPOS, GERARDO
LCPL	CANHAM, DUSTIN LEE
PO3	CANNON, MARK RUSSELL
PFC	CANTU, SHANE WILLIAM
SSG	CARABALLO PIETRI, JOSE MANUEL
LTCOL	CARAZO, MARIO DELOSANGELES
PO2	CARBULLIDO, ANTHONY MARK
SSG	CARDENAZ, MICHAEL DAVID P
SPC	CARDOZA, KEVIN
SPC	CARLSON, DANIEL LEWIS
SSG	CARNES, NICHOLAS RAY
MSG	CARNEY, SCOTT MICHAEL
SPC	CARON, JOSEPH THIERRY
LCPL	CARPENTER, ANDREW PAUL
SPC	CARROLL, JACOB CHARLES
SGT	CARROLL, PATRICK RYAN
MAJ	CARRON, PAUL DOUGLAS
CPL	CARSE, NATHAN BROCK
PO1	CARSON, SEAN PATRICK
SPC	CARTER, CURTISS ANTHONY
CW4	CARTER, DAVID RUDOLPH
CW4	CARTER, JAMES
SGT	CARTWRIGHT, CHARLES ISSAC
CPL	CARVER, JACOB RUSSELL
LCPL	CARVER, ROSS STEVEN
1LT	CARWILE, DONALD CLAYTON
SGT	CASEY, NICHOLAS ANTHONY
PFC	CASILLAS, JUSTIN AARON
SGT	CASKEY, JOSEPH DAVIS
LCPL	CASSADA, JESSIE ADAM
HN	CASTIGLIONE, BENJAMIN PHILLIP

SPC	CASTRO, ANDREW JORDAN
SGT	CASTRO, JOHN PAUL
SFC	CATHCART, MICHAEL ANTHONY
LCPL	CATHERWOOD, ALEC ERNST
SPC	CATLETT, MATTHEW RYAN
SPC	CAULEY, GEORGE WALTER
CPL	CAZAREZ, ROBERTO
SFC	CELIZ, CHRISTOPHER ANDREW
SPC	CEMPER, JOSEPH BRIAN
LCPL	CENICEROS, IRVIN MARTIN
LCPL	CENTANNI, RICK JOSEPH
SPC	CERROS, RICARDO JR
SFC	CERVANTES, VICTOR HUGO
CPT	CHAFFIN, JAMES EDWARD III
SGT	CHAMBERS, DAVID JAMES
SPC	CHANDLER, CHRISTIAN JACOB
CPT	CHANDLER, JEREMY ALAN
SFC	CHAPLEAU, KRISTOPHER DAVID
MSGT	CHAPMAN, JOHN ALLAN
SFC	CHAPMAN, NATHAN ROSS
SPC	CHARLTON, ROBERT KEITH
PO3	CHARPENTIER, ANDREW SCOTT
CPL	CHARTE, PHILIP GERALD EICHNER
SGT	CHASE, JULIAN CLEMENT
SGT	CHAVERS, BROCK HENRY
SSG	CHAY, KYU HYUK
SGT	CHECO, STEVEN
CPO	CHECQUE, NICOLAS DAVID
PV2	CHEN, DANNY
SSG	CHERRY, CRAIG WILLIAM
SPC	CHIHUAHUA, SHANNON
LCPL	CHILDERS, CODY STEVEN
MSG	CHILDS, GREGORY LAMONT
SSG	CHIOMENTO, ROBERT JOSEPH II

PFC	CHISHOLM, BENJAMEN GLEN
LT	CHOE, FLORENCE BACONG
SSG	CHRISTEN, JAMES MICHAEL
SSGT	CHRISTIAN, ERIC DAMON
SSG	CHRISTIAN, RUSTY HUNTER
LCPL	CHROBOT, JORDAN LEE
LCPL	CIARAMITARO, DOMINIC JOHN
SSGT	CINCO, MICHAEL ANTHONY
CPT	CLARK, BRUCE KEVIN
SPC	CLARK, CHAZRAY CLEA-ANTOINE
SGT	CLARK, CORY LUTTREL SR
LCPL	CLARK, JEFFERY LANE
LCPL	CLARK, PHILIP P
SPC	CLARK, RYANE GLENN
GYSGT	CLARK, THEODORE JR
LTC	CLARK, TODD JOHN
SGT	CLARKSON, JOEL DAVID
1SG	CLAUNCH, HERBERT RONALD
SPC	CLAYTON, HILDA IVELIS
SSG	CLEAVER, JOHN JAMES
SPC	CLEMENS, BRIAN MICHAEL
SSG	CLEMENS, SHAWN MICHAEL
SPC	CLEMENTS, CHAD DEREK
CPT	CLIFF, RICHARD GORDON JR
LCPL	CLORE, PETER JAMES
CPL	CLOUSE, JUSTIN ROBERT
SSG	CLOWERS, JESSE GLADDEN JR
SPC	COCHILUS, JUNOT M L
LCPL	COCHRAN, KENNETH ELDREN
CPL	COFFEY, KEATON GRANT
CPL	COFFLAND, CHRISTOPHER JAMES
SSGT	COHEE, WALTER FRANCIS III
CW4	COLE, BRENT SCOTT
CPL	COLE, JEREMIAH SCOTT

SPC	COLEMAN, CHAD DEREK
SPC	COLEMAN, JUSTIN DEAN
MSG	COLEMAN, MARK WAYNE
PFC	COLIN, MATTHEW CHRISTOPHER
SGT	COLLETTE, JOSEPH PETER
LCPL	COLLINS, JEREMIAH MICHAEL JR
SGT	COLLINS, SEAN MARTIN
PFC	COLVIN, JULIAN LEE
SSG	COMBS, CASEY DEAN
CPT	COMFORT, KYLE AARON
CPL	COMMONS, MATTHEW ALLEN
SPC	CONDE, GABRIEL DAVID
PFC	CONLON, PAUL EDWARD JR
MAJ	CONNOLLY, DAVID SCOTT
SGT	CONNOLLY, RYAN JAMES
SGT	CONRAD, TIMOTHY JOHN JR
SPC	CONTRERAS, KORAN PULIDO
PFC	COOK, NICHOLAS SCOTT
SPC	COOK, ROBERT JAMES
SPC	COOK, RYAN JAMES
SPC	COOPER, KEENAN ALEXANDER
CPL	COOPER, WILLIAM JUSTIN LEE
SSGT	COPES, GREGORY TODD
PFC	CORDO, DOUGLAS LEONARD
TSGT	CORLEW, SEAN MITCHELL
SFC	CORLEY, CLARK ARNOLD JR
1LT	CORMA, SALVATORE SIMPLICIO II
LCPL	CORNELIUS, KEVIN MICHAEL
CPL	CORPUZ, BERNARD PAUL
LCPL	CORRAL, JOSHUA DANIEL
PFC	CORTEZ, CESAR
LTC	CORTEZ, WILLIAM EUGENE
LCPL	CORZINE, KENNETH A
LCPL	COTISEARS, NIALL WILLIAM

SGTMAJ	COTTLE, ROBERT JAMES
SPC	COUMAS, KYLE ANDREW
CPL	COURCY, PETER JOHN
PFC	COUTU, KYLE JOSEPH
SSG	COWDREY, ROBERT BRIAN
CPL	COX, DANIEL LEE
SSG	COX, NATHAN MATTHEW
SGT	COX, NATHAN WILLIAM
SGT	CRAIG, ADAM DANIEL
SSG	CRAIG, BRIAN THOMAS
SSG	CRAIG, HEATHE NATHANNIEL
SPC	CRANE, RICHARD MICHAEL
LCPL	CRASS, LAYTON BRADLY
SGT	CREAMER, ZAINAH CAYE
SGT	CREIGHTON, ANDREW JAMES
SFC	CRIBBEN, STEPHEN BAXTER
1SG	CRISOSTOMO, JOSE SAN
SGT	CROSE, BRADLEY STEPHEN
PFC	CROSS, PETER KYLE
CPL	CROUSE, WILLIAM HARRY IV
SGT	CROW, ROBERT WAYNE JR
SPC	CRUMPLER, JOSIAH DENNIS
SGT	CRUTTENDEN, AARON BRETT
PFC	CRUZ, JOSEPH
CPL	CUETO, KEVIN ALEXANDER
SGT	CULBRETH, JUSTIN ERIC
SSG	CULLERS, ARI RICHARD
SSGT	CULLINS, JOSHUA JAMES
SRA	CUNNINGHAM, JASON DECASTRO
2LT	CUNNINGHAM, JOE LEE
SSG	CURRERI, JOSEPH FRANCESCO
PFC	CURRIER, ERIC DENNIS
1SG	CURRY, MICHAEL SEAFRED JR
SPC	CURTIS, JONATHAN MICHAEL

SSG	CURTISS, KURT ROBERT
SPC	CUTSFORTH, SEAN RUSSELL
PFC	CUZZUPE, PAUL ORAZIO II
CAPT	CYR, BRANDON LEE
SPC	DAEHLING, MITCHELL KIRK
SPC	DAHL, MICHAEL ANTHONY JR
SSG	DAHLKE, JASON SEAN
CPL	DAMAS, LEOPOLD FRED
CPT	DAMON, PATRICK DANIEL
SGT	DANIELS, DEVIN JAMES
LCPL	DANIELS, NICKOLAS ALAN
SPC	DANYLUK, KERRY MICHAEL GEORGE
SGT	DARROUGH, JAMES MICHAEL
SSGT	D'AUGUSTINE, JOSEPH
SPC	DAVIS, ADAM JAMES
MMFR	DAVIS, BRYANT LEROY
SGT	DAVIS, DAVID ALAN
MSG	DAVIS, JEFFERSON DONALD
SPC	DAVIS, JOHNATHON FRANK
SSGT	DAVIS, JONATHAN DALE
LCPL	DAVIS, JOSHUA MICHAEL
PFC	DAVIS, JUSTIN RAY
SPC	DAVIS, NATHAN TYLER
SGT	DAVIS, ROBERT GENE
SSGT	DAVIS, TIMOTHY PETER
SGT	DAWSON, EZRA
CPL	DAWSON, JOHN MICHAEL
PFC	DAWSON, WILLIAM BRANDON
SSGT	DAY, DAVID PIRIE
PO1	DAY, JARED WILLIAM
SSG	DAZACHACON, EDWIN HERBERT
SSG	DE ALENCAR, MARK ROCHETTO
SSG	DE LA PENA-HERNANDEZ, ESAU IVAN
SGT	DE LA ROSA, FERNANDO

CPL	DEANS, PATRICK DAVID
CPL	DEBOER, DAANE ADAM
MSG	DEBOSE, COATER BERNARD
SPC	DECOTEAU, MARC PAUL
SPC	DEFAZIO, ROBERT WILLIAM
MSG	DEGHAND, BERNARD LEE
1LT	DEL CASTILLO, DIMITRI ALEJANDRO
MSG	DELEON-FIGUEROA, LUIS FELIPE
SGT	DELUZIO, STEVEN JOSEPH
SPC	DEMARSICO, MICHAEL ROBERT II
LCPL	DENIER, ANTHONY JOSEPH
PFC	DENNIS, JACOB ANTHONY
PV2	DENNIS, JEROD RHOTON
CPL	DENNIS, PRESTON JOHN
SGT	DEPOTTEY, JEREMY EDWARD
1LT	DEPRIMO, JEFFREY FRANK
PFC	DERONDE, LEROY III
SGT	DESFORGES, JOSHUA DAVID
CPT	DESOLENNI, BRUNO GIANCARLO
PFC	DEVOE, PATRICK ALLEN II
LCPL	DEW, VICTOR ANTHONY
PFC	DEWATER, RICHARD ALLEN
1LT	DEWHIRST, NICK A
SGT	DEYOUNG, MATTHEW JAMES
PFC	DEYSIE, ARA TYLER
SGT	DIAZ BORIA, ROBERTO EFRAIN
SSGT	DIAZ, CHRISTOPHER
CPL	DIAZ, ISAAC EDWARD
SGT	DICKHUT, NICHOLAS MICHAEL
SSGT	DICKINSON, SCOTT EDWARD
SSG	DICKMYER, ADAM LYNN
SSGT	DICKSON, RICHARD ANDREW
PFC	DIENER, JACKIE LEE II
SPC	DIETRICH, JESSE WAYNE

PO2	DIETZ, DANNY PHILLIP JR
CDR	DIFEDERICO, ALBERT EDWARD
SPC	DIKCIS, ALAN NATHAN
LCPL	DILISIO, ANTHONY ATTILIO
PFC	DILLON, JAMES ROBERT JR
SPC	DIMOCK, JOSEPH WHITING II
CPL	DIMOND, SCOTT GENE
PFC	DINTERMAN, MICHAEL RICHARD
PFC	DION, JOHN PHILLIP
SPC	DISNEY, JASON A
MAJ	DIVELY, DUANE WILLIAM
SSG	DIXON, EDWARD FRED III
PFC	DOBEREINER, ADAM EUGENE
SSGT	DODDS DUDLEY, THOMAS JOSEPH
SSG	DOLES, JOHN GLEN
SSGT	DOLPHIN, PATRICK RYAN
SFC	DOMEIJ, KRISTOFFER BRYAN
CPL	DOMION, ALEX FRANK
CPL	DONAHUE, MAX WILLIAM
MAJ	DONAHUE, MICHAEL JOSEPH
CW2	DONALDSON, CHRISTOPHER BRIAN
SPC	DONEVSKI, ROBERT JOHN
1STLT	DONNELLY, WILLIAM JAMES IV
SSG	DORRITY, JAMES PAUL
PO1	DOUANGDARA, JOHN
TSGT	DOUVILLE, DANIEL LEE
SPC	DOWNER, MARK JORDON
SPC	DRAKE, CHRISTOPHER RE'SHAWN
PFC	DRAKE, DAVID ANDREW
SGT	DRAKULICH, DAVID JOSEPH
SPC	DRAWL, ROBERT EUGENE JR
PFC	DREES, STEVEN THOMAS
CAPT	DRONET, BRANDON RYAN
LCPL	DUARTE, CURTIS JOSEPH

TSGT	DUFFMAN, SCOTT ERIC
CPL	DUMAW, JOSHUA ROBERT
SGT	DUMONT, PAUL EDMOND JR
SPC	DUNCAN, SPENCER COLSON
LCPL	DUNN, KIELIN TERRELL
SSGT	DUNNING, STEPHEN JOEL
MSG	DUPONT, KEVIN ALLAN
SPC	DUPONT, STEVEN LLOYD
SGT	DURGIN, RUSSELL MEADE
SGT	DURHAM, PATRICK KEITH
CPL	DURKIN, CIARA MARIE
SGT	DURKIN, SEAN MICHAEL
CW2	DUSKIN, MICHAEL STEPHEN
CPL	DUTCHER, MICHAEL JOSEPH
SGT	DUTTON, JAMES EVAN
SPC	DYAS, ROBERT ESTLE JR
LCPL	DYCUS, EDWARD JOE
CW2	DYER, SCOTT WILLIAM
GYSGT	EASTMAN, CHRISTOPHER LUCAS
PV2	EBBERS, JAMES HENRY
PO1	EBBERT, KEVIN RICHARD
GYSGT	ECKARD, CHRISTOPHER WILLIAM
SPC	EDENS, JASON KYLE
SGT	EDGERTON, DONALD ROCKY
PFC	EDGIN, KEVIN FINCH
SPC	EDMUNDS, JONN JOSEPH
CPT	EGGERS, DANIEL WILLIAM
SSG	EGGLESTON, BRANDON FORREST
CW2	EGNOR, JODY LYNN
SRA	EISCHEN, NICHOLAS DWAIN
SSG	ELAM, GREGORY LOWELL
SSGT	ELCHIN, DYLAN JAMES
MSG	ELIZARRARAS, EMIGDIO EFRAIN
SPC	ELLIS, ROBERT WAYNE

PFC	ELLIS, VINCENT JAMES
SPC	ELM, MICHAEL DAVIS
1SG	ELWELL, KENNETH BRIAN
SPC	EMMONS, RICHARD CHARLTON III
SFC	EMOND, ERIC MICHAEL
SSGT	EMRICK, JORDAN BLAKE
CPL	ENDSLEY, ZACHARY RYAN
PO1	ENOS, DARREL LYNN
SSG	EPPINGER, GARRICK LOUIS JR
CPL	ERICKSON, CALEB LANE
LCPL	ESPINOZA, DAVID LEE
SGT	ESPOSITO, MICHAEL JOHN JR
CPL	ESSARY, KEITH ERIC
SGT	ESSEX, RICHARD ALLEN
MAJ	ESTELLE, RAYMOND GRAY II
SFC	ESTLE, BOBBY LEE
PFC	ESTOPINAL, JASON HILL
PO3	ESTRADA, KYLER LAVON
SGT	EUGENIO, CARLO FRANCISCO
SGT	EVANS, JERRY RANDALL JR
1LT	EWENS, FORREST PINKERTON
2LT	EWY, JERED WAYNE
SSG	EZERNACK, TROY SHANE
CPO	FAAS, JOHN WESTON
LCPL	FABBRI, RALPH JOHN
SFC	FABRIZI, JASON JOHN
SPC	FAHEY, DAVID RICHARD JR
PFC	FAIRBAIRN, AARON ELI
SSG	FALKEL, CHRISTOPHER MATTHEW
SSGT	FANKHAUSER, JOSEPH HENRY
SSGT	FANNIN, DANIEL NEIL
SGT	FANNIN, SHAWN DEE
SPC	FANT, GARRETT ANTHONY
LCPL	FARIAS, JOHN FELIX

1LT	FARKAS, DANIEL
SSG	FARLEY, BRANDON WADE
SSG	FARLEY, DEREK JOHN
SGT	FARRELL, SHAWN MICHAEL II
SPC	FARRIS, JOSHUA RAY
SGT	FASTUCA, LOUIS ROBERT
PFC	FAULKNER, JEREMY PAT
CPL	FAUST, AARON MATTHEW
1LT	FAZZARI, MATHEW GREGORY
MSGT	FEDDER, DANIEL LOUIS
PO1	FEEKS, PATRICK DELANEY
MAJ	FEISTNER, CURTIS DONALD
SGT	FEJERAN, GREGORY DUENAS
SPC	FELDHAUS, DUSTIN JAMES
SGT	FELICIANO GUTIERREZ, KELVIN EDGAR
LTC	FENTY, JOSEPH JAMES JR
SGT	FERNANDEZ, CHRISTOPHER JAMES CEPEDA
CPL	FERNANDEZ, KYLE KA EO
CPT	FERRARA, MATTHEW CHARLES
LCPL	FERRELL, BRUCE EARNEST
SPC	FIELDS, ARRONN DAVID
SFC	FIKE, ROBERT JAMES
SPC	FINGAR, JASON DAVID
SPC	FINLEY, JAMES MATTHEW
SPC	FINNIGINAM, ERIC MABTONG
SSG	FIRTAMAG, JEROME
CPT	FISCUS, MICHAEL TODD
SGT	FISHER, ZACHARY MICHAEL
SPC	FITTS, KRYSTAL MARIE
PFC	FITZGIBBON, PATRICK SCOTT
PO1	FITZMORRIS, JOSEPH PATRICK-NEWMAN
CW3	FLANIGAN, WILLIAM TIMOTHY
SSG	FLANNERY, SEAN MICHAEL

CPL	FLEISCHER, JACOB RUDELOFF
1STLT	FLEMING, SCOTT JOSEPH
CPL	FLEURY, GREGORY MICHAEL WILLIAM
SPC	FLORES, DWAYNE WESTFALL
SPC	FLORES, JESUS OLAR JR
TSGT	FLORES, MICHAEL PAUL
CW3	FLYNN, JOHN MICHAEL
SSG	FOGARTY, THOMAS KENT
CPO	FONTAN, JACQUES JULES
SSG	FORAKER, RYAN DANE
SFC	FORDE, OMAR WILFRED
SGT	FORDYCE, JAMES FLOYD
SRA	FORESTER, MARK ANDREW
SPC	FORTUNATO, STEPHEN ROBERT
SGT	FOSHEE, JEREMY DALE
LCPL	FOWLKES, CHRISTOPHER SCOTT
SGT	FOXX, DILLON B
CPL	FRACKER, DALE EDWIN JR
CPL	FRAISE, DAVID MAURICE
PO3	FRALISH, JOHN THOMAS
SSG	FRAMPTON, GREGORY MICHAEL
LCPL	FRANCESCONI, ALBERTO
SGT	FRANK, EDWARD J II
PFC	FRANKLIN, BENNY SHANTELL
SGT	FRAZIER, DANIEL ALEXANDER
SSGT	FRAZIER, JACOB LEE
SSG	FREDSTI, NICHOLAS CHARLES
CPL	FREEMAN, DANIEL JASON
SGT	FREEMAN, JAMEEL TALIB
CAPT	FREEMAN, MATTHEW CHARLES HAYS
LCPL	FREEMAN, MICHAEL LOUIS JR
LCPL	FREEMAN, RONALD DOUGLAS
CPO	FREIWALD, JASON RICHARD
SSG	FRENCH, ALEX IV

1LT	FRISON, DEMETRIUS MONTAZ
SSG	FRITH, KERRY WAYNE
SSG	FRITSCHE, WILLIAM RYAN
SGT	FROKJER, CHAD DENNIS
CW2	FUCHIGAMI, KIRK TAKESHI JR
SSG	FUERST, JOSEPH FREDERICK III
SFC	FUGA, MICHAEL TAUAE
SPC	FULLER, CHAD EDWARD
SSG	GABEL, MICHAEL JOHN
CPL	GAFFNEY, CHARLES PATRICK JR
SGT	GAILEY, CHRISTOPHER DREW
SPC	GALARZAHERNANDEZ, VILMAR
SSG	GALEWSKI, JUSTIN JOSEPH
SSG	GALLEGOS, JUSTIN TIMOTHY
HN	GALLINGER-LONG, RILEY
SGT	GALVAN, DANIEL LEE
LCPL	GAMBLE, GARRETT WILLIAM
PFC	GAMMONE, VINCENT EMMANUEL III
CPL	GARABRANT, BRANDON JOHN
SPC	GARBS, RYAN CLARK
HN	GARCIA, ANTHONY CHRISTIAN
SGT	GARCIA, ISRAEL
PV2	GARCIA, JAIR DEJESUS
SSG	GARCIA, MICHAEL JONATHAN
CPT	GARNER, MARK ANDESS
SGT	GARRISON, JOSEPH MICHAEL
SPC	GARTNER, RYAN ANTHONY
SGT	GARVER, COREY EDWIN
SPC	GARVIN, NATHANIEL DOUGLAS
PFC	GARZA, DAMIAN JAMES
CPL	GARZA, ROGELIO ROLANDO JR
SSG	GASS, GIRARD DAVID JR
PFC	GASSEN, JACOB ALEXANDER
A1C	GATES BENSON, AUSTIN HARPER

SPC	GATHERCOLE, CHRISTOPHER
CW2	GAUDET, BRADLEY JUSTIN
LCPL	GEARY, DANIEL JOSEPH
LCPL	GEARY, MICHAEL ERICK
SGT	GEE, NICOLE LEEANN
SGT	GEIGER, CHRISTOPHER PATRICK
SGT	GELIG, IAN TIMOTHY DAGDAGAN
1STLT	GENTZ, JOEL CHRISTOPHER
SPC	GEORGE, MATTHEW ERIC
LCPL	GEORGE, PHILLIP CARSON
SSGT	GERMOSEN, SCOTT NELSON
CW3	GIBBONS, THOMAS JOSEPH
CWO-3	GIBSON, JONATHAN SHELBY
PFC	GIDEON, NICOLAS HUGH JOSEPH
LCPL	GIESE, JOSEPH RYAN
GYSGT	GIFFORD, JONATHAN WILLIAM
SPC	GILBERT, KYLE EUGENE
GYSGT	GILBERT, ROBERT LEE II
SPC	GILBERT, WILLIAM JOSEPH
SGT	GILL, CARLOS EDWARD
MSGT	GILLESPIE, RANDY JOE
SGT	GILMAN, BENJAMIN LEWIS
TSGT	GINETT, ADAM KENNETH
2LT	GIRDANO, MICHAEL ROBERT
SSG	GIRE, JOSHUA SETH
SPC	GLENDE, THEODORE MATTHEW
SFC	GLOYER, RYAN ALLEN
SSG	GOARE, SHAMUS OTTO
SFC	GOBLE, MICHAEL JAMES
1LT	GOEKE, CHRISTOPHER SHULTZ
CPT	GOETZ, DALE ALAN
CAPT	GOLDEN, JONATHAN JOSEPH
SGT	GOLDING, NICHOLES DARWIN
SFC	GOLDSMITH, WYATT ANDREW

SFC	GOLIN, MIHAIL
SGT	GOLLNITZ, JONATHAN ALAN
CPL	GOMEZ, BILLY
PFC	GONCALO, ETHAN LOUIS
SFC	GONSALVES, CHAD AYRON
SGT	GONZALES, ADAN JR
PV2	GONZALES, JOSEPH FRANCISCO
HN	GONZALEZ, EDWIN
SGT	GONZALEZ, JAIME JR
MSG	GONZALEZ, JOSE JUAN
SFC	GONZALEZ, LUIS MANUEL
SGT	GONZALEZ, MOISES JESUS
SGT	GONZALEZ-GARZA, RODRIGO
SSG	GONZALEZ-O'MALLEY, ARACELY
SPC	GOOCH, GARY LEE JR
SRA	GOOD, ALECIA SABRINA
CPL	GOODE, JORDAN EMIL
PFC	GOODINE, BRANDON DWAYNE
CPL	GOODIRON, NATHAN JOEL
SRA	GOODMAN, ASHTON LYNN MARIE
CW3	GOODNATURE, COREY JAMES
SSG	GOODWIN, ROBERT STACEY
SPC	GORDON, BRANDON DREW
SPC	GORDON, BRITTANY BRIA
SGT	GORDON, ROBERT DAVID II
SPC	GORDON, TERRY KISHAUN
PFC	GORHAM, BRIAN LEE
SGT	GORNEWICZ, BRETT EDWARD
SGT	GORRA, MARCOS ANTONIO
SGT	GOULD, KRISTOPHER JAMES
CPL	GOYET, MARK RAYMOND
SGT	GRACE, EDWARD SAVY
SPC	GRACE, KEITH ERIN JR
SN	GRADY, KATRINA RENEE

SPC	GRADY, RYAN JOHN
SPC	GRAHAM, KEVIN JAMES
CAPT	GRAMITH, THOMAS JOSEPH
SFC	GRANADO, ALEJANDRO III
LCPL	GRANT, CHRISTOPHER OBRYAN
PFC	GRAY, JOSHUA ALLEN
MAJ	GRAY, WALTER DAVID
SGT	GREEN, ANTHONY GABRIEL
SPC	GREEN, DOUGLAS JAY
MAJ	GREEN, MICHAEL LEE
SSGT	GREEN, STACY ANDRU
MG	GREENE, HAROLD JOSEPH
SGT	GREENE, JEREMY RICHARD
CPL	GREER, KRISTOPHER DANIEL
LCPL	GRENIGER, ROBERT STEPHEN
SFC	GRIDER, RONALD AARON
SSG	GRIECO, KEVIN DOUGLAS
SPC	GRIEMEL, JARRETT PEARSON
SGT	GRIFFIN, CHRISTOPHER TODD
SGT	GRIFFIN, DALE RUSSEL
SFC	GRIFFIN, JEREMY WAYNE
CSM	GRIFFIN, KEVIN JAMES
LCPL	GRIFFIN, TYLER OWEN
SGT	GRIFFITH, JOHN CRIPE
MAJ	GRIFFITH, SAMUEL MARK
SSG	GRINDEY, JESSE JAMES
CPL	GRINER, AARON MATTHEW
SFC	GRISSOM, JAMES FLOYD
SSG	GROCHOWIAK, CASEY JAMES
CW2	GROGAN, TRAVIS WAYNE
PFC	GROSS, DUSTIN DEAN
CPL	GROSS, FRANK ROBERT
SGT	GROSSPANIAGUA, WILLIAM BENJAMIN
CW3	GROVES, JAMES EDISON III

SSG	GUERRA, RAUL MADRIGAL
SGT	GUILLORY, MICHAEL JAMES
CPL	GULLETT, JEREMY RAYMOND
SGT	GURR, DANIEL DAVID
SPC	GUTIERREZ, AGUSTIN
SSG	GUTIERREZ, DAVID HECTOR
SFC	GUTIERREZ, JAVIER JAGUAR
SPC	GUTOWSKI, STEVEN EDWARD
CPL	GUZMAN RIVERA, CHRISTIAN ARMANDO
SGT	GUZMAN, GABRIEL
SGT	HADAWAY, BRANDON EUGENE
LCPL	HAGER, ROGER GARY MICHAEL
MAJ	HAGERTY, SCOTT ALAN
SFC	HAIRSTON, SAMUEL CARLOS
1LT	HALL, BENJAMIN JOHN
SPC	HALL, BLAKE WADE
SPC	HALL, DAVID EUGENE
LCPL	HALL, DAVID RAY
SSG	HALL, JEFFREY ALAN
PFC	HALL, JONATHON DAVID
CAPT	HALL, RYAN PRESTON
CPT	HALLETT, JOHN LOUIS III
SSG	HAMBURGER, PATRICK DOUGLAS
SPC	HAMILTON, ADAM SCOTT
SPC	HAMILTON, DONNELL ANTWAIN JR
SSG	HAMMAR, CARL ERIK
SSGT	HAMMOND, RYAN DAVID
SSGT	HAMSKI, JOSEPH JOHN
SPC	HAN, KIMBLE ANDRUS
SPC	HAND, ANDREW LEE
LCPL	HAND, NICHOLAS JOEL
SSG	HANEY, RANDY MICHEAL
MSG	HANNON, SHAWN THOMAS
SSGT	HANSEN, DANIEL LOUIS

SSG	HANSEN, DENNIS JOE
SSG	HANSEN, JOHN ERIC
SGT	HANSEN, JUSTIN MICHAEL
LCPL	HANSON, MATTHIAS NUMON
SGT	HARDIN, ETHAN CARROLL
SGT	HARDISON, JEREMY FRANKLIN
SPC	HARDT, ADAM JEFFERY
SGT	HARDT, JOSHUA MITCHELL
SSG	HARGROVE, ZACHARY HAYDEN
PFC	HARIO, ERIC WILLIAM
SSG	HARLEY, WILLIE JAMES JR
SGT	HARMON, MATTHEW ALLEN
PFC	HARPER, ANDREW MARTIN
LCPL	HARPER, SCOTT DANIEL
CW2	HARRIMAN, STANLEY LORN
SPC	HARRIS, CHRISTOPHER MICHAEL
PFC	HARRIS, DEVON JEMAIL
PFC	HARRIS, JOSEPH GRAHAM
PO1	HARRIS, JOSHUA THOMAS
SGT	HARRIS, JOSHUA WILLIAM
CPL	HARRIS, LARRY DONELL JR
SGT	HARRIS, TAUREAN TRAVANTI
SFC	HARRIS, TODD MONROE
SFC	HARRISON, CALVIN BERNARD
COL	HARRISON, JAMES WARREN JR
SSG	HART, BRADLEY CHARLES
SFC	HARTMAN, DAVID JAMES
CPL	HARTON, JOSHUA ALEXANDER
SSGT	HARVELL, ANDREW WILLIAM
SGT	HARVEY, JAMES WILLIAM II
PFC	HASENAUER, JASON DANIEL
SSG	HASENFLU, WILLIAM EARL
MSGT	HATFIELD, JEROME DAVID
SGT	HAWKINS, PATRICK CHRISTOPHER

MSGT	HAYES, JOHN ERIC
CPT	HAYS, BRUCE EVAN
SGT	HAYS, NATHAN PAUL
SCPO	HEALY, DANIEL RICHARD
SGT	HEALY, JAMES KALEB
LCPL	HECK, RANDY MICHAEL
SGT	HEEDE JR, MICHAEL WAYNE
LCPL	HEFNER, SHAWN PATRICK
SPC	HELTON, JUSTIN RYAN
SPC	HEMAUER, KYLE MATTHEW
SFC	HENDERSON, AARON ARTHUR
CW2	HENDERSON, BRYAN JAMES
SFC	HENDERSON, CHRISTOPHER DALE
PV2	HENDERSON, JOHN MCKENZIE JR
SGT	HENDRIKS, ROBERT ANDREW
SFC	HENNEN, JOHN MICHAEL
SGT	HENNIGAN, MATTHEW ROBERT
SPC	HENSLEY, NICHOLAS CHARLIE
SPC	HERCULES, RUSSELL SHANE JR
SSGT	HEREDIA, EDGAR ALBERTO
SSG	HERMANSON, MATTHEW DANIEL
SGT	HERMOGINO, KEN KING
SGT	HERNANDEZ CHAVEZ, JOSUE EMMAN
SPC	HERNANDEZ, ALEX III
LCPL	HERNANDEZ, DEREK
SGT	HERNANDEZ, EDELMAN LEONARDO
CPL	HERNANDEZ, EMMANUEL
LCPL	HERNANDEZ, JOSE ALONZO
CPL	HERNANDEZ, JOSEPH MICHAEL
SPC	HERNANDEZ, ROBERTO ANTONIO II
SSG	HERRERA, OCTAVIO
SGT	HERRERA, PERNELL JOHNNIE
SFC	HERRERA, ROCKY H
SGT	HERSHEY, BRETT MICHAEL

SGT	HESELTON, EDWARD RALPH
SPC	HESS, DAVID ALAN
SGT	HESS, JACOB MICHAEL
1LT	HESS, ROBERT JOSEPH
SPC	HICKEY, JULIE ROCHELLE
SFC	HICKMAN, JASON OMAR BRADLEY
SGT	HICKS, CHANNING BO
CPL	HICKS, DARRION TERRELL
SGT	HICKS, JAMAR AVERY
SSGT	HICKS, JASON CARLYLE
1LT	HIDALGO, DAREN MIGUEL
SGT	HIERHOLZER, DAVID MICHAEL
MSG	HIESTER, MICHAEL THOMAS
SGT	HIETT, ANTON JESEAN
SGT	HIGGINS, TANNER STONE
PV2	HIGH, CHARLES MILTON IV
SGT	HIGH, STEPHEN CORRELL
SGT	HIKE, ADRIAN EDWARD
SPC	HILAMAN, KEVIN JOSEPH
BG	HILDNER, TERENCE JOHN
LCPL	HILL, JASON DANIEL
SPC	HILL, JOSHUA LEE
SPC	HILL, KEVIN OLSEN
SGT	HILL, SHAWN FITZGERALD
SFC	HILTON, MATTHEW LEE
SSGT	HINES, BENJAMIN SCOTT
1LT	HINES, DEREK STEVEN
SPC	HIZON, RUDOLPH RYAN
SSG	HOBBS, BRIAN SCOTT
LCPL	HOGAN, DONALD JAMES
LCPL	HOGAN, HUNTER DALTON
CPT	HOLBROOK, JASON ELLIS
PFC	HOLDER, KYLE MATTHEW
SPC	HOLLAND, DEREK DAVID

GYSGT	HOLLEY, FLOYD EARL COURTNEY
SSG	HOLMAN, ERIC SCOTT
SGT	HOLMES, DAVID ALEXANDER
SPC	HOLMES, MIGUEL LORENZO
SGT	HOLTZ, TYLER NICHOLAS
PO1	HOLZEMER, MATTHEW I
SPC	HONAKER, CHRISTOPHER STEVEN
LCPL	HONEYCUTT, TERRY EDWARD JR
SFC	HOOVER, BRYAN ALAN
SSGT	HOOVER, DARIN TAYLOR
TSGT	HORNBARGER, JAMES ROBERT
SPC	HORNE, PATRICIA LEE
PFC	HORNS, CHRISTOPHER ALEXANDER
CW3	HORNSBY, BRIAN DANIEL
SPC	HORSLEY, JUSTIN LOUIS
SPC	HORTON, CHRISTOPHER DAVID
SSG	HOSEY, MICHAEL WESLEY
SGT	HOSFORD, CHESTER WAYNE
SGT	HOSKINS, JAY MICHAEL
PFC	HOSTETTER, JONATHON MICHAEL DEAN
PFC	HOTCHKIN, GUNNAR RANDALL
SGT	HOUCK, ERIC MICHAEL
CPO	HOUSTON, KEVIN ARTHUR
CPL	HOVATER, JASON DANE
LCPL	HOWARD, ABRAM LARUE
SGT	HOWARD, BRYCE DANIEL
SFC	HOWARD, MERIDETH LEIGH
SSG	HOWICK, CHRISTOPHER THOMAS
SGT	HRBEK, CHRISTOPHER RICHARD
LCPL	HTAIK, MAUNG PHYOTHU
SFC	HUGHES, BRADLEY SCOTT
SPC	HUGHIE, BUDDY JAMES
SGT	HULING, JOHN PATRICK
SSG	HUNSBERGER, TRAVIS KENT

SSG	HUNTER, JAMES PATRICK
SGT	HUNTER, JONATHON MICHAEL
SPC	HURNE, TERRY JOHN
MSG	HURT, DAVID LEE
LCPL	HUSE, DAKOTA RAY
SPC	HUSTON, MATTHEW DAVID
CPL	HUTCHINS, ANDREW LEWIS
1LT	HYLAND, JOSHUA MICHAEL
CAPT	IANNELLI, RYAN KENNETH
PFC	IBARRA, JOSUE
SPC	IBARRIA, VINCENT SEBASTIAN
SSG	IDE, JAMES ROGER V
CAPT	IMLAY, FRANCIS DEE JR
SSG	INFANTE, JESSE
SSGT	INGHAM, MATTHEW NEVIN
SGT	INGRAM, MATTHEW LEE
SGT	INGRAM, MICHAEL KEITH JR
SGT	ISENHOWER, BRET DANIEL
SGT	ISLIP, BRANDON TAYLOR
CPT	ISTRE, AARON DALE
PFC	IUBELT, TYLER RAY
LCPL	JACKSON, FRANCISCO RAFAEL
SGT	JACKSON, ISSAC BRANDON
LCPL	JACKSON, JOE MICHAEL
SFC	JACKSON, MARK WAYNE
LCPL	JACKSON, TIMOTHY MATTHEW
SGT	JACKSON, WAKKUNA ALMIRA
SPC	JACOBS, KEDITH LAMONT JR
1LT	JACOBS, SEAN ROBERT
SGT	JACOBY, KIP ALLEN
EMFA	JAKES, MICHAEL JAMEL JR
CSM	JALLAH, DENNIS JR
SPC	JAMES, DENNIS JR
SSG	JAMES, ERROL MELVIN

PO2	JAMES, LAQUITA PATE
CPL	JANKIEWICZ, MICHAEL DOUGLAS
SSG	JARBOE, JAMIE DARRELL
SFC	JARRELL, JOHN HASKELL
SFC	JARVIS, BARRY EDWARD
SGT	JASSO, LEANDRO ANTONIO SLEEPER
PFC	JAVIER, CONRADO DIAZ JR
SPC	JAYNE, RYAN PAUL
PFC	JEFFERSON, DAVID ANTHONY
TSGT	JEFFERSON, WILLIAM HAYWOOD JR
SPC	JEFFRIES, DOUGLAS JAY JR
SPC	JEFFRIES, JOSEPH ALLEN
CPT	JENKINS, CORY J
SPC	JENKINS, GERALD ROBERT
MAJ	JENRETTE, KEVIN MICHAEL
SPC	JENSEN, DENNIS GREGORY
GYSGT	JESCHKE, RYAN
PFC	JETTON, JOSHUA LYNN
SPC	JIRTLE, CHARLES SCOTT
PFC	JOHNS, JASON DOUGLAS
SFC	JOHNSON, ALLEN CORNELIUS
PO3	JOHNSON, BENJAMIN ALAN
SGT	JOHNSON, CLIFTON DAVID
SRA	JOHNSON, DANIEL JAMES
1LT	JOHNSON, DAVID ANDREW
SSG	JOHNSON, DONNA RAE
GYSGT	JOHNSON, EDWIN WAYNE JR
SPC	JOHNSON, ISAAC LEE JR
CPL	JOHNSON, JEFFREY WARREN
PFC	JOHNSON, JOHN COREY
SGT	JOHNSON, JOSEPH DENNIS
SSG	JOHNSON, JUSTIN RASARD SR
PFC	JOHNSON, KALIN CHRISTOPHER LEE
LCPL	JOHNSON, LARRY MICHAEL

SPC	JOHNSON, MATTHEW JAMES
1STLT	JOHNSON, MICHAEL EDWARD
CW2	JOHNSON, NICHOLAS SCOTT
LCPL	JOHNSON, RAYMON LEE ALLEN
SPC	JOHNSON, TIMOTHY LAMAR
SGT	JOHNSON, TRAVON TRAVIS
SGT	JOHNSON, TREVOR JERIMIAH
SRA	JOHNSONHARRIS, QUINN LAMAR
SGT	JOHNSTON, JAMES GREGORY
SPC	JOHNSTON, JASON MICHAEL
CPL	JONES, ADAM DOUGLAS
CAPT	JONES, ERIC ALTON
CPT	JONES, JASON BENJAMIN
LCDR	JONES, LANDON LE
SGT	JONES, OMAR ALEJANDRO
SPC	JONES, PAYTON ALEXANDER
PFC	JONES, RICHARD KELVIN
SGT	JONES, RICKY DEWAYNE
SGT	JORDAN, JEFFREY WILLIAM
LCPL	JOYCE, KEVIN BOYD
LCPL	JUAREZ, MARK DAVID
SGT	JUDEN, TYLER AUSTIN
PFC	JUSTESEN, ANTHONY T
SSG	JUSTICE, JAMES ALAN
SPC	JUSTICE, JAMES AUSTIN
SFC	KAHLER, MATTHEW RYAN
LCPL	KAIPAT, RAMON TAISAKAN
CDR	KALAFUT, CHRISTOPHER EDWARD
SGT	KANCLER, DENNIS EDWARD
LCPL	KANE, JEREMY MITCHELL
PO2	KANTOR, MATTHEW GEOFFREY
SGT	KARCH, CHRISTOPHER NEAL
CPL	KARELLA, JASON ANTHONY
SGT	KASSIN, ROBERT PAUL

SPC	KATZENBERGER, CHRISTOPHER M
SSG	KATZENBERGER, JEREMY ANDREW
SGT	KEARNEY, JAMES CHARLES III
CPT	KEATING, BENJAMIN DAVID
PFC	KELLER, ANDREW JAMES
SGT	KELLEY, MICHAEL JASON
SSG	KELLY, NIGEL DAVID
1STLT	KELLY, ROBERT MICHAEL
LCDR	KELSALL, JONAS B
GYSGT	KENEFICK, AARON MICHAEL
SPC	KENNEDY, JOSEPH ALAN
SGT	KENNEDY, NATHAN PATRICK
MAJ	KENNEDY, THOMAS ELLIOTT
SPC	KERN, KURT WILLIAM
MSGT	KERWOOD, WILLIAM JO
SSG	KESSLER, KEVIN JAMES
MCPO	KESSLER, RICHARD JAMES JR
SFC	KETTLE, JEFFREY DUANE
PFC	KIHM, JOHN FRANCIS
SGT	KIMBALL, BRANDEN TYME
LTC	KIMBROUGH, PAUL WAYNE
PFC	KING, BRANDON MICHAEL
CPL	KING, JARRID LEE
SPC	KING, RYAN CHARLES
SPC	KINSER, ADAM GARETH
SGT	KIRK, JOSHUA JOHN
PFC	KIRKPATRICK, HANSEN BRADEE
SGT	KIRSPEL, MICHAEL DANA JR
CPL	KIRTON, BRANDON MICHAEL
CPL	KIRVEN, NICHOLAS CAIN
SSG	KISLING, DANIEL LEON JR
SGT	KISSELOFF, DENIS DELEON
SGT	KITOWSKI, CHARLES BERNARD III
CPL	KLEINWACHTER, CHRIS K

SGT	KLUSACEK, ERICK JUSTIN
CW2	KNADLE, DAVID CHARLES
SGT	KNAPP, MICHAEL JOSEPH
SSG	KNAUSS, RYAN CHRISTIAN
SPC	KNIGHT, MARQUES IRVING
SGT	KNOX, JABRAUN STEVEN
CPT	KNUTSON, SARA MARIE
CPL	KOCH, STEVEN ROBERT
SGT	KOEHLER, EDWARD WILLIAM III
SSG	KOELE, SHANE MARION
CPL	KOPP, BENJAMIN STEPHEN
SSG	KORTE, NOAH MARK
SPC	KOWALL, COREY JOSEPH
SGT	KRAMER, AARON KEITH
CW2	KRAUSE, SURESH NIRANJAN ABA
SPC	KREINZ, TYLER RICHARD
PFC	KREISCHER, BRANDON JAY
CPL	KRIDLO, DALE JUSTIN
PFC	KRIPPNER, ANDREW MARK
LCDR	KRISTENSEN, ERIK SAMSEL
PFC	KROPAT, JASON MICHAEL
PFC	KROPOV, SERGE
SGT	KUBIK, RONALD ALAN
MSGT	KUHSE, GREGORY THOMAS
SPC	KULIGOWSKI, ADAM MICHAEL
SSG	KUTSCHBACH, PATRICK FRANCIS
CSM	LABORDE, JOHN KEITH
SFC	LACEY, WILLIAM KELLY
SMSGT	LACKEY, JAMES BERTRAND
SSG	LAGMAN, ANTHONY SANTOS
SPC	LALLIER, JARROD ALLEN
SGT	LAMAR, DONALD JAMES II
1LT	LAMBKA, TODD WILLIAM
SSG	LAMMERTS, MICHAEL SCOTT

SPC	LANCASTER, JOSHUA TREVYN
SPC	LANCOUR, JOSEPH MICHAEL
CPL	LAND, BRETT WILLIE
SPC	LANDIS, CHRISTOPHER ANDREW
1LT	LANDRUM, BRANDON JAMES
SFC	LANE, MITCHELL ARTHUR
SSG	LANE, RANDALL RAY
SGT	LANE, RYAN H
CPL	LANGEVIN, SEAN KANAE-ALDRIQUE
SCPO	LANGLAIS, LOUIS JAMES
PFC	LANINGHAM, IRA BENJAMIN IV
LCPL	LARGE, SAMUEL WAYNE JR
PFC	LARSON, RYAN JEFFREY
LCPL	LASHER, JEREMY SCOTT
CPL	LATORRE, XHACOB
CPT	LAWRENCE, JOSHUA SEAN
SPC	LAWSON, DANIEL COURTNEY
SSG	LAWSON, ERIC TIMOTHY SR
CAPT	LAWTON, GARRETT TUCKER
SPC	LAY, PATRICK LEWIS II
PO3	LAYTON, JAMES RAY
SSG	LEACH, MATTHEW JOHN
1LT	LECHOWICH, IVAN DEREK
SGT	LEE, CARLIE MATTISON III
SSG	LEE, DANIEL TYLER
SSG	LEE, DICK ALSON JR
SGT	LEE, JAMES SHAWN
SPC	LEE, JINSU
SPC	LEE, ROGER
1LT	LEEHAN, DAMON THOMAS
SFC	LEGGETT, MATTHEW IVAN
SPC	LEHMILLER, MICHAEL ROBERT
CPL	LEICHT, JACOB CARL
SGT	LEIMBACH, DAVID LEE

MAJ	LELI, KELLIANN
SPC	LEMBKE, ERIC NATHANIEL
CPL	LEMBKE, MATTHEW RYAN
TSGT	LEMM, JOSEPH GERARD
SGT	LENGSTORF, JOSHUA ALLEN
SGT	LEON GUERRERO, BRIAN STEVEN
LTC	LEONARD, JAIMIE ELIZABETH
SGT	LEONHARDT, BRIAN JEFFERY
SGT	LEVENS, DONNIE LEO FORD
LCPL	LEVY, CHRISTOPHER PHOENIX JACOB
LCPL	LEW, HARRY
CPT	LEWIS, DARRELL CORNELIUS
SPC	LEWIS, JOSEPH MICHAEL
SSG	LEWIS, LEX LEE
CPL	LEWIS, TIMOTHY DALE
SSG	LEWSADER, ROY PERSIMMON JR
SPC	LIBBY, GEORGE VERANUS
SPC	LIGHTFOOT, ANTHONY MARQUIS
2LT	LILES, STUART FORREST
SPC	LILLARD, NATHAN EDWARD
MSG	LILLEY, ARTHUR LEROY
SGT	LILLY, JOSEPH MICHAEL
SGT	LIM, DANIEL
SFC	LINDE, DARREN MICHAEL
MAJ	LINDENAU, ROBERT DUANE
SFC	LINDSAY, WILL DUSTON
SSG	LINDSEY, NATHANIEL BRADLEY
SPC	LINDSKOG, JAMESON LYNN
SSG	LINDSTROM, ERIC JAMES
CPL	LINNABARY, DANIEL LEE II
SFC	LIPARI, KEVIN ERNEST
SSG	LOBOSCO, ANDREW THOMAS
SSGT	LOBRAICO, TODD JAMES JR
LTCOL	LOCHT, GWENDOLYN ANN

SSG	LOEZA, ROBERTO JR
LTCOL	LOFTIS, JOHN DARIN
CPL	LOGAN, JOSEPH DANIEL
SGT	LONEY, YOUVERT
SSG	LONGSWORTH, CHRISTIAN
SGT	LOONEY, ANDREW RICHARD
LT	LOONEY, BRENDAN JOHN
SPC	LOPEZ, ANGEL LUIS
CPL	LOPEZ, HUNTER
PFC	LOPEZ, JESUS JONATHAN
LCPL	LOPEZ, JOSEPH CHARLES
PFC	LOPEZ, RUEBEN JESUS
LCPL	LOPEZ-CASTANEDA, JUAN
SSG	LOREDO, EDWARDO
SSG	LORENZO, KRISTOFFERSON BERNARDO
A1C	LOSANO, RAYMOND
PFC	LOVEJOY, ZACHARY GEORGE
CPL	LOWE, JAMIE RUSSEL
SPC	LOWELL, JACOB MICHAEL
CPL	LOWRY, CONNER THOMAS
CPL	LUCAS, JASON ALLEN
PO1	LUCAS, JEFFREY ALAN
SSGT	LUCAS, LEON HORACE JR
CPT	LUCE, RONALD GEORGE JR
SGT	LUGO, MARTIN ANTHONY
SGT	LUKEALA, JOSHUA AKONI
SPC	LUMLEY, RYAN MICHAEL
2LT	LUNDELL, SCOTT BLANCHARD
PO2	LUNDY, BRIAN KEITH JR
SPC	LUSCHER, JONATHON LUKE
SPC	LUTES, DAVID CHRISTOPHER
CPL	LUXMORE, BRYANT JORDAN
SSG	LYBERT, PATRICK LEE
LCPL	LYNCH, SCOTT ALBERT

SGT	LYNCH, TERRY JAY
CAPT	LYON, DAVID IRVIN
SGT	LYONS, JOHN ALDEN
CW3	LYONS, NIALL DAMIEN
SPC	MACE, STEPHAN LEE
CPT	MACFARLANE, BRUCE ANDREW
CPL	MACIEL, JOSEPH
TSGT	MACKEY, HERMAN III
SGT	MACPHERSON, THOMAS RAYMOND
SPC	MADDEN, RUSSELL EDWARD
SGT	MADDOX, ANTHONY RANEL
1STLT	MADRAZO, NICHOLAS AARON
MSGT	MAGNANI, PATRICK DANIEL
SGT	MAHER, BRENT MATTHEW
MSG	MAHOLIC, THOMAS DONALD
PFC	MAHR, MICHAEL CHRISTOPHER
SSGT	MALACHOWSKI, JAMES MICHAEL
SPC	MALDONADO, ALEXIS VICENTE
LCPL	MALDONADO, JOSE LUIS
SPC	MALDONADO, PEDRO ANTONIO
LCPL	MALONE, JOHN JOEL
MSGT	MALTZ, MICHAEL HARRY
SFC	MANCINI, CURTIS
SPC	MANGANO, ANTHONY LEONARD
1STLT	MANN, JASON DANIEL
CAPT	MANOUKIAN, MATTHEW PATRICK
CPL	MARCELLUS, MATTHIEU
MAJ	MARCHANTI, ROBERT JOSEPH II
SCPO	MARCUM, JOHN WAYNE
PV2	MARIA, GIOVANNY
CPL	MARLER, DONALD MATTHEW
SSG	MARQUEZ, JUSTIN CAMERON
SPC	MARQUIS, CHRISTOPHE J
SPC	MARTA, CHASE STONE

SPC	MARTIN, ETHAN JACOB
SSG	MARTIN, JACK MAYFIELD III
LCPL	MARTIN, SHANE ROBERT
SSG	MARTIN, VERNON WILLIAM
SPC	MARTIN, WYATT JOSEPH
PFC	MARTINEK, MATTHEW M
CPL	MARTINEZ, ALEX
SGT	MARTINEZ, RAFAEL JR
CPO	MASON, MATTHEW DAVID
SSG	MASSARELLI, ROBERT ANTHONY
CPL	MASTERSON, CONOR GERARD
MSG	MATOS COLON, EDWIN ANTONIO
SGT	MATTEONI, ANTHONY DENNIS
PFC	MATTOX, JOHN ALEXANDER
SGT	MAUGANS, JAMIE ODELL
SGT	MAY, ERIK NATHANIEL
SGT	MAY, KENNETH BLAINE JR
SPC	MAYBERRY, THOMAS JAMES
SSG	MAYS, CHAUNCY RYAN
PO1	MAZUR, ALEC FRANK
CW3	MCADAMS, ANDREW LANGSTON
SSG	MCANINCH, KENNETH KEITH
SSGT	MCBRIDE, CHESTER JAMICHEAL
SFC	MCCAIN, JOHNATHAN BRYANT
CW3	MCCANTS, HERSHEL DANIEL JR
SGT	MCCLAIN, CHARLES JOHN
SGT	MCCLAIN, KYLE BRENTON
SGT	MCCLARY, JASON MITCHELL
CW2	MCCLELLAN, JONAH DAVID
PFC	MCCLENNEY, DANIEL BRADLEY
CPT	MCCLIMANS, JOSHUA MICHAEL
SFC	MCCLINTOCK, MATTHEW QUINN
SFC	MCCLOSKEY, SHAWN PATRICK
SPC	MCCLURE, CHARLES PATRICK

SGT	MCCLUSKEY, JASON JAMES
SGT	MCCOLLEY, JONATHAN ERIC
CAPT	MCCOLLUM, DANIEL GARDNER
LCPL	MCCOLLUM, RYLEE JAMES
SGT	MCCONNELL, ANDREW HARRON
SSG	MCDANIEL, MECOLUS CHEVETTE
MSGT	MCDANIEL, WILLIAM LOUIS II
LCPL	MCDANIELS, JOSHUA BRENT
SGT	MCDONALD, EDMUND WAYNE
SSG	MCDONALD, JASON ANDREW
SFC	MCDOWELL, DAVID LOREN
CAPT	MCDOWELL, MARK RUSSELL
2LT	MCGAHAN, MICHAEL EVERETT
SPC	MCGARRAH, CLAYTON DWAYNE
CPL	MCGEATH, PHILIP DAINE
SFC	MCGEE, ROBERT KEITH
SGT	MCGEE, THOMAS PATRICK
SSG	MCGILL, TIMOTHY RAYMOND
LT	MCGREEVY, MICHAEL MARTIN JR
CAPT	MCHONE, NATHAN RONALD
COL	MCHUGH, JOHN MICHAEL
SFC	MCKAY, JOSEPH A
SSG	MCKENNA, ALLEN ROBERT JR
1SG	MCKENNA, PETER ANDREW JR
PFC	MCLAIN, BUDDY WENDALL
SSG	MCLAUGHLIN, IAN PAUL
SGT	MCLAWHORN, WILLIE ATLAS JR
SCPO	MCLENDON, DAVID BLAKE
SGT	MCLEOD, JASON ADAM
SGM	MCLOCHLIN, JEFFREY ALLEN
CPT	MCMAHON, JASON THOMAS
LTC	MCMAHON, MICHAEL JEROME
SFC	MCNABB, BARETT WAMBLI
SSG	MCNABB, SHAWN HENRY

SPC	MCNAIR, ANDRE DEVON JR
PFC	MCNEIL, SPENCE ALEXANDER
PO2	MCNELEY, JUSTIN JACOB
SPC	MCNULTY, RICHARD LEWIS III
SGT	MCQUEARY, JEREMY RYAN
SGT	MEADOR, JOHN DAVID II
PV2	MEADOWS, COLMAN JOSEPH III
CAPT	MEADOWS, JOSHUA STEWART
LCPL	MEANS, DALE WAYNE
PFC	MEARI, ANDREW NIMR MAHMOUD
SGT	MEDDOCK, CAMERON ALEXANDER
SGT	MEDLEY, PRESTON RAY
CPL	MEHRER, CURTIS ROBERT
CPL	MEHRINGER, DANIEL FREDERICK
LCPL	MEINERT, JACOB ALEXANDER
LCPL	MEIS, CHRISTOPHER STEELE
1SG	MEISTER, TOBIAS CORBIN
SSGT	MELENDEZ-SANCHEZ, LUIS MANUEL
SPC	MELTON, BRADLEY LOUIS
CAPT	MELTON, JESSE III
SSG	MELTON, JOSHUA ALLEN
SSG	MEMON, KASHIF MOHAMMED
LCPL	MENDEZ HERNANDEZ, NORBERTO
SPC	MENDOZA, HUGO VICTOR
SGT	MENDOZA, MATTHEW ELIAS
1STSGT	MERCARDANTE, LUKE JOHN
PFC	MEREDITH, WILLIAM L
LCPL	MEROLA, DYLAN RYAN
SSG	MERRIWEATHER, DANIEL DEWAYNE
SGT	MERSMAN, JEFFERY SCOTT
MAJ	MESCALL, BRIAN MICHAEL
PFC	METCALF, MICHAEL JOSEPH
SFC	METCALFE, DANIEL THOMAS
SFC	METZGER, DAVID ELIAH

SSG	METZGER, JONATHAN MATTHEW
CAPT	MICHAUD, SETH ROBERT
PFC	MICHEL, DEVIN JAY
SGT	MICKLER, DONALD RAY JR
CPL	MIDDLETON, WILLIAM KYLE
CPL	MIHALO, ANTHONY GARY
PFC	MIKEASKY, JOSHUA
PO2	MILAM, CHARLES LUKE
SPC	MILLER, ALEXANDER JOEL
PFC	MILLER, CALE CLYDE
SFC	MILLER, DANIEL EDWARD
PFC	MILLER, DAVID TAYLOR
SPC	MILLER, HARLEY D R
SPC	MILLER, JAMES LEE
A1C	MILLER, JEROME DAVID JR
PFC	MILLER, MYKEL FILIP
CPL	MILLER, PAUL JAMES
SSG	MILLER, ROBERT JAMES
SPC	MILLET MELETICHE, PEDRO ANTONIO IV
1LT	MILLEY, SCOTT FRANCIS
PFC	MILLIARD, ERROL DURAN ASTER
CPO	MILLIKEN, KYLE JEFFREY
SSG	MILLS, EDWARD DAVID JR
LCPL	MILLS, EUGENE CLIFTON III
SSG	MILLS, JOSHUA M
CPO	MILLS, STEPHEN MATTHEW
PFC	MIRACLE, JOSEPH ALAN
PO3	MIRANDA, DENIS
SGT	MISENER, GARRETT ANDERSON
SPC	MISSMAN, GREGORY JAMES
CAPT	MITCHELL, DAVID SETH
SFC	MITCHELL, SEAN KERRY
SSG	MITTLER, SHAUN MICHAEL
SPC	MIXON, KELLY JOSEPH

CW2	MOEHLING, TIMOTHY WAYNE
SPC	MOFFITT, THOMAS ADAM
SFC	MOGENSEN, ROBERT JOSEPH
SGT	MOLINA, JACOB
CPL	MONAHAN, CHRISTOPHER MICHAEL JR
SGT	MONDRAGON, ENRIQUE
PFC	MONROE, JEREMIAH JAMES
CW2	MONTENEGRO, JOSE LUIS JR
LCPL	MONTES DE OCA, OSBRANY
CW4	MONTGOMERY, MICHAEL PATRICK
SSG	MONTGOMERY, THADDEUS SCOTT II
SFC	MONTI, JARED CHRISTOPHER
PFC	MONTOYA, DIEGO MIGUEL
SGT	MONTROND, ALBERTO DASILVEIRA
SGT	MOODY, WILLIAM ROBERT
MAJ	MOOLDYK, EVAN JAN
SPC	MOON, CHRISTOPHER JAMES
SPC	MOORE, BENJAMIN GERALD
LTCOL	MOORE, JOSEPH ARTHUR
SPC	MOOSMAN, CODY OTHO
PFC	MOQUIN, BRIAN MICHAEL JR
SSG	MORA, CONRAD ADRIAN
SGT	MORA, SAMSON AUGUSTO
SSG	MORALES, ORLANDO
SGT	MORALES, RAYMUNDO PORRAS
PFC	MORALESDELVALLE, GIL ISAI
PO3	MORENO, FABRICIO ALEXANDER
CPT	MORENO, JENNIFER MADAI
2LT	MORGADO, TRAVIS ALAN
SSGT	MORGAN, DWIGHT JASON
SGT	MORIN, DARBY TODD
SPC	MORRIS, JORDAN MATTHEW
SFC	MORRIS, RAMON SHELDON
SPC	MORRISON, DONALD SCOTT

SFC	MORTON, JOHN DAVID
SGT	MOSES, SONNY JADE
LT	MOSKO, CHRISTOPHER E
SSGT	MOTE, SKY RUSSELL
SSG	MOWERY, BRIAN KEITH
SSG	MOWRIS, JAMES DOUGLAS
PO3	MUDGE, DAVID MICHAEL
SGT	MUELLER, NICKOLAS ANTHONY
SPC	MUHR, SHAWN ANDREW
SGT	MULALLEY, CHRISTOPHER WAUGH
CPL	MULLEN, SCOTT JAMES
WO1	MULLEN, SEAN WILLIAM
CPL	MULLER, IAN MATTHEW
SPC	MULLINS, BRANDON SCOTT
SPC	MULVIHILL, WILLIAM JOSEPH
SFC	MUNDEN, RAYMOND JOHN
SGT	MUNGUIARIVAS, RODRIGO AMILCA
LTC	MUNIER, CHARLES EARL
SGT	MUNIZ, CHRISTOPHER LEE
SFC	MUNOZ, PEDRO ANTONIO
SPC	MURACH, THOMAS PAIGE
SFC	MURALLES, MARCUS VINICIO
PV2	MURDOCK, MICHAEL WAYNE
SSG	MURPHREY, MICHAEL CHANCE
MAJ	MURPHY, EDWARD JOHN
LT	MURPHY, MICHAEL PATRICK
SFC	MURRAY, DENNIS RAY
TSGT	MYERS, PHILLIP ANDREW
SGT	MYRIE, MARLON E
SPC	NAGORSKI, SCOTT THOMAS
SPC	NANCE, MICHAEL ISAIAH
PFC	NAPIER, DUSTIN PAUL
1LT	NAQVI, MOHSIN A
LCPL	NASS, RYAN JOHN

SGT	NAVARRO, JUAN PANTOJA
CPL	NEAL, BENJAMIN HAROLD
PFC	NEAR, ROBERT JAMES
CPL	NECOCHEA, KENNETH EDWARD JR
PFC	NEENAN, BRENDAN PATRICK
SPC	NEFF, RANDY LJ JR
SPC	NEGRON, CARLOS JAVIER
CPT	NEHL, JAMES DOMINIC
SSG	NEIL, WILLIAM ROBERT JR
PO1	NELSON, CALEB ANDREW
SPC	NELSON, JOSHUA NATHANIEL
LCPL	NELSON, TRAVIS MICHAEL
SGT	NENA, SAPURO BRIGHTLEY
SSG	NETTLETON, ERIC MARCEL
SSG	NEVINS, LIAM JULES
SSG	NEW, STEPHEN MICHAEL
PO2	NEWLOVE, JAROD PAUL
SSG	NEWMAN, CHRISTOPHER ROD
SSG	NEWMAN, CLINTON THOMAS
SGT	NEWMAN, ERIC COLBY
SSG	NEWMAN, JAIME CARLOS
PFC	NEWTON, ALAN HOWARD JR
CPT	NEWTON, MICHAEL WRAY
LCPL	NEWTON, ROBERT JOHN
PFC	NGO, TAN QUOC
SGT	NGUYEN, LONG NGOC
CPL	NGUYEN, TEVAN LEE
SFC	NICHOLAS, JAMIE SCOTT
CW2	NICHOLS, BRYAN JOSEPH
SPC	NICHOLS, DONALD LEE
SGT	NICHOLS, KENNETH RAY JR
SPC	NICHOLS, ROB LEE
SGT	NICOL, ANDREW COTE
SPC	NIEVES, RAFAEL ANGEL JR

LCPL	NIKOUI, KAREEM MAELEE GRANT
CAPT	NISHIZUKA, REID KIJIRO
SSG	NIXON, TRAVIS WAYNE
SGT	NOLEN, JAMES MICHAEL
CPL	NOLEN, MICHAEL CONRAD
PFC	NORRIS, CODY ROBERT
SGT	NOUV, CARYN ELAINE
PV2	NOVAK, ADAM JACOB
SSG	NOWACZYK, DAVID PAUL
1LT	NOZISKA, MARK ANTHONY
SSG	NUANES, ISRAEL PAUL
CPO	NULL, NICHOLAS HEATH
SPC	NUNCIO, LEVI EFRAIN
SFC	NUNEZ, DAVID
SSG	NUNEZRODRIGUEZ, JOE ABRAHAM
PFC	NUNN, ANTHONY MICHAEL
CAPT	NYLANDER, NATHAN JAY
LCPL	O`BRIEN, NICHOLAS SHEA
LCPL	O`CONNOR, SEAN MICHAEL NICHOLAS
SSG	OAKES, CURTIS ALLEN
SGT	OBAKRAIRUR, JASPER KID
PFC	OBOD, ALBERTO LUSTRE JR
PO3	O'BRYANT, MATTHEW JAMES
PFC	OCEGUERA, ALEX
LCPL	OCHOA, ALFONSO JR
SFC	OCHSNER, JAMES SCOTT
SPC	O'DONOHOE, JUSTIN LEE
MAJ	OFECIAR, HENRY SAN NICOLAS
SGT	OFFICER, JUSTIN ADAM
PFC	OGDEN, MATTHEW DWIGHT
SSG	OLAES, TONY BRUCE
CPL	O'LEARY, TANNER JAMES
LCPL	OLESKI, BLAISE ADAM
CPL	OLIVAS, NICHOLAS HENRY

SSG	OLIVEIRA, JORGE MIGUEL
SGT	OLIVER GALBREATH, LUIS ANTONIO
SSG	OLLIS, MICHAEL HAROLD
LCPL	OLSEN, NIGEL KENTON
LCPL	OLVERA, JAVIER
PFC	O'NEILL, EVAN WILLIAM
SPC	O'NEILL, JONATHAN CHARLES
SGT	O'NEILL, MICHAEL CHRISTOPHER
SPC	O'QUIN, JAMES JOSEPH JR
LCPL	ORATOWSKI, KEVIN EDWARD
SPC	ORGAARD, TYLER JOHN
HN	ORTEGA, WILLIAM F
SSGT	ORTIZ RIVERA, JAVIER ORLANDO
CPL	OSBORN, BENJAMIN DOUGLAS
SGT	OSBORN, KYLE BRUCE
SPC	OSBORNE, JEROD HEATH
LCPL	OSE, JOSHUA SCOTT
SSG	OSMAN, ERGIN VEDAT
CW3	O'STEEN, MARK STEVEN
CPL	OSTERMAN, SEAN ANDREW
CPL	OTT, NICHOLAS STEPHEN
PO1	OUELLETTE, BRIAN JOSEPH
CPL	OUELLETTE, MICHAEL WEBSTER
SSG	OWEN, KIRK AVERY
CPT	OWENS, BARTT DEREK
SPC	OWENS, BRANDON ANDRE
SGT	OWENS, GREGORY JR
SGT	OWENS, VINCENT LEE CARSON
CPT	OZBAT, JESSE AARON
CPT	PACE, SCOTT PATRICK
SGT	PACI, ANTHONY AMERICO
SGT	PADGETT, TIMOTHY PAUL
SPC	PAGAN, BOBBY JUSTIN
CPL	PAGE, DAEGAN WILLIAM-TYELER

SPC	PAGE, JAMES ANTHONY
CAPT	PAIRSH, JOSHUA COLE
CPL	PALACIO, MICHAEL JEREMY
SPC	PALLARES, RONNIE JOSEPH
SGT	PALMATEER, MARK CHARLES
LTCOL	PALMER, BENJAMIN JAMES
PFC	PALMER, CHRISTOPHER LLOYD
SGT	PALMERTON, JASON T
SGT	PALOMAREZ, ISAAC
SSG	PAPE, KEVIN MATTHEW
SSG	PAQUET, DAVID LAWRENCE
CPL	PARADARODRIGUEZ, NICHOLAS DIMAS
SGT	PARANZINO, MICHAEL FRANCIS
SPC	PARDO, ALEJANDRO JOSE
PFC	PARK, BENJAMIN J
SFC	PARK, DAE HAN
PO1	PARKER, VINCENT E
SGT	PARSONS, JASON RAY
1LT	PARTEN, TYLER EDWARD
SFC	PASKER, TERRYL LYNN
SGT	PATCH, SCHUYLER BRENT
GYSGT	PATE, RALPH EARL JR
CPL	PATINO, CLAUDIO IV
SGT	PATRON, DANIEL JAMES
SPC	PATTERSON, CHRISTOPHER ALEXANDER
SPC	PATTERSON, CODY JAMES
SPC	PATTON, ADAM JAMES
PFC	PATTON, MICHAEL ROBERT
PO2	PATTON, SHANE ERIC
SSG	PAUL, ROBERT JOSEPH
CPL	PAYNE, RONALD RAYMOND JR
LCPL	PEAK, ADAM DANIEL
LCPL	PEARSON, BRANDON WILLIAM
CPT	PEDERSEN-KEEL, ANDREW MICHAEL

SGT	PEDRO, BRIAN JOSEPH
SPC	PELHAM, JOHN ALEXANDER
MAJ	PELKY, PHYLLIS JOY
SPC	PELLERIN, JUSTIN REID
CPT	PENA, PAUL WENCESLAUS
SGT	PENA, ROGER PINA JR
SPC	PENA-SUAREZ, PEDRO LAZARO
SGT	PENEY, JONATHAN KELLY LEE
SGT	PENICH, JOHN MICHAEL
LCPL	PENNY, RICHARD REES
SSG	PEPPER, BRANDON ROBERT
SPC	PEREDA, CALVIN MATTHEW
SPC	PEREZ, SERGIO EDUARDO
SSGT	PERKINS, ADAM LEVI
SPC	PERKINS, ADRIAN MICHAEL
SGT	PERREAULT, THEODORE LOUIS
SGT	PERROTT, DUSTIN JOHN
SSG	PERRY, JOHN WILLIAM
SGT	PETERS, JOSEPH MICHAEL
SGT	PETERSON, ANTHONY DEL MAR
SFC	PETITHORY, DANIEL HENERY
SGT	PETO, JASON DARREN
PFC	PETREE, JAYSINE PILAR SUCGANG
PFC	PFEIFER, CHRISTOPHER FRANKLIN
SPC	PHANEUF, JOSEPH EDGAR II
CAPT	PHANEUF, RYAN SCOTT
SFC	PHARRIS, ROBERT WAYNE
SSG	PHILLIPS, ANTON RAMESH
SSG	PHILLIPS, FRANCIS GENE IV
CPL	PHILLIPS, MATTHEW BRITTEN
SGT	PHILPOT, EDWARD OTIS
PFC	PICKERING, BRANDON THOMAS
LCPL	PIER, NOAH MILES
SPC	PIERCE, ROBERT ALLAN

SSG	PIERCY, BRIAN FRANCIS
SGT	PIERRE, LINDA LAMOUR
CAPT	PIERSON, JORDAN BRADFORD
PFC	PIETREK, DAWID
CPO	PIKE, CHRISTIAN MICHAEL
SPC	PILGERAM, JONATHAN ADAM
CAPT	PINCKNEY, VICTORIA ANN
SPC	PINNICK, TREVOR ADAM
SSG	PIPER, CHRISTOPHER NEAL
SGT	PIRTLE, JAMES DEWEL
PO1	PITTMAN, JESSE DARYL
LCPL	PLANK, MICHAEL GEE
SPC	PLEITEZ, BENJAMIN CARLOS
SRA	PLITE, JASON THOMAS
MAJ	PLUMHOFF, STEVEN
SPC	PLUNK, JARED CLIFTON
SGT	PLUTINO, ALESSANDRO LEONARD
MSGT	POIRIER, DAVID LUCIEN
1LT	POLING, WILLIAM COMPTON JR
MSG	PONDER, JAMES WILLIAMS III
LCPL	POOLE, TIMOTHY JAMES JR
ENS	POPE, JERRY OREALL II
CPL	PORTO, JONATHAN DANIEL
LCPL	POSEY, GREGORY ALAN
PFC	POTTER, TONY JOE JR
PO1	POUGH, PARIS SHAWN
SPC	POULIN, DENNIS CULLEN
SSG	POVILAITIS, ALEXANDER GEORGE JR
SSG	POWELL, JOSHUA DAVID
SPC	POWELL, MATTHEW CHRISTOPHER
SSG	PRANGE, BENJAMIN GILL
1LT	PRASNICKI, STEPHEN CHASE
CW2	PRATHER, CLINT JEFFREY
SPC	PRATT, DENNIS JOSEPH

CW5	PRATT, JOHN CASTLE
LCPL	PREACH, KEVIN THOMAS
SPC	PRENTLER, JOSEPH THOMAS
SPC	PRESCOTT, BRANDON JOSEPH
PFC	PRESSLEY, CHEIZRAY LASHAWN
CW3	PRICE, BRUCE EDWARD
MSG	PRICE, CHARLES LEVAN III
GYSGT	PRICE, DANIEL JOSEPH
CDR	PRICE, JOB WILSON
PFC	PRIDHAM, MICHAEL SHANE JR
SGT	PRINCE, MYCAL LEE
SPC	PROCTOR, DAVID TYLER
PO3	PROFITT, JASON ALLEN
SSG	PROSSER, BRIAN CODY
MSGT	PRUITT, SCOTT EUGENE
SSG	PUCINO, MATTHEW ALBERT
CPL	PYEATT, LUCAS TODD
SPC	PYRON, MICHAEL WAYNE
PO2	QI, XIN
CW3	QUINLAN, JOHN ANDREW
SGT	QUINN, ADAM DAVID
SSG	QUINN, PATRICK HOWARD
SSG	QUINTANA, DANIEL ANTHONY
SSG	RABJOHN, THOMAS DUANE
SGT	RABON, LUTHER WILLARD JR
SFC	RADA MORALES, JEFFREY MICHAEL
1SG	RAFFERTY, CHRISTOPHER CONRAD
SGT	RAI, BARUN
LTCOL	RAIBLE, CHRISTOPHER KEITH
CPL	RAINEY, PRUITT ALLEN
SPC	RAMIREZ, JOEL ALVAREZ
SPC	RAMIREZ, RAY ANTHONY
CW2	RAMIREZ, THALIA SUZANNE
SGT	RAMOSVELAZQUEZ, LOUIE A

SRA	RAMSEY, JACOB ISRAEL
SPC	RAMSEY, MATTHEW WAYNE
CPT	RAMSEY, WAID CHARLES
PO2	RANDOLPH, TONY MICHAEL
LCPL	RANEY, DANIEL GABRIEL
LCPL	RANGEL, CHRISTOPHER
SGT	RANKEL, JOHN KENNETH
MAJ	RANSOM, CHARLES ANTHONY
SGT	RAO, ELIJAH JOHN MILES
SGT	RAPP, ROBERT THEODORE
SPC	RAPPUHN, BRADLEY DAVID
CW2	RASMUSSEN, DERIC MICHAEL
HN	RAST, BENJAMIN DAVID
SSG	RATH, JOSHUA LEE
SCPO	RATZLAFF, THOMAS ARTHUR
SPC	RAVER, BRYN TODD
1LT	RAWL, RYAN DAVIS
SGT	RAY, ADAM JAMES
1LT	RAY, CLOVIS TIM
SSG	RAY, JOSEPH RANDALL
PFC	RAYMUNDO, MARIANO MARTIN
CW5	REAGAN, CURTIS SCOTT
SPC	REDDING, BLAINE EDWARD
SSG	REED, JERRY DON II
SPC	REED, JESSE DAVID
SSG	REEVES, JASON ALLEN
SCPO	REEVES, ROBERT JAMES
PO1	REGELIN, CHAD ROBERT
MAJ	REICH, STEPHEN CHARLES
SSG	REID, NICHOLAS JOHN
PFC	REIFERT, SHANE MICHAEL
CPL	REIFF, ZACHARY CHRISTOPHER
SSG	REIGOUX, JOB MATTHEW
SSG	REINERS, JOHN ALLEN

CPL	REINHARD, KEVIN JAMES
PFC	REPKIE, ROBERT KELSEY LEVI
PFC	RESTREPO, JUAN SEBASTIAN
HN	RETMIER, MARC ALLEN
PO1	RETZER, THOMAS EUGENE
SGT	REYES, JOSE JOEL
SGT	REYNOLDS, TITUS RODERICK
LCPL	REZA, MATTHEW GREGORY
SFC	RHEA, TRENTON LOCKARD
PFC	RHOADS, WILLINGTON MITCHELL
PFC	RICE, JEFFREY LEON
CPL	RICHARD, MATTHEW THOMAS
LCPL	RICHARDS, WILLIAM TAYLOR
SGT	RICHARDSON, JONATHAN JEROME
SGT	RICHARDSON, JOSEPH ALVIN
CWO2	RICHARDSON, RICKY LINN JR
SGT	RICHMOND, COLBY LEE
SSG	RICKETTS, WILLIAM SETH
MSGT	RIDDICK, TRAVIS WILLIAM
CPT	RIDGLEY, CHARLES EDWARD JR
SSGT	RIDOUT, JUAN MIGUEL
MSG	RIECK, JEFFREY JAMES
SPC	RILEY, BRIAN DAVID JR
SPC	RILEY, JOSEPH WILLIAM
MSG	RILEY, MICHEAL BERNARD
SGT	RIMER, JOSHUA JAMES
SGT	RINEY, DOUGLAS JAMES
PFC	RIOS ORDONEZ, GUSTAVO ADOLFO
SGT	RISTAU, MICHAEL EUGENE
SSG	RIVADENEIRA, JUAN LUIS
SSG	RIVERA, EDWIN
SGT	RIVERA, PAUL ANDREW
CPL	RIVERA, RICHARD ANTHONY JR
SPC	RIVERS, DAQUANE DEMETRIS

LCPL	RIVERS, THOMAS EDWARD JR
LCPL	ROADS, TYLER ALLAN
SFC	ROBBINS, ELLIOTT JEROME
CPL	ROBERSON, JEFFREY GORDON
LCPL	ROBERTS, CODY ALLEN
PO2	ROBERTS, DION RASHUN
SFC	ROBERTS, EDGAR NATHANIEL JR
SSG	ROBERTS, KEVIN CASEY
SPC	ROBERTS, MICHAEL CHRISTOPHER
PO1	ROBERTS, NEIL CHRISTOPHER
SFC	ROBERTSON, FORREST WARREN
SGT	ROBERTSON, NICHOLAS ALAN
PFC	ROBINSON, ANTIONE VINCENT
SSG	ROBINSON, CARLO MONTELL
CPT	ROBINSON, CHARLES DANIEL
SFC	ROBINSON, CHRISTOPHER LEE
SGT	ROBINSON, DAVID SCOTT
CPL	ROBINSON, FERNANDO DANIEL
SCPO	ROBINSON, HEATH MICHAEL
SGT	ROBINSON, JAMES CHRISTOPHER JR
SGT	ROBINSON, JOSHUA JAMES
LTCOL	ROBINSON, MICHAEL ALAN
SGT	ROBINSON, SIMONE ASIA
LCDR	ROBINSON, THOMAS LEWIS
SPC	ROBLES SANTA, WILBEL ALEXANDER
CPL	ROBLES, ADRIAN
LCPL	RODEWALD, JOSEPH EARL
LCPL	RODGERS, CHRISTOPHER BLAKE
SGT	RODGERS, JOSHUA PATRICK
CW2	RODGERS, JOSHUA ROBERT
SSG	RODGERS, KRISTOPHER DAN
SGT	RODRIGUEZ RAMIREZ, NELSON D
SFC	RODRIGUEZ, ANTONIO REY
PFC	RODRIGUEZ, ARTURO EMMANUEL

SSG	RODRIGUEZ, DANIEL ANTHONY
SFC	RODRIGUEZ, GREGORY ALLEN
SGT	RODRIGUEZ, JOSE
SGT	RODRIGUEZ, MARIO JR
LCPL	RODRIGUEZ, MATTHEW ROLANDO
MAJ	RODRIGUEZ, RODOLFO IVAN
SGT	RODRIGUEZ, RODOLFO JR
SGT	RODRIGUEZ, RONALD ARIEL
LCPL	ROEBUCK, OMAR GREGDORIAN
SGT	ROELLI, JAKOB JAMES
SSG	ROGERS, ALAN LEE
SSGT	ROGERS, JASON AARON
PFC	ROGERS, JESSY SCOTT
SGT	ROGERS, JOHN MICHAEL
SGT	ROGERS, JUSTIN RICHARD
SPC	ROJAS, DANIELA
CAPT	ROLAND, MATTHEW DAVID
SFC	ROMERO, DANIEL AARON
SPC	ROMIG, CHRISTIAN JOSEPH
SPC	ROOKEY, KYLE ROBERT
CPL	ROQUE, LESTER GOMEZ
LCPL	ROSA, ANTHONY JAMES
SGT	ROSARIO PICHARDO, JOHANNY
PFC	ROSS, ADAM COREY
CPT	ROSS, ANDREW PATRICK
LCPL	ROSS, JACOB ALLEN
CPL	ROSS, JUSTIN DAVID
SGT	ROSS, KENNETH GRANT
SPC	ROUGHTON, ANDREW JAY
SSG	ROUGLE, LARRY ISMAEL
CPL	ROUSH, NICHOLAS RYAN
1SG	ROWE, BLUE CHARLES
SGT	ROY, MICHAEL CURRIE
CPT	ROZANSKI, NICHOLAS JAN

SSG	RUDD, KEITH FREEMAN
SSG	RUDZINSKI, CHRISTOPHER MICHAEL
CW3	RUFFNER, MATTHEW PAUL
SGT	RUIZ, CESAR BOCANEGRA
SGT	RUIZ, CLINTON KEITH
SRA	RUIZ, XCEY ELENA
MSG	RUIZ, PABLO ALLENDE III
1LT	RUNKLE, JOHN MARSHALL JR
SSG	RUSHFORTH, BRUCE ALAN JR
PFC	RUSHING, THEODORE BOYKIN
PFC	RUSK, COLTON WESLEY
CPT	RUSSELL, DREW EDWARD
1LT	RUSSELL, JONAM JOSUE
SFC	RUSSELL, MICHAEL LYNN
2LT	RYLANDER, DAVID E
MSG	SABALU, WILBERTO JR
SGT	SACZEK, LUKASZ DARIUSZ
SFC	SADELL, CHARLES MONTAGUE
SGT	SAENZ, JOSE LUIS III
SPC	SALAZAR, BRENDEN NEAL
PO2	SALDANA, SLAYTON RICHARD
PFC	SALMON, ZACHARY STEVEN RICHARD
PFC	SALVACION, JR
A1C	SAMEK, JESSE MONROE
SSG	SAN AGUSTIN, DIOBANJO SORIANO
SRA	SANCHEZ, DANIEL RAY
CPL	SANCHEZ, HUMBERTO ABIEL
SGT	SANCHEZ, IAN THOMAS
SGT	SANCHEZ, JAVIER JR
MAJ	SANCHEZ, MARIA VICTORIA
SGT	SANCHEZ, ROBERTO DANIEL
SPC	SANCHO, JEREMIAH THOR
SSG	SANDERS, CHARLES RAY JR
PFC	SANNICOLAS, CHRISTIAN RILEY

SGT	SANTIAGO, ANIBAL JR
SPC	SANTIAGO, TRINIDAD JR
SGT	SANTORA, JASON ANTHONY
CPL	SANTOS, DAVE MICHAEL MALIKSI
SGT	SANTOS, DELFIN MONTEMAYOR JR
1LT	SANTOS, TIMOTHY GEORGE JR
SFC	SANTOS-SILVA, CARLOS MARCELINO
SRA	SARTAIN, NATHAN COLE
SGM	SARTOR, JAMES GREGORY
SFC	SAVARD, RYAN JAMES
SFC	SAWYER, RONALD WAYNE
SGT	SAYNE, TIMOTHY DOUGLAS
SSG	SCHAD, REX LLOYD
SSG	SCHAFER, MICHAEL WAYNE
CW4	SCHERKENBACH, CHRIS JON
SPC	SCHILLER, PHILIP CHANNING SIPE
LCPL	SCHIMMEL, PATRICK WAYNE
WO1	SCHIRO, JOSEPH LEE
GYSGT	SCHMALSTIEG, JUSTIN EDWARD
LCPL	SCHMIDT, BENJAMIN WHETSTONE
SSG	SCHMIDT, JONATHAN PHILIP
LCPL	SCHMITZ, JARED MARCUS
CPL	SCHNEIDER, KYLE RICHARD
CPL	SCHOENER, RICHARD PHILLIP
SRA	SCHOLTEN, JULIAN SEIJI
SSG	SCHOONHOVEN, MARK HENRY
1STLT	SCHULTE, ROSLYN LITTMANN
CPT	SCHULTZ, JOSEPH WILLIAM
LCPL	SCHULTZ, NATHANIEL JOSEPH AUGUSTUS
SPC	SCHUMANN, JORDAN CHRISTOPHER
SGT	SCHWALLIE, JACOB MICHAEL
TSGT	SCHWARTZ, MATTHEW SCOTT
SSG	SCIALDO, MARC ANTHONY
SGT	SCOBIE, DREW MICHAEL

PFC	SCOTT, BRICE MURRILL
SPC	SCOTT, CHRISTOPHER JOHN
SGT	SCOTT, JUSTIN ANDREW
LCPL	SCOTT, LUCAS CHRISTOPHER
SGT	SCUSA, MICHAEL PATRICK
SGT	SEABROOKS, ANDREW
SPC	SEALS, JOSHUA MICHAEL
A1C	SEIDLER, MATTHEW RYAN
SSG	SEIJA, RICARDO
SGT	SEITSINGER, DANTON KYLE
SSG	SELF, DAVID DWAYNE
SSG	SENFT, DAVID PAUL
SRA	SERVAIS, ADAM PETER
CPL	SERVIN, ANTHONY RAMON
LCPL	SERWINOWSKI, TIMOTHY GILES
SGT	SHAFFER, DEAN RUSSELL
SGT	SHANFIELD, DEREK LEE
SSG	SHANK, MICHAEL ALLEN
SFC	SHANNON, MICHAEL PAUL DAVID
SPC	SHANNON, ZACHARY LEE
LCPL	SHARP, CHARLES SETH
SGT	SHARP, RYAN DAVID
SFC	SHAW, CHRISTOPHER DONNELL
SSG	SHAW, ERIC BYRON
CPL	SHEA, KURT STEVEN
SGT	SHERER, JEFFREY CHUL SOON
SGT	SHERMAN, BENJAMIN WILLIAM
SSGT	SHERO, ANISSA ANN
PFC	SHIELDS, ANDREW JON
SPC	SHOECRAFT, JUSTIN BLUE
SPC	SHUMAKER, KEVIN ROGER
SSGT	SIBLEY, FORREST BRENT
1SG	SIERCKS, BILLY JOE
SGT	SIGLEY, RANDOLPH ALONZO JR

SSG	SILK, BRANDON MARK
SPC	SILVA, EDUARDO SOSA
CW2	SILVERMAN, JOSHUA BENJAMIN
LCPL	SIM, SAN
PFC	SIMMONS, ANTHONY WARREN
MSG	SIMMONS, SHAWN ELLIOT
CPL	SIMONETTA, DEREK TODD
SGT	SIMPSON, MARK ALLEN
SSG	SIMPSON, MICHAEL HARRISON
CW3	SIMS, JACOB MICHAEL
PFC	SIMS, MARKIE TYRELL
CPL	SINGER, CHRISTOPHER GREG
CPL	SINGH, GURPREET
PFC	SINKLER, AMY RENEE
SPC	SIPPLE, ANDREW HOLLAND
2LT	SISSON, JUSTIN LEE
SGT	SISSON, ROBERT CURTIS JR
CPL	SITTON, CHRISTOPHER FRANKLIN
SSG	SITTON, MATTHEW STEVEN
SGT	SKALBERG, JAMES LYN JR
SFC	SKELT, ROBERTO CARLOS
CPT	SKLAVER, BENJAMIN A
SPC	SLACK, WADE ALAN
SGT	SLAPE, JAMES ALLEN
CW4	SLEBODNIK, MICHAEL
CPL	SLEDD, ANTONIO JAMES
MAJ	SLOAN, DOUGLAS EMORY
SFC	SLUSS-TILLER, MATTHEW STEPHEN
SSGT	SLUTMAN, CHRISTOPHER-KENLEY ALDRIC
PFC	SMALL, ANDREW RICHARD
SSG	SMALL, MARC JOSEPH
1STLT	SMALL, SARAH KATHERINE
SGT	SMITH, AARON MICHAEL
PO2	SMITH, ADAM OLIN

SRA	SMITH, BRADLEY RANDALL
SSGT	SMITH, DAVID CAZZIE
SGT	SMITH, DAVID JAMES
SSG	SMITH, EDWARD BERNARD
SGT	SMITH, GERRICK D
PO1	SMITH, JAMES LEE
SGT	SMITH, JASON THOMAS
SSGT	SMITH, JEREMY DANIEL
CW2	SMITH, JOHN DAREN
SSG	SMITH, PAUL GENE
SGT	SMITH, SCOTT DANIEL
SGT	SMITH, STEFAN MARC
SFC	SMITH, TARA JEAN
SSG	SMITH, TYLER JAMES
LCPL	SMITH, ZACHARY DYLAN
SPC	SNOW, DEANGELO BARNELL
SPC	SNOW, JESSE ADAM
MSGT	SNOW, TERESA MICHELLE
SSG	SNYDER, ALAN LEIGH
SGT	SNYDER, DEVIN ARIELLE
SPC	SNYDER, NORMAN KYLE
CPL	SOCKALOSKY, STEPHEN COTY
SGT	SODERLUND, CHRISTOPHER PAUL
SSG	SOJA, MAREK ANDRZEJ
TSGT	SOLESBEE, KRISTOFFER MICHAEL
SGT	SOLORZANO VALDOVINOS, DIEGO ALBERTO
SPC	SOLTERO, OMAR
CPL	SONKA, DAVID MICHAEL
PFC	SOUFRINE, ERIC DANIEL
1LT	SOUTHWORTH, JARED WILLIAM
SGT	SOUTHWORTH, TRISTAN HOWARD
PO3	SOVIAK, MAXTON WILLIAM
LCPL	SOVIE, NICHOLAS JOSEPH

LCPL	SPARKS, JOHN TRAVIS
SSG	SPARKS, ORION NELSON
SPC	SPAULDING, RILEY SHERIDAN
SFC	SPEER, CHRISTOPHER JAMES
PO2	SPEHAR, NICHOLAS PATRICK
GYSGT	SPICER, DAVID SHANE
SSG	SPINO, RONALD JAY
SGT	SPITZER, THOMAS ZACHARY
SPC	SPIVEY, MICHAEL KEITH
PFC	SPRINGER, CLINTON EDWARD II
PFC	SPRINGMANN, TYLER MICHAEL
SSGT	SPROVTSOFF, NICHOLAS ADAM
SSG	STAATS, CHRIS NEIL
SGT	STACEY, WILLIAM CHAPMAN
LCPL	STACK, JAMES BRAY
SSG	STACY, DONALD VINCENT
PFC	STAGGS, AUSTIN GARRETT
SPC	STAMBAUGH, CAMERON JAMES
CPL	STANDFEST, JEFFREY ROBERT
SPC	STANKER, JARED DONALD
SGT	STANLEY, CHASE BRENNEN
LCPL	STANLEY, CODY ROBERT
CPL	STANLEY, DEREK ANTHONY
CN	STANLEY, TREVOR JOVANNE
SPC	STANSBERY, MICHAEL LANE JR
CPL	STANTON, JORDAN ROBERT
1SG	STAPLEY, TRACY LANE
SPC	STARK, CHRISTOPHER GLENN
SGT	STEEDLEY, CAMELLA MARCHETT
CAPT	STEEL, JAMES MICHAEL
CPT	STEELE, JOSHUA ERIC
1LT	STEELE, TIMOTHY JAMES
SPC	STEFFEY, BRANDON KEITH
LTC	STEIN, JOHN HENRY

SGT	STEPHENS, DAVID ALEXANDER
SFC	STEPHENS, RILEY GENE
SSG	STETS, MARK ALAN JR
LCPL	STEVENS, STEVEN PRINCE II
MSG	STEVENSON, BENJAMIN ALLEN
SSGT	STEWART, DAVID HAMILTON
SGT	STEWART, PATRICK DANA
CPL	STEYART, MATTHEW PAUL
SGT	STILES, JONNIE LEE
SSG	STILTZ, MATTHEW HENRICK
CPL	STITES, JESSE WADE
SSG	STIVISON, GLEN HALE JR
SFC	STODDARD, JAMES JOHN JR
SPC	STOECKLI, KYLE PASCAL
MSG	STONE, JOHN THOMAS
PFC	STONESIFER, KRISTOFOR TIF
SSG	STOUT, CHRISTOPHER TODD
SPC	STOUT, CHRYSTAL GAYE
SGT	STOUT, KYLE BRANDON
SGT	STRACHOTA, MICHAEL JOSEPH
PO1	STRANGE, MICHAEL JOSEPH
LTCOL	STRATTON, MARK EDWARD II
SGT	STREAM, SCOTT BRADLEY
SSGT	STRICKLAND, CHRISTOPHER DEWAYNE
PO3	STRICKLAND, EICHMANN ANTONIO
SGT	STRICKLAND, JOSHUA JACOB
SGT	STRONG, CHARLES CALVIN
LCPL	STROUD, JONATHAN FULTON
CPL	STRUBLE, SASCHA
SSG	STUDENMUND, SCOTT RICHARD
SSG	STUDER, BRIAN EDWARD
CPL	STULTZ, GREGORY SCOTT
WO1	STUMP, ADRIAN BOVEE
PFC	STYER, BRANDON MICHAEL

SPC	SUGGS, CODY DALTON
CW4	SUGGS, MILTON ERIC
PO2	SUH, JAMES ERIK
CPO	SULLIVAN, SEAN PATRICK
SGT	SUMMERS, JEREMY RUSSELL
SFC	SUMMERS, SEVERIN WEST III
SFC	SUPLEE, DANIEL ADRIAN
PFC	SUTER, JAKE WILLIAM
SPC	SUTER, PRESTON J
SFC	SUTTON, BILLY ALBERT
LCPL	SUTTON, STEVEN GENE
SGT	SVITAK, PHILIP JAMES
LCPL	SWANSON, AARON MICHAEL
LCPL	SWANSON, JUSTIN JAMES
CPL	SWANSON, MATTHEW KALEN SAMUEL
SSG	SWEENEY, PAUL ANTHONY
CPL	SWENSON, CURTIS MICHAEL
SGT	SWINDLE, JASON MICHAEL
PO3	SWINK, JAMES MICHAEL II
SPC	SYKES, PENDELTON LIDELL II
CDR	SZWEC, ADRIAN BASIL
SPC	TABADA, BRIAN
SFC	TABB, DONALD THERRONNIE
SGT	TALBERT, CHRISTOPHER MAXWELL
PO1	TAPPER, DAVID MARTIN
LCPL	TARWOE, ABRAHAM
AN	TATE, DARREN ETHAN
CPL	TATE, JACOB ALLEN
SSG	TATE, SHELDON LEON
CPO	TATHAM, MICHAEL REX
SSGT	TAUB, PETER WAGNER
SPC	TAUTERIS, ROBERT JOSEPH JR
SGT	TAUTOLO, TOFIGA JOSHUA
SGT	TAWNEY, IAN MATTHEW

SSGT	TAYLOR, AARON JAMES
SSGT	TAYLOR, ARCHIE ANDREW
MAJ	TAYLOR, BRENT RUSSELL
SSG	TAYLOR, CYNTHIA RENEA
SPC	TAYLOR, DAVID WAYNE
SGT	TAYLOR, DEON LAMARR
SFC	TAYLOR, HOUSTON MARK
PO1	TAYLOR, JEFFREY SCOTT
SFC	TAYLOR, JOHN EDWARD
CPL	TAYLOR, JOHNATHAN WESLEY
LCPL	TAYLOR, JONATHAN ANDREW
SPC	TAYLOR, MATHEW DONALD
SPC	TAYLOR, NICHOLAS ANDREW
SSGT	TEAL, JOHN MICHAEL
SGT	TELLIER, ZACHARY DANIEL
CAPT	TERHUNE, ERIC DANIEL
LCPL	TERWISKE, ALEC ROBERT
LCPL	THACKER, JUSTON TYLER
1LT	THEINERT, JOSEPH JAMES
CW2	THIBODEAU, CHRISTOPHER ROY
SFC	THODE, JAMES EARL
PFC	THOMAS, ADAM LEE
SSG	THOMAS, ADAM SAMUEL
SGT	THOMAS, CAMERON HARRISON
CPO	THOMAS, COLLIN TRENT
SGT	THOMAS, DAVID WILLIAM
SSG	THOMAS, JESSE LAMAR JR
PFC	THOMAS, KRISTOFER DOUGLAS SCOTT
SFC	THOMAS, MATTHEW BRADFORD
SSG	THOMAS, MICHAEL DUANE
SSG	THOMAS, ROBERT EDWARD JR
1LT	THOMPSON, ALEJO RENE
SPC	THOMPSON, BLAIR DANIEL
SGT	THOMPSON, DANIEL JAMES

CPT	THOMPSON, DAVID J
LCPL	THOMPSON, JABARI NKOSI
SSG	THOMPSON, MATTHEW VAIL
PFC	THOMSON, KEVIN CHRISTOPHER
SSG	THROCKMORTON, JOSHUA ADAM
SSG	TIEMAN, RICHARD JAMES
CPL	TILLMAN, PATRICK DANIEL
SGT	TILTON, JESSE RICHARD
SPC	TIMMONS, DAVID NELSON JR
CPT	TINSLEY, JOHN
CDR	TIU, JOEL DEL MUNDO
SGT	TOBIN, ANDREW ROBERT
SFC	TODD, DAVID JAMES JR
1LT	TOGI, JASON
PO1	TOLES, ROSS LAVAL III
SGT	TOM, TROY ORION
SGT	TOMLINSON, JOSHUA ABRAM
SSG	TOMPKINS, TRAVIS MARTIN
LTJG	TONER, FRANCIS LAWRENCE IV
PFC	TOPPEN, AARON SCOTT
CPL	TORBERT, ERIC MICHAEL JR
MSGT	TORIAN, AARON CARL
SPC	TORRES, JUAN MANUEL
SGT	TORRES, LOUIS RAMON
CW3	TOTTEN, ERIC WILLIAM
LCPL	TOVES, JACOB JOSEPH
PFC	TOWNSEND, JON ROSS
SSG	TOWNSEND, JOSHUA RHEA
SPC	TOWSE, CODY JAMES
SGT	TRACY, WILLIAM JOHN
SFC	TRANSFIGURACION, REYMUND RAROGAL
SGT	TREBER, JAMES MATTHEWS
MSG	TRENT, GREGORY RAY
SFC	TRENT, NELSON DAVID

PFC	TRIMBLE, CHAD MICHEAL
SSG	TRUEBLOOD, ERIC STANLEY
PV1	TUCKER, LAMAROL JEROME
PFC	TUCKER, STEVEN CHARLES
CPO	TUMILSON, JON THOMAS
CPL	TURBETT, JACOB HENRY
SSG	TURNBULL, LYLE DERVIN
1SG	TURNER, EDDIE
SPC	TURNER, ESTELL LEE
PFC	TURNER, NEIL ISAAC
SGM	TURNER, WARDELL BENJAMIN
PO3	TURPIN, EMORY JASON
LCPL	TUTTLE, BENJAMIN WAYNE
LCPL	TWIGG, JOSHUA THOMAS
SFC	TYCZ, PETER PAUL II
PFC	TYNES, MARCUS ALLAN
HN	ULLOM, AARON DAVID
CPL	UZENSKI, NICHOLAS KELLY
CPL	VACCARO, ANGELO JOSEPH
LCPL	VALDEZ, STEVEN ARMANDO
MSG	VAN AALST, JARED NEVILLE
SGT	VAN AALTEN, ALEXANDER
SGT	VAN ZOEST, TRAVIS ALLEN
SSG	VANCE, GENE ARDEN JR
CAPT	VANDEGIESEN, KYLE ROLF
CPL	VANDREUMEL, JOSEPH ANDREW
SSG	VANGIESEN, KENNETH ROWLAND
PFC	VAQUERANO, JALFRED DAVID
SPC	VARGAS, ANTHONY
CPL	VARGAS, JULIO
CW2	VARNADORE, TERRY LEE II
SFC	VASQUEZ, GARY JOSEPH
SPC	VASQUEZ, MANUEL JOSEPH
SGT	VASSELIAN, DANIEL MARK

CPO	VAUGHN, AARON CARSON
SPC	VAUGHN, TRAVIS RYAN
LCPL	VAZQUEZ, FREDERIK ERIK
SSG	VAZQUEZ, JASON ANTHONY
SSG	VAZQUEZ, RICHARD LEE
PO2	VELASQUEZ, JORGE LUIS
SPC	VELEZ, ANDREW
SFC	VENETZ, ANTHONY JR
SSG	VENNE, DAIN TAYLOR
LCPL	VERBEEK, JARED CAMERRON
SPC	VICARI, AUGUSTUS JAMES
CPO	VICKERS, KRAIG MICHAEL KALEOLANI
PFC	VIEYRA, BARBARA
SSG	VILE, WILLIAM DAVID
CPL	VILLACIS, JORGE EMMANUEL
SPC	VILLALON, MIGUEL ANGEL
PFC	VILLANUEVA, JONATHAN MICHAEL
CPL	VILLARREAL, JORGE JR
PFC	VIMOTO, TIMOTHY RAY
PFC	VINCENT, DONALD WAYNE
LCPL	VINNEDGE, PHILLIP DAVID
SSG	VIOLA, ALEX ANTHONY
CW2	VIRAY, DON CAYETANO
SPC	VOAKES, ROBERT LEE JR
MAJ	VOAS, RANDELL DUNTON
MAJ	VOELKE, PAUL CLARKE
SFC	VOGELER, LANCE HERMAN
SGT	VOID, DEMETRIUS LAMAR
SPC	VON ZERNECK, JASON ERIC
MAJ	VORDERBRUGGEN, ADRIANNA MARIA
CW2	VOSE, DOUGLAS M III
CAPT	VOSS, MARK TYLER
LTCOL	VOSS, PAUL KENNETH
SPC	WADE, ANDREW PAUL

CPL	WADE, CHAD STAFFORD
SGT	WADE, TRISTAN MYKAL
PFC	WADMAN, BRANDON JAMES
CW3	WAGSTAFF, MATTHEW GABRIEL
SGT	WALKER, BRIAN LLOYD
1LT	WALKER, LAURA MARGARET
SPC	WALKER, MATTHEW HERBERT
PFC	WALKER, MORRIS LEWIS
SSGT	WALKUP, THOMAS ALVA JR
SGT	WALLACE, DANIEL WAYNE
SGT	WALLACE, DAVID WILLIAM III
CPT	WALLACE, ELLERY R
SFC	WALLS, JOHNNY CARL
SGT	WALLS, JONATHAN MICHAEL
1LT	WALSH, JONATHAN PATRICK
SPC	WALSH, SEAN MICHAEL
SPC	WALSHE, TYLER ROBERT
TSGT	WALTERS, HOWARD ARLEN
SGT	WALTERS, ZACHARY JOE
LTC	WALTON, JAMES JOSEPH
PFC	WALZ, CHRISTOPHER IAN
SSG	WARD, CHRISTOPHER MICHAEL
LCPL	WARD, ERIC LEVI
SGT	WARE, ALBERT DONO
HN	WARREN, ERIC DEAN
SSG	WARREN, KYLE RAY
PFC	WARRINER, CHRISTIAN MICHAEL KADE
PO2	WARSEN, DAVID JOHN
SGT	WASHINGTON, MICHAEL TOUSSIANT-HYLE
SPC	WATERS, JAMES ALLEN
LCPL	WATSON, FRANKLIN NAMON
PFC	WATSON, JASON RYAN
SPC	WATTS, SAMUEL THOMAS
SFC	WEATHERS, ANDREW TARRANT

MSG	WEAVER, DAVY NATHANIEL
SGT	WEAVER, JASON MICHAEL
1LT	WEAVER, TODD WILLIAM
SGT	WEICHEL, DENNIS PAUL JR
SSG	WEIGLE, DAVID JEE
SSG	WEIKERT, MATTHEW WARD
SGT	WEINGER, ROBERT MARTIN
MAJ	WEIS, JAMES MATTHEW
SPC	WELCH, JONATHAN DAVID
SPC	WELCH, NICKOLAS SHANE
1LT	WELCH, ROBERT FORREST III
SSG	WELLS, MARK CHRISTOPHER
SPC	WELLS, WESLEY ROBERT
SSG	WEST, MATTHEW J
SFC	WESTBROOK, KENNETH WARREN
MAJ	WESTON, MICHAEL EDWARD
SPC	WHEELER, ABRAHAM SHERROD III
SFC	WHETTEN, GLEN JACOB
SPC	WHIPPLE, BLAKE DANIEL
LCPL	WHITACRE, ANDREW FRANCIS
SSG	WHITAKER, JOSHUA ROBERT
1LT	WHITE, ASHLEY IRENE
SRA	WHITE, BENJAMIN DANIEL
PFC	WHITE, JAMES PAUL JR
SPC	WHITE, JEFFREY LEE JR
SPC	WHITE, JOSEPH VALERE
CW3	WHITE, KENNETH RYAN
SGT	WHITE, KEVIN WILSON
PFC	WHITE, ROBERT CHARLES III
SSG	WHITE, ROBERT FRANK
LCPL	WHITE, RUSSELL PATRICK
CPL	WHITEHEAD, JOSEPH CHARLES
CAPT	WHITLOCK, NICHOLAS SCHADE
PFC	WHITMIRE, JUSTIN MICHAEL

SPC	WHITSITT, GEOFFREY ALEXANDER
CPT	WHITTEN, DANIEL PRESTON
LCPL	WHITTLE, JOSHUA RAY
SGT	WICHMANN, GRANT ARTHUR
SPC	WICKLIFF CHACIN, JAMES TAYLOR
SGT	WIEKAMP, JEFFERY SCOTT
SSG	WILBUR, CHRISTOPHER ALEXANDER
PFC	WILDES, MATTHEW EVERETT
SPC	WILDRICK, RONALD HERBERT JR
LTC	WILEY, JAMES LEON JR
CPL	WILFAHRT, ANDREW CHARLES
1STLT	WILKENS, JUSTIN JAMES
SGT	WILKINSON, ADAM ALEXANDER
CPL	WILKS, KYLE WESTON
CAPT	WILLARD, BRYAN DOUGLAS
CPL	WILLIAMS, ANTHONY LEE
PFC	WILLIAMS, CHARLES ALVIN II
SPC	WILLIAMS, CLARENCE III
SGT	WILLIAMS, DAVID VINCENT
PFC	WILLIAMS, DENNIS MICHAEL
1LT	WILLIAMS, DERWIN ISAAC
SGT	WILLIAMS, ERIC EDWARD
SSG	WILLIAMS, JESSE LEE
PFC	WILLIAMS, KEITH MICHAEL
TSGT	WILLIAMS, LESLIE DOMINIC
SSG	WILLIAMS, WESLEY ROSS
SGT	WILLIAMSON, PATRICK OLIVER
SGT	WILSON, CHRISTOPHER M
LCPL	WILSON, IVAN IRL
LCPL	WILSON, JUSTIN J
PFC	WILSON, MATTHEW WILLARD
PO1	WILSON, RYAN JAMES
PFC	WILSON, SHANE GREGORY
PFC	WILSON, THOMAS RANDOLPH

SGT	WILSON, WADE DANIEL
SSG	WILSON, WILLIAM ROBERT III
LCPL	WIMPEY CAGLE, JOHN ROBERT
SSG	WING, JESSICA MARIE
SPC	WINKLEMAN, DAMON GABRIEL
PV2	WINSTON, VINCENT CORTEZ JR
SGT	WINTERS, JEANNETTE LEE
SSG	WINTERS, LESTON MICHAEL
SFC	WISE, BENJAMIN BRIAN
CAPT	WISNIEWSKI, DAVID ANTHONY
SGT	WITKOWSKI, PHILIP LAWRENCE
LCPL	WITSMAN, JOSHUA ELI
SGT	WITTMAN, AARON XAVIER
SGT	WITTMAN, JEREMIAH THOMAS
SGT	WOITOWICZ, WILLIAM JOSEPH
SGT	WOLF, EDUVIGES GUADALUPE
CPL	WOLFF, ADAM FRANKLIN
PFC	WOLVERTON, BRIAN MICHAEL
PFC	WOOD, BRETT EVERETT
PFC	WOOD, EDWIN COBELLEE
SGT	WOOD, ROY ALVIN
PO3	WOOD, ZARIAN ANDRE
SSG	WOODARD, ROMANES LEE
CPL	WOODS, TRAVIS MARTIN
SFC	WOODS, WILLIAM BRIAN JR
SGT	WORKMAN, CHRIS JOHN
CPO	WORKMAN, JASON RAY
SGT	WORLD, FRANK JOSEPH-ALFONSO
CPL	WREN, CHARLES JEFFREY
SPC	WRIGHT, CHRISTOPHER SHANE
1LT	WRIGHT, DAVID TIMOTHY II
SGT	WRIGHT, JEREMY ROBERT
SPC	WRIGHT, KYLE JAMES
LCPL	WRIGHT, TERRY CARL

SGT	WRIGHTSMAN, JOE LEE
SGT	WRINKLE, CHRISTOPHER MATTHEW
CPL	WYATT, DEREK ALLEN
SPC	WYATT, STERLING WILLIAM
SGT	WYCKOFF, CHARLES EDWARD JR
PFC	WYKSTRA, JACOB HENRY
SSG	WYRICK, NATHAN LEE
LCPL	XAVIER, PATRICK JR
CPL	XIARHOS, NICHOLAS GEORGE
PFC	YANNEY, JONATHAN CHRISTOPHER
1LT	YATES, ERIC DAVID
LCPL	YAZZIE, ALEJANDRO JAY
SRA	YELNER, JONATHAN ANTONIO VEGA
CPT	YLLESCAS, ROBERTO JOSE
CW2	YODER, JARETT MICHAEL
CPL	YOUNG, JAMES CHAD
MSG	YOUNG, MITCHELL WAYNE
SFC	YOUNG, RICARDO DEANDRELL
CAPT	YURISTA, TREVOR JON
SGT	ZAEHRINGER, FRANK RIDDELL III
CPL	ZANOWICK, PAUL WILLIAM II
TSGT	ZERBE, DANIEL LEE
1LT	ZERMENO, ANDRES
1STLT	ZIMMERMAN, JAMES RUSSELL
SSG	ZIMMERMAN, SONNY CHRISTOPHER
SPC	ZIZUMBO, DANIEL
CPL	ZWILLING, GUNNAR WILLIAM

ACKNOWLEDGEMENTS

First and foremost, I want to acknowledge and pay tribute to the 2,448 service members that have given their lives in support of our mission in Afghanistan.

To all of those who volunteered to have their stories shared in this book and the forthcoming book, I wholeheartedly thank you for allowing me to share your story with the world.

A big thank you goes out to Charles as well for bringing it to my attention that my list was incomplete.

Lastly, to my family and my support system who endured my long hours buried in research, incessant ramblings, frustrations and excitement.

BIBLIOGRAPHY

- briefing on Operation Moshtarak in Helmand Province, Afghanistan. Accessed July 9, 2022. https://www.govinfo.gov/content/pkg/CHRG-111shrg64644/html/CHRG-111shrg64644.htm.

"11 Seals, 8 Army Night Stalkers Killed 14 Years Ago Today in Operation Red Wings." American Military News, June 28, 2019. https://americanmilitarynews.com/2019/06/11-seals-8-army-night-hawks-killed-14-years-ago-today-in-operation-red-wings/.

2, Daphne EviatarOctober, Daphne Eviatar, and Daphne Eviatar. "Here's the New U.s.-Afghanistan Bilateral Security Agreement." Just Security, October 2, 2014. https://www.justsecurity.org/15843/u-s-afghanistan-bilateral-security-agreement/.

2022-07-08, 2022-07-07, 2022-07-06, and 2022-07-05. "IEC Everywhere for a Safer and More Efficient World." IEC, July 8, 2022. https://www.iec.ch/homepage.

ABC News. "Five Arrested in Afghanistan over Involvement in Pakistan School Massacre." ABC News. ABC News, January 15, 2015. https://www.abc.net.au/news/2015-01-15/five-men-arrested-for-pakistan-massacre-involvement/6018048.

"Abdul Raziq Achakzai." Historica Wiki. Accessed July 9, 2022. https://historica.fandom.com/wiki/Abdul_Raziq_Achakzai.

"About First Read." August deadliest month for U.S. military - First Read - msnbc.com. Accessed July 9, 2022. https://web.archive.org/web/20090928234410/http://firstread.msnbc.msn.com/archive/2009/08/31/2048560.aspx.

"Afghan Civilians." The Costs of War. Accessed July 9, 2022. https://watson.brown.edu/costsofwar/costs/human/civilians/afghan.

"Afghan Conflict: Special Forces 'Free' Prisoners of Taliban." BBC News. BBC, May 6, 2016. https://www.bbc.com/news/world-asia-36230668.

"Afghan Forces Raid Another Taliban 'Prison' in Helmand." FDD's Long War Journal. Accessed July 9, 2022. https://www.longwarjournal.org/archives/2016/02/afghan-forces-raid-another-taliban-prison-in-helmand.php.

"Afghan Taliban Abducts 40 Passengers on Kunduz Highway." Taliban News | Al Jazeera. Al Jazeera, June 8, 2016. https://www.aljazeera.com/news/2016/6/8/afghan-taliban-abducts-40-passengers-on-kunduz-highway.

"Afghan Taliban Launch Spring Offensive as U.S. Reviews Strategy," Reuters (Thomson Reuters, April 28, 2017), https://www.reuters.com/article/us-afghanistan-taliban/afghan-taliban-launch-spring-offensive-as-u-s-reviews-strategy-idUSKBN17U0E9.

"Afghan Taliban Seize Dozens of Hostages in Kunduz." BBC News. BBC, June 8, 2016. https://www.bbc.com/news/world-asia-36478081.

"Afghanistan 2004 Constitution." Constitute. Accessed July 9, 2022. https://www.constituteproject.org/constitution/Afghanistan_2004?lang=en.

"Afghanistan Is Head Killed in RAID - US and Afghan Officials." BBC News. BBC, May 8, 2017. https://www.bbc.com/news/world-asia-39839339.

"Afghanistan War." Encyclopædia Britannica. Encyclopædia Britannica, inc. Accessed July 9, 2022. https://www.britannica.com/event/Afghanistan-War#ref292844.

"Afghanistan: The New Constitution." Council on Foreign Relations. Council on Foreign Relations. Accessed July 9, 2022. https://www.cfr.org/backgrounder/afghanistan-new-constitution.

"Afghanistan's Security Forces Take over from NATO." The Guardian. Guardian News and Media, June 18, 2013. https://

www.theguardian.com/world/2013/jun/18/afghan-forces-take-security-lead-from-nato.

"After Afghan Massacre, How Deep Are the Wounds?" US-ATODAY.COM, March 12, 2012. https://web.archive.org/web/20120323201905/https://www.usatoday.com/news/world/afghanistan/story/2012-03-12/panjwai-afghanistan-killings/53503494/1.

"Agreement for Bringing Peace to Afghanistan as a State and Is Known as ..." Accessed July 9, 2022. https://www.state.gov/wp-content/uploads/2020/02/Agreement-For-Bringing-Peace-to-Afghanistan-02.29.20.pdf.

Al Jazeera, "Afghan President Ghani Flees Country as Taliban Enters Kabul," Ashraf Ghani News | Al Jazeera (Al Jazeera, August 16, 2021), https://www.aljazeera.com/news/2021/8/15/afghan-president-ghani-flees-country-as-taliban-surrounds-kabul.

Al Jazeera, "Full Transcript of Bin Ladin's Speech," News | Al Jazeera (Al Jazeera, November 1, 2004), https://www.aljazeera.com/news/2004/11/1/full-transcript-of-bin-ladins-speech.

Al Jazeera. "US-Taliban Afghan Peace Talks at 'Important Stage': Khalilzad." Taliban News | Al Jazeera. Al Jazeera, December 19, 2019. https://www.aljazeera.com/news/2019/12/19/us-taliban-afghan-peace-talks-at-important-stage-khalilzad.

"Al-Qaeda's Kandahar Training Camp 'Probably the Largest' in Afghan War." FDD's Long War Journal. Accessed July 9, 2022. https://www.longwarjournal.org/archives/2015/10/al-Qaedas-kandahar-training-camp-probably-the-largest-in-afghan-war.php.

"Al-Qaeda's Kandahar Training Camp 'Probably the Largest' in Afghan War." FDD's Long War Journal. Accessed July 9, 2022. https://www.longwarjournal.org/archives/2015/10/al-Qaedas-kandahar-training-camp-probably-the-largest-in-afghan-war.php.

Andersson, Hilary. "Red Cross Confirms 'Second Jail' at Bagram, Afghanistan." BBC News. BBC, May 11, 2010. http://news.bbc.co.uk/2/hi/south_asia/8674179.stm.

Anusha, "Iec.org.af Election Types : Independent Commission of Afghanistan," – www.electionin.org, accessed July 12, 2022, https://www.electionin.org/2639.html.

Ap. "U.S. Hands over Bagram Prison to Afghans." The Huffington Post, September 12, 2012. https://web.archive.org/web/20120913225753/http://www.huffingtonpost.com/2012/09/10/us-hands-over-bagram-prison-afghanistan_n_1869671.html.

Army completes investigations of deaths at Bagram and forwards to respective commanders for action. Accessed July 9, 2022. https://web.archive.org/web/20071224110128/http://www4.army.mil/ocpa/read.php?story_id_key=6450.

Ayaz Gul, "At Least 140 Killed in Taliban Assault on Afghan Army Base," VOA (At Least 140 Killed in Taliban Assault on Afghan Army Base, April 22, 2017), https://www.voanews.com/a/more-than-100-killed-in-taliban-assault-on-afghan-army-base/3821184.html.

"Bagram Prison Handed over to Afghan Forces despite US Concerns over Future of Inmates," CBS News (CBS Interactive), accessed July 12, 2022, https://www.cbsnews.com/news/bagram-prison-handed-over-to-afghan-forces-despite-us-concerns-over-future-of-inmates/.

"Battle of Darzab." DBpedia. Accessed July 9, 2022. https://dbpedia.org/page/Battle_of_Darzab.

"Biography of Dr. Abdullah Abdullah," Afghanistan Online, September 13, 2020, https://www.afghan-web.com/biographies/biography-of-dr-abdullah-abdullah/.

"Bomber in Afghanistan Kills 15, Including Six Americans." Reuters. Thomson Reuters, May 16, 2013. https://www.reuters.com/article/us-afghanistan-attack/bomber-in-afghanistan-kills-15-including-six-americans-idUSBRE94F06320130516.

"Bonn Conference Could Mark Formal Start of Afghan Peace Process." The Guardian. Guardian News and Media, June 20, 2011. https://www.theguardian.com/world/julian-borger-global-security-blog/2011/jun/20/afghanistan-taliban-talks-bonn.

"Bowe Bergdahl Exchange." Ballotpedia. Accessed July 9, 2022. https://ballotpedia.org/Bowe_Bergdahl_exchange.

Bowman, Tom, Steve Inskeep, and Renee Montagne. "U.S. Gen. Urges Release of Bagram's Detainees." NPR. NPR, August 20, 2009. https://www.npr.org/templates/story/story.php?storyId=112051193.

"Briefing," Time (Time Inc., March 26, 2012), https://content.time.com/time/subscriber/article/0,33009,2109142,00.html.

Brown, Daniel. "The Life of Afghan Gen. Abdul Raziq, Whose Assassination Thursday Was a Huge Taliban Victory." Business Insider. Business Insider, October 19, 2018. https://www.businessinsider.com/afghan-gen-abdul-raziq-whose-assassination-was-a-taliban-victory-2018-10#in-the-last-few-years-of-his-life-raziq-often-disregarded-the-chain-of-command-criticized-afghan-president-ghani-and-would-walk-around-without-his-uniform-on-ghani-considered-firing-him-but-the-us-dissuaded-him-arguing-it-would-bring-instability-7.

Browne, Ryan, and Zachary Cohen. "2 US Service Members Killed in Afghanistan." CNN. Cable News Network, April 28, 2017. https://edition.cnn.com/2017/04/27/politics/us-special-operations-forces-soldiers-afghanistan/index.html.

Carter, Chelsea J., Masoud Popalzai, and Joe Sterling. "Official: Man in Afghan Security Uniform Kills 3 U.S. Troops." CNN. Cable News Network, August 10, 2012. https://www.cnn.com/2012/08/10/world/asia/afghanistan-us-casualties.

"Central Intelligence Agency - CIA." Accessed July 9, 2022. https://www.cia.gov/readingroom/docs/0006555318.pdf.

Central Intelligence Agency. Central Intelligence Agency. Accessed July 9, 2022. https://www.cia.gov/legacy/museum/exhibit/on-the-front-lines-cia-in-afghanistan/.

Clark, James. "For Those Who Fought in Marjahh, It Was More than Just a Battle." Task & Purpose, July 8, 2021. https://taskandpurpose.com/leadership/fought-Marjahh-just-battle/.

Constable, Pamela, and Sayed Salahuddin. "Taliban Rival Claims Kabul Blast That Kills at Least 15, Including Two U.S. Troops." The Washington Post. WP Company, May 16, 2013. https://www.washingtonpost.com/world/bomb-in-kabul-kills-4-nato-forces-6-afghans/2013/05/16/baa60108-be0c-11e2-89c9-3be8095fe767_story.html.

Constable, Pamela. "Former Afghan Leader Hamid Karzai Grew Estranged from His American Allies during 10 Years in Power. Here's What He Says about the Afghanistan Papers." The Washington Post. WP Company, December 18, 2019. https://www.washingtonpost.com/world/former-afghan-leader-hamid-karzai-grew-estranged-from-his-american-allies-during-10-years-in-power-heres-what-he-says-about-the-afghanistan-papers/2019/12/18/ef4ccb32-20dc-11ea-b034-de7dc2b5199b_story.html.

Cooper, Helene. "2 U.S. Service Members Killed in Afghanistan, Pentagon Says." The New York Times. The New York Times, April 27, 2017. https://www.nytimes.com/2017/04/27/us/politics/two-us-service-members-killed-in-afghanistan-pentagon-says.html?_r=0.

Cooper, Helene. "'Friendly Fire' May Have Killed 2 U.S. Soldiers in Afghanistan Raid." The New York Times. The New York Times, April 28, 2017. https://www.nytimes.com/2017/04/28/world/middleeast/american-soldiers-afghanistan.html?_r=0.

"Country Reports on Terrorism 2015 - FDD's Long War Journal." Accessed July 9, 2022. https://www.longwarjournal.org/wp-content/uploads/2016/06/2016-State-Department-Country-Report-on-Terrorism.pdf.

"The Culture & Conflict Review - Naval Postgraduate School." Accessed July 9, 2022. https://nps.edu/documents/105988371/107571254/Dearing.pdf/ca006709-3aa1-46ed-b252-c84ebfc17b97.

Davis, Julie Hirschfeld, and Mark Landler. "Trump Outlines New Afghanistan War Strategy with Few Details." The New York Times. The New York Times, August 22, 2017. https://www.nytimes.com/2017/08/21/world/asia/afghanistan-troops-trump.html.

"Deadly Insider Attack That Left 3 U.S. Marines Dead Was Work of an Afghan Teenager." Washington Post, August 17, 2012. https://web.archive.org/web/20131023122113/http://articles.washingtonpost.com/2012-08-17/world/35493178_1_afghan-local-police-afghan-security-afghan-officials.

Defense Casualty Analysis System. Accessed July 9, 2022. https://dcas.dmdc.osd.mil/dcas/.

Desk, News. "Operation Mansouri: Afghan Taliban Launch Deadliest Spring Offensive." Times of Islamabad. Times of Islamabad, April 28, 2017. https://timesofislamabad.com/28-Apr-2017/operation-mansouri-afghan-taliban-launch-deadliest-spring-offensive.

Diamond, Jeremy, Jim Sciutto, Elise Labott, Pamela Brown, Jamie Crawford, Jim Acosta, and Gloria Borger. "U.S. Drone Strike Accidentally Killed 2 Hostages - Cnnpolitics." CNN. Cable News Network, April 23, 2015. https://edition.cnn.com/2015/04/23/politics/white-house-hostages-killed/index.html.

Dpmmurphadmin. "Operation Red Wings." LT Michael P. Murphy Navy SEAL Museum, June 26, 2022. https://murphsealmuseum.org/about/operation-red-wings/.

Dr. Rajkumar Singh, "Chasing Peace in Afghanistan: Dynamics and Dilemmas," Daily Outlook Afghanistan, the Leading Independent Newspaper., July 12, 2021, http://outlookafghanistan.net/topics.php?post_id=29792.

Druzin, Zubair Babakarkhail Heath, and stripes Administrator. "Afghan Forces Take over Responsibility for Security from NATO." Stars and Stripes, June 18, 2013. https://www.stripes.com/theaters/middle_east/afghan-forces-take-over-responsibility-for-security-from-nato-1.226391.

Eidenmuller, Michael E. George W. Bush - address to the nation on 9-11-01 - The Rhetoric of 9/11. Accessed July 9, 2022.

https://www.americanrhetoric.com/speeches/gwbush911ad-dresstothenation.htm.

Evans, John R. "Bilateral Security Agreement: A New Era of Afghan-U.S. Cooperation." Brookings. Brookings, July 29, 2016. https://www.brookings.edu/blog/up-front/2014/09/30/bi-lateral-security-agreement-a-new-era-of-afghan-u-s-coopera-tion/.

Faiez, Jason Straziuso And Rahim. USA today. Gannett Satellite Information Network, August 24, 2008. https://usatoday30.us-atoday.com/news/world/2008-08-23-1051356149_x.htm.

France-Presse, Agence. "Controversial Afghan Cop, 'Tor-turer-in-Chief', Killed in Taliban Attack." NDTV.com. NDTV, October 19, 2018. https://www.ndtv.com/world-news/kandahar-afghanistan-general-abdul-raziq-afghanistans-tor-turer-in-chief-killed-in-taliban-attack-1934262.

"Fresh Claims Us Is Running Secret Prison in Afghanistan." BBC News. BBC, October 15, 2010. https://www.bbc.com/news/world-south-asia-11551409.

Gall, Carlotta. "Convoy CRASH Sparks Kabul Riots - Asia - Pa-cific - International Herald Tribune." The New York Times. The New York Times, May 29, 2006. https://www.nytimes.com/2006/05/29/world/asia/29iht-afghan.1843499.html.

Carlotta Gall, "Karzai Orders Investigation of U.S. Attack," The New York Times (The New York Times, May 24, 2006), https://www.nytimes.com/2006/05/24/world/asia/karzai-orders-in-vestigation-of-us-attack.html.

Gamio, Lazaro, Karen Yourish, Lauren Leatherby, and Sarah Kerr. "Chaos and Desperation at the Kabul Airport." The New York Times. The New York Times, August 16, 2021. https://www.nytimes.com/interactive/2021/08/16/world/asia/ka-bul-airport-maps-photos.html.

Gannon, Kathy. "US Left Afghan Airfield at Night, Didn't Tell New Commander." AP NEWS. Associated Press, July 6, 2021. https://apnews.com/article/bagram-afghanistan-airfield-us-tr oops-f3614828364f567593251aaaa167e623.

Garland, Chad. "US Special Operator Was 1st US Casualty in Fight against Islamic State in Afghanistan." Stars and Stripes, October 5, 2016. https://www.stripes.com/theaters/middle_east/us-special-operator-was-1st-us-casualty-in-fight-against-islamic-state-in-afghanistan-1.432343.

Gary Berntsen and Ralph Pezzullo, Jawbreaker: The Attack on Bin Laden and Al-Qaeda: A Personal Account by the CIA's Key Field Commander (New York: Three Rivers Press (CA), 2006).

"General John F. Campbell ISAF-Resolute Support Transition Ceremony Address," American Rhetoric: The Power of Oratory in the United States (American Rhetoric, December 28, 2014), https://www.americanrhetoric.com/speeches/johncampbell-resolutesupportceremony.htm.

"General Kenneth F. McKenzie Jr.. Commander of U.S. Central Command and Pentagon Press Secre." U.S. Department of Defense. Accessed July 9, 2022. https://www.defense.gov/News/Transcripts/Transcript/Article/2780738/general-kenneth-f-mckenzie-jr-commander-of-us-central-command-and-pentagon-pres/.

Gibbons-Neff, Thomas, and Missy Ryan. "Two U.S. Troops Die Battling Islamic State Militants in Eastern Afghanistan." The Washington Post. WP Company, April 28, 2017. https://www.washingtonpost.com/world/national-security/two-us-troops-die-battling-islamic-state-militants-in-eastern-afghanistan/2017/04/27/14879ad8-2b55-11e7-be51-b3fc6ff7faee_story.html.

"Giovanni Lo Porto, Killed in US Drone Strike, Was 'Incredibly Loyal' Friend." The Guardian. Guardian News and Media, April 23, 2015. https://www.theguardian.com/world/2015/apr/23/giovanni-lo-porto-killed-us-drone-strike-incredibly-loyal-friend.

Goldman, Adam. "AP INVESTIGATION: Cautionary Tale From CIA Prison." AP investigation: Cautionary tale from CIA prison. ABC News. Accessed July 9, 2022. https://web.archive.org/web/20101123050959/https://abcnews.go.com/print?id=10222080.

"The Haqqani Network." Institute for the Study of War. Accessed July 9, 2022. https://www.understandingwar.org/report/haqqani-network.

"Headlines from around the World – MSN News UK." MSN. Accessed July 9, 2022. https://www.msn.com/en-gb/news/world/2-us-army-soldiers-killed-fighting-isis-in-afghanistan/ar-BBAs1fW?li=AA59G2&ocid=spartanntp.

History.com Editors. "Osama Bin Laden." History.com. A&E Television Networks, December 16, 2009. https://www.history.com/topics/21st-century/osama-bin-laden.

History.com Editors. "September 11 Attacks." History.com. A&E Television Networks, February 17, 2010. https://www.history.com/topics/21st-century/9-11-attacks.

Holland, Steve. "Obama Plans to End U.S. Troop Presence in Afghanistan by 2016." Reuters. Thomson Reuters, May 27, 2014. https://www.reuters.com/article/us-usa-afghanistan-obama/obama-plans-to-end-u-s-troop-presence-in-afghanistan-by-2016-idUSKBN0E71WQ20140527.

"How Mass Killings by US Forces after 9/11 Boosted Support for the Taliban." The Guardian. Guardian News and Media, September 10, 2021. https://www.theguardian.com/us-news/2021/sep/10/how-mass-killings-by-us-forces-after-911-boosted-support-for-the-taliban.

"ICasualties Iraq: ICASUALTIES Home Page." iCasualties Iraq: iCasualties Home Page. Accessed July 9, 2022. http://icasualties.org/.

"International Community Responds." International Community Responds | National September 11 Memorial & Museum. Accessed July 9, 2022. https://www.911memorial.org/learn/resources/digital-exhibitions/digital-exhibition-revealed-hunt-bin-laden/international-community-responds.

"Is in Afghanistan 'Kills 30 Abducted Civilians'." BBC News. BBC, October 26, 2016. https://www.bbc.com/news/world-asia-37772200.

"Islamic Movement of Uzbekistan Security Council." United Nations. United Nations Accessed July 9, 2022. https://www.un-.org/securitycouncil/sanctions/1267/aq_sanctions_list/summaries/entity/islamic-movement-of-uzbekistan.

James Vicini, "U.S. Court Rejects Appeal by Afghanistan Prisoners," Reuters (Thomson Reuters, May 21, 2010), https://www.reuters.com/article/us-usa-security-bagram/u-s-court-rejects-appeal-by-afghanistan-prisoners-idINTRE64K4EI20100521.

"Joint Declaration of the United States-Afghanistan ... - Govinfo.gov." Accessed July 9, 2022. https://www.govinfo.gov/content/pkg/WCPD-2005-05-30/pdf/WCPD-2005-05-30-Pg863.pdf.

"Joint Statement from the Department of State and Department of Defense: Update on Afghanistan - United States Department of State." U.S. Department of State. U.S. Department of State, August 16, 2021. https://www.state.gov/joint-statement-from-the-department-of-state-and-department-of-defense-update-on-afghanistan/.

Josh Rothman, "Bin Laden's (Fictional) Mountain Fortress," Boston.com (The Boston Globe), accessed July 12, 2022, http://archive.boston.com/bostonglobe/ideas/brainiac/2011/05/bin_ladens_fict.html.

Julie Pace, "President Obama Looks to Start 'New Chapter' in U.S. Foreign Policy," PBS (Public Broadcasting Service, May 23, 2014), https://www.pbs.org/newshour/politics/president-obama-looks-start-new-chapter-u-s-foreign-policy.

"July 2022 Monthly Forecast." Security Council Report. Accessed July 9, 2022. https://www.securitycouncilreport.org/.

"Karzai Widens Lead in Afghan Poll." BBC News. BBC, August 26, 2009. http://news.bbc.co.uk/2/hi/south_asia/8221709.stm.

Ken Silverstein, "The Charmed Life of a CIA Torturer: How Fate Diverged for Matthew Zirbel, Aka CIA Officer 1, and Gul Rahman," The Intercept (The Intercept, December 15, 2014), https://theintercept.com/2014/12/15/charmed-life-cia-torturer/.

"Kidnapped German Aid Worker Freed in Afghanistan." AP NEWS. Associated Press, October 10, 2014. https://apnews.com/article/7ba7e94f57f643c9a0c8e5ab98df9ea9.

Knowlton, Brian, and International Herald Tribune. "Rumsfeld Rejects Planto Allow Mullah Omar 'to Live in Dignity' : Taliban Fighters Agree to Surrender Kandahar." The New York Times. The New York Times, December 7, 2001. https://www.nytimes.com/2001/12/07/news/rumsfeld-rejects-planto-allow-mullah-omar-to-live-in-dignity-taliban.html.

Lamothe, Dan. "Senior ISIS Leader Killed in Northern Afghanistan, Highlighting Shifting Militant Allegiances." The Washington Post. WP Company, October 26, 2021. https://www.washingtonpost.com/news/checkpoint/wp/2018/04/09/senior-isis-leader-killed-in-northern-afghanistan-highlighting-shifting-militant-allegiances/.

LANDAY, CAROL ROSENBERG and JONATHAN. "Washington: Prosecutors Probing Deaths of Two CIA Captives - Guant." The Miami Herald, January 2, 1970. https://web.archive.org/web/20121006181941/http://www.miamiherald.com/2011/06/30/2293780/justice-department-investigating.html.

Dr Anna Larson and Astri Suhrke, "Afghanistan," Lessons from Bonn: Victors' peace? | Conciliation Resources, June 1, 2018, https://www.c-r.org/accord/afghanistan/lessons-bonn-victors%E2%80%99-peace.

"Listen." The Costs of War. Accessed July 9, 2022. https://watson.brown.edu/costsofwar/.

Mahsud, Ishtiaq. "Al-Qaeda: U.S. Drones Kill 2 Leaders in Pakistan." USA Today. Gannett Satellite Information Network, April 12, 2015. https://www.usatoday.com/story/news/world/2015/04/12/al-Qaeda-drone-strikes/25668307/.

"March 2017 Online Exclusive Article." i. Accessed July 9, 2022. https://www.armyupress.army.mil/Journals/Military-Review/Online-Exclusive/2017-Online-Exclusive-Articles/Operation-Anaconda-Shah-i-Khot-Valley-Afghanistan/.

"Marine Tape Reaction Sets Taliban Fighters against Commanders." Reuters. Thomson Reuters, January 20, 2012. https://www.reuters.com/article/us-afghanistan-pakistan-taliban-idUSTRE-80J0D320120120.

Mashal, Mujib, and Thomas Gibbons-neff. "How a Taliban Assassin Got Close Enough to Kill a General." The New York Times. The New York Times, November 2, 2018. https://www.nytimes.com/2018/11/02/world/asia/taliban-attack-raziq-alliance.html.

Mashal, Mujib. "Afghan Mosque Suicide Bombing Kills at Least 20." The New York Times. The New York Times, August 1, 2017. https://www.nytimes.com/2017/08/01/world/asia/herat-afghanistan-mosque-bombing.html.

Miriam Arghandiwal, "Bomber in Afghanistan Kills 15, Including Six Americans," Reuters (Thomson Reuters, May 16, 2013), https://www.reuters.com/article/us-afghanistan-attack/bomber-in-afghanistan-kills-15-including-six-americans-idUS-BRE94F06320130516.

Mirwais Harooni and Laura Myers, "Karzai Slams Us over Afghan Massacre, Soldier Identified," Reuters (Thomson Reuters, March 17, 2012), https://www.reuters.com/article/afghanistan/karzai-slams-us-over-afghan-massacre-soldier-identified-idINDEE82E0JY20120317.

"MMP: Tehrik-i-Taliban Pakistan." FSI. Accessed July 9, 2022. https://cisac.fsi.stanford.edu/mappingmilitants/profiles/tehrik-i-taliban-pakistan.

Motlagh, Jason. "As the Taliban Return, Afghanistan's Past Threatens Its Future." History. National Geographic, June 20, 2022. https://www.nationalgeographic.com/history/article/as-the-taliban-rise-again-afghanistans-past-threatens-its-present.

Murphy, Brett. "Inside the U.S. Military's Raid against Its Own Security Guards That Left Dozens of Afghan Children Dead." USA Today. Gannett Satellite Information Network, August 17, 2021. https://www.usatoday.com/in-depth/news/investigations/2019/12/29/security-guards-afghan-warlords-mass-civilian-casualties/2675795001/.

Myers, Meghann, and Andrew deGrandpre. "Army Rangers Killed in Afghanistan Were Possible Victims of Friendly Fire." Army Times. Army Times, August 8, 2017. https://www.armytimes.com/news/your-army/2017/04/28/army-rangers-killed-in-afghanistan-were-possible-victims-of-friendly-fire/.

Nakamura, David, and Abby Phillip. "Trump Announces New Strategy for Afghanistan That Calls for a Troop Increase." The Washington Post. WP Company, August 21, 2017. https://www.washingtonpost.com/politics/trump-expected-to-announce-small-troop-increase-in-afghanistan-in-prime-time-address/2017/08/21/eb3a513e-868a-11e7-a94f-3139abce39f5_story.html.

"Nathan R. Chapman." Green Beret Foundation, January 5, 2020. https://greenberetfoundation.org/memorial/nathan-ross-chapman/.

National Archives and Records Administration. National Archives and Records Administration. Accessed July 9, 2022. https://georgewbush-whitehouse.archives.gov/infocus/bushrecord/.

National Archives and Records Administration. National Archives and Records Administration. Accessed July 9, 2022. https://georgewbush-whitehouse.archives.gov/news/releases/2004/10/20041008-6.html.

"NATO Ends Combat Operations in Afghanistan." The Guardian. Guardian News and Media, December 28, 2014. https://www.theguardian.com/world/2014/dec/28/nato-ends-afghanistan-combat-operations-after-13-years.

Nato. "ISAF's Mission in Afghanistan (2001-2014)." NATO. Accessed July 9, 2022. https://www.nato.int/cps/en/natohq/topics_69366.htm.

Nato. "NATO and Afghanistan." NATO, June 10, 2022. https://www.nato.int/cps/en/natohq/topics_8189.htm.

Nctc. "National Counterterrorism Center: Groups." National Counterterrorism Center | Groups. Accessed July 9, 2022. https://www.dni.gov/nctc/groups/afghan_taliban.html.

Nctc. "National Counterterrorism Center: Groups." National Counterterrorism Center | Groups. Accessed July 9, 2022. https://www.dni.gov/nctc/groups/haqqani_network.html.

Nctc. "National Counterterrorism Center: Groups." National Counterterrorism Center | Groups. Accessed July 9, 2022. https://www.dni.gov/nctc/groups/hezb_e_islami.html.

Nctc. "National Counterterrorism Center: Groups." National Counterterrorism Center | Groups. Accessed July 9, 2022. https://www.dni.gov/nctc/groups/ttp.html.

"'No Losers, Only Partners' with Afghan Unity Government, Security Council Told | | UN News." United Nations. United Nations. Accessed July 9, 2022. https://news.un.org/en/story/2014/09/477732-no-losers-only-partners-afghan-unity-government-security-council-told.

"Obama: 8,400 U.S. Troops to Remain in Afghanistan through January," U.S. Department of Defense, accessed July 12, 2022, https://www.defense.gov/News/News-Stories/Article/Article/827640/obama-8400-us-troops-to-remain-in-afghanistan-through-january/.

"Obama Administration Backs Bush, Grants No Rights to Bagram Prisoners | CBC News." CBCnews. CBC/Radio Canada, February 21, 2009. https://www.cbc.ca/news/world/obama-administration-backs-bush-grants-no-rights-to-bagram-prisoners-1.860853.

"Obama Announces Plan to Keep 9,800 US Troops in Afghanistan after 2014." The Guardian. Guardian News and Media, May 27, 2014. https://www.theguardian.com/world/2014/may/27/obama-us-afghanistan-force-2014.

"Obama Details Afghan War Plan, Troop Increases." NBCNews.com. NBCUniversal News Group, December 1, 2009. https://www.nbcnews.com/id/wbna34218604.

"Obama Pushes Back Troop Drawdown in Afghanistan until after 2015." The Guardian. Guardian News and Media, March 24, 2015. https://www.theguardian.com/us-news/2015/mar/24/us-troop-levels-afghanistan-2015.

"One More Step." archive.ph. Accessed July 9, 2022. https://archive.ph/20130131194943/http://www.philstar.com/Article.aspx?articleid=498012.

"Operation Moshtarak: Preparing for the Battle of Marjahh." Institute for the Study of War. Accessed July 9, 2022. https://www.understandingwar.org/report/operation-moshtarak-preparing-battle-Marjahh.

"Operation Moshtarak: Taking and Holding Marjahh." Institute for the Study of War. Accessed July 9, 2022. https://www.understandingwar.org/report/operation-moshtarak-taking-and-holding-Marjahh.

"Operation Neptune Spear." Operation Neptune Spear | National September 11 Memorial & Museum. Accessed July 9, 2022. https://www.911memorial.org/learn/resources/digital-exhibitions/digital-exhibition-revealed-hunt-bin-laden/operation-neptune-spear.

"Operation Sleigh Ride." DVIDS. Accessed July 9, 2022. https://www.dvidshub.net/video/8550/operation-sleigh-ride.

"Operation Sleigh Ride." DVIDS. Accessed July 9, 2022. https://www.dvidshub.net/video/8550/operation-sleigh-ride.

"Osama Bin Laden Dead," National Archives and Records Administration (National Archives and Records Administration), accessed July 12, 2022, https://obamawhitehouse.archives.gov/blog/2011/05/02/osama-bin-laden-dead.

"Pakistan School Attack: Suspects Arrested in Afghanistan." BBC News. BBC, January 14, 2015. https://www.bbc.com/news/world-asia-30818347.

PaolaFarer, "Kerry Statement on Bin Laden Tape," KUSA.com (KUSA, October 29, 2004), https://www.9news.com/article/news/kerry-statement-on-bin-laden-tape/73-344859151.

Person, and Patricia Zengerle Ahmad Elhamy. "Kabul Attacks Put Bitter Adversary Islamic State Back into U.S. Sights." Reuters. Thomson Reuters, August 26, 2021. https://www.reuters.com/world/islamic-state-claims-responsibility-kabul-airport-attack-2021-08-26/.

"President Bush on Friday: 'We Will Not Be Intimidated' ," National Archives and Records Administration (National Archives and Records Administration), accessed July 12, 2022, https://georgewbush-whitehouse.archives.gov/news/releases/2004/10/text/20041029-18.html.

"President Bush's Speech on Terrorism," The New York Times (The New York Times, September 6, 2006), https://www.nytimes.com/2006/09/06/washington/06bush_transcript.html.

"President Obama on The Way Forward in Afghanistan." National Archives and Records Administration. National Archives and Records Administration. Accessed July 9, 2022. https://obamawhitehouse.archives.gov/blog/2011/06/22/president-obama-way-forward-afghanistan.

Press, Associated. "Taliban Kill 12 Captives in Front of Hundreds of People, Official Says." Fox News. FOX News Network, June 8, 2016. https://www.foxnews.com/world/taliban-kill-12-captives-in-front-of-hundreds-of-people-official-says.

Press, Jason Straziuso The Associated. "Afghan Raid Blamed on False Tip." Tribune. Sarasota Herald-Tribune, September 15, 2008. https://www.heraldtribune.com/news/20080915/afghan-raid-blamed-on-false-tip.

Press, Khaama. "Taliban Kill 17 Passengers after Kidnapping around 185 in Kunduz." The Khaama Press News Agency, May 31, 2016. https://www.khaama.com/taliban-kill-17-passengers-after-kidnapping-around-185-in-kunduz-01124/.

Press, The Associated. "Germany: Abducted Aid Worker Freed (Published 2014)." The New York Times. The New York Times, October 11, 2014. https://www.nytimes.com/2014/10/11/world/europe/germany-abducted-aid-worker-freed.html.

"Prison Officials Visited CIA 'Dungeon,'" but Kept No Record of the Trip." CBS News. CBS Interactive, November 22, 2016. https://www.cbsnews.com/news/bureau-of-prisons-officials-visited-cia-salt-pit-dungeon/.

"The Prophet Muhammad and the Origins of Islam ." Metmuseum.org. Accessed July 9, 2022. https://www.metmuseum.org/learn/educators/curriculum-resources/art-of-the-islamic-world/unit-one/the-prophet-muhammad-and-the-origins-of-islam.

Rahim, Najim, and Rod Nordland. "Taliban Surge Routs ISIS in Northern Afghanistan." The New York Times. The New York Times, August 1, 2018. https://www.nytimes.com/2018/08/01/world/asia/afghanistan-taliban-isis.html.

"Rasul v. Bush, 542 U.S. 466 (2004)." Justia Law. Accessed July 9, 2022. https://supreme.justia.com/cases/federal/us/542/466/.

Rayment, Sean, and Kabul. "How the SAS Freed Hostages from Taliban Caves." The Sydney Morning Herald. The Sydney Morning Herald, June 3, 2012. https://www.smh.com.au/world/how-the-sas-freed-hostages-from-taliban-caves-20120603-1zq1s.html.

"Read 'Disrupting Improvised Explosive Device Terror Campaigns: Basic Research Opportunities: A Workshop Report' at Nap.edu," SUMMARY | Disrupting Improvised Explosive Device Terror Campaigns: Basic Research Opportunities: A Workshop Report |The National Academies Press, accessed July 12, 2022, https://nap.nationalacademies.org/read/12437/chapter/2.

"Remarks by President Biden on Afghanistan." The White House. The United States Government, August 16, 2021. https://www.whitehouse.gov/briefing-room/speeches-remarks/2021/08/16/remarks-by-president-biden-on-afghanistan/.

"Remarks by President Biden on the Terror Attack at Hamid Karzai International Airport," The White House (The United States Government, August 27, 2021), https://www.whitehouse.gov/briefing-room/speeches-remarks/2021/08/26/remarks-by-president-biden-on-the-terror-attack-at-hamid-kar-zai-international-airport/.

"Remarks by President Biden on The Way Forward in Afghanistan." The White House. The United States Government, April 14, 2021. https://www.whitehouse.gov/briefing-room/speeches-remarks/2021/04/14/remarks-by-president-biden-on-the-way-forward-in-afghanistan/.

"Remarks by the President on The Way Forward in Afghanistan," National Archives and Records Administration (National Archives and Records Administration), accessed July 12, 2022, https://obamawhitehouse.archives.gov/the-press-cffice/2011/06/22/remarks-president-way-forward-Afghanistan.

"Remembering Warren Weinstein, the American Hostage Accidentally Killed in U.S. Drone Strike | CBC Radio." CBCnews. CBC/Radio Canada, April 23, 2015. https://www.cbc.ca/radio/asithappens/as-it-happens-thursday-edition-1.3045833/remembering-warren-weinstein-the-american-hostage-accidentally-killed-in-u-s-drone-strike-1.3046275.

"Results Leave Karzai One Step from Victory," The Guardian (Guardian News and Media, October 25, 2004), https://www.theguardian.com/world/2004/oct/25/afghanistan?CMP=gu_com.

"The Rhetoric of 9/11 - President Bush Delivers Operation Enduring ..." Accessed July 9, 2022. https://www.americanrhetoric.com/speeches/gwbush911intialafghanistanops.htm.

"Rise, Fall and Resurgence of Taliban in Afghanistan." Anadolu Ajansı. Accessed July 9, 2022. https://www.aa.com.tr/en/asia-pacific/rise-fall-and-resurgence-of-taliban-in-afghanistan/1750222.

Roggio, Bill. "Al-Qaeda Leader Killed in Eastern Afghanistan, NDS Claims ." Equipo Nizkor - al-Qaeda leader killed in eastern Afghanistan, NDS claims. The Long War Journal. Accessed July 9, 2022. http://www.derechos.org/nizkor/iraq/doc/afg608.html.

Rosenberg, Matthew, and Eric Schmitt. "U.S. Is Escalating a Secretive War in Afghanistan." The New York Times. The New York Times, February 12, 2015. https://www.nytimes.com/2015/02/13/world/asia/data-from-seized-computer-fuels-a-surge-in-us-raids-on-al-Qaeda.html.

Rotondi, Jessica Pearce. "9 Unexpected Things Navy Seals Discovered in Osama Bin Laden's Compound." History.com. A&E Television Networks, April 8, 2021. https://www.history.com/news/bin-laden-compound-abbottabad-belongings.

Ryan, Missy, and Karen DeYoung. "Biden Will Withdraw All U.S. Forces from Afghanistan by Sept. 11, 2021." The Washington Post. WP Company, August 17, 2021. https://www.washingtonpost.com/national-security/biden-us-troop-withdrawal-afghanistan/2021/04/13/918c3cae-9beb-11eb-8a83-3bc1fa69c2e8_story.html.

Sahak, Matin. "Families Flee as Taliban Battle Islamic State in Northern Afghanistan." Reuters. Thomson Reuters, July 20, 2018. https://www.reuters.com/article/us-afghanistan-taliban-islamic-state/families-flee-as-taliban-battle-islamic-state-in-northern-afghanistan-idUSKBN1KA231.

Sameen, Ismail. "Taliban Commander Dadullah Killed in Afghan Clash." Reuters. Thomson Reuters, May 13, 2007. https://www.reuters.com/article/us-afghan-taliban/taliban-commander-dadullah-killed-in-afghan-clash-idUSISL29013220070513.

Sarah Pruitt, "Islam's Sunni-Shia Divide, Explained," History.com (A&E Television Networks, July 31, 2019), https://www.history.com/news/sunni-shia-divide-islam-muslim.

Savage, Charlie. "Detainees Barred from Access to U.S. Courts." The New York Times. The New York Times, May 21, 2010. https://www.nytimes.com/2010/05/22/world/asia/22detain.html.

Schogol, Jeff. "Marine Who Pissed on Dead Taliban Wins in Court." Marine Corps Times. Marine Corps Times, November 9, 2017. https://www.marinecorpstimes.com/news/your-marine-corps/2017/11/09/marine-who-urinated-on-dead-taliban-wins-in-court/.

Scott, Andrea. "Here Are the Names of the 13 U.S. Service Members Killed in Afghanistan Attack." Military Times. Military Times, August 28, 2021. https://www.militarytimes.com/news/your-marine-corps/2021/08/28/here-are-the-names-of-the-13-service-members-who-died-in-afghanistan-attack/.

"Secret Prisons: Obama's Order to Close 'Black Sites'." The Guardian. Guardian News and Media, January 23, 2009. https://www.theguardian.com/world/2009/jan/23/secret-prisons-closure-obama-cia.

"Senior Al-Qaeda Leader Reported Killed in US Airstrike in Eastern Afghanistan." FDD's Long War Journal, October 19, 2014. https://www.longwarjournal.org/archives/2014/10/senior_al_qaeda_lead_12.php.

Shah, Taimoor, and Graham Bowley. "U.S. Sergeant Is Said to Kill 16 Civilians in Afghanistan." The New York Times. The New York Times, March 11, 2012. https://www.nytimes.com/2012/03/12/world/asia/afghanistan-civilians-killed-american-soldier-held.html.

Sidner, Sara. "U.S. Soldier Accused of Afghan Killing Spree." CNN. Cable News Network, March 12, 2012. https://edition.cnn.com/2012/03/11/world/asia/afghanistan-us-service-member/index.html.

Somade, Jesutofunmi E. "Bacha Bazi: Afghanistan's Darkest Secret." Human Rights and discrimination. Human Rights and discrimination, August 21, 2017. https://humanrights.brightblue.org.uk/blog-1/2017/8/18/bacha-bazi-afghanistans-darkest-secret.

"Soviet Invasion of Afghanistan," Encyclopædia Britannica (Encyclopædia Britannica, inc.), accessed July 12, 2022, https://www.britannica.com/event/Soviet-invasion-of-Afghanistan.

"Special Forces Rescue Aid Workers - Details Emerge," british special forces, accessed July 12, 2022, https://www.eliteukforces.info/uk-military-news/030612-british-special-forces-rescue-details.php.

Starr, Barbara, and Jake Tapper. "US Military Ordered to Begin Planning to Withdraw about Half the Troops in Afghanistan | CNN Politics." CNN. Cable News Network, December 21, 2018. https://www.cnn.com/2018/12/20/politics/afghanistan-withdrawal/index.html.

"Statement by the President on the Signing of the Bilateral Security Agreement and NATO Status of Forces Agreement in Afghanistan." National Archives and Records Administration. National Archives and Records Administration. Accessed July 9, 2022. https://obamawhitehouse.archives.gov/the-press-office/2014/09/30/statement-president-signing-bilateral-security-agreement-and-nato-status.

"Still under the IS's Black Flag: Qari Hekmat's ISKP Island in Jawzjan after His Death by Drone." Afghanistan Analysts Network - English, March 9, 2020. https://www.afghanistan-analysts.org/en/reports/war-and-peace/still-under-the-iss-black-flag-qari-hekmats-iskp-island-in-jawzjan-after-his-death-by-drone/.

"Stripes," Stars and Stripes, accessed July 12, 2022, https://www.stripes.com/.

"Sunnis and Shia: Islam's Ancient Schism." BBC News. BBC, January 4, 2016. https://www.bbc.com/news/world-middle-east-16047709.

"Taliban Announces Start of 'Operation Mansouri.'" FDD's Long War Journal, April 28, 2017. https://www.longwarjournal.org/archives/2017/04/taliban-announce-start-of-operation-mansouri.php.

"Taliban Defy Bush Ultimatum." The Guardian. Guardian News and Media, September 21, 2001. https://www.theguardian.com/world/2001/sep/21/september11.usa15.

"Taliban Rejects President Bush's Demands." PBS. Public Broadcasting Service, September 21, 2001. https://www.pbs.org/newshour/world/terrorism-july-dec01-taliban_09-21.

"Taliban, Islamic State Continue Battle in Northern Afghanistan." FDD's Long War Journal, July 19, 2018. https://www.longwarjournal.org/archives/2018/07/taliban-islamic-state-con-tinue-battle-in-northern-afghanistan.php.

The New York Times, "Full Transcript and Video: Trump's Speech on Afghanistan," The New York Times (The New York Times, August 22, 2017), https://www.nytimes.com/2017/08/21/world/asia/trump-speech-afghanistan.html.

"The Strategic Benefits of Minimizing Civilian Harm in Counter-terrorism Strikes," Human Rights First, accessed July 12, 2022, https://www.humanrightsfirst.org/resource/strategic-bene-fits-minimizing-civilian-harm-counterterrorism-strikes.

"The Taliban." The Taliban | Mapping Militant Organizations. Accessed July 9, 2022. https://web.stanford.edu/group/map-pingmilitants/cgi-bin/groups/print_view/367.

Tamkin, Hamid. "Jawzjan Elders Save Woman from Taliban Stoning." Pajhwok Afghan News Jawzjan elders save woman from Taliban stoning Comments. Accessed July 9, 2022. https://pajhwok.com/2015/11/12/jawzjan-elders-save-woman-tali-ban-stoning/.

Taylor, Rob, and Jack Kimball. "U.S. Soldier Charged with 17 Murders in Afghan Killings." Reuters. Thomson Reuters, March 24, 2012. https://www.reuters.com/article/us-afghanistan-usa-charges/u-s-soldier-charged-with-17-murders-in-afghan-killings-idUSBRE82M0ZU20120324.

"Timeline: U.S. War in Afghanistan." Council on Foreign Re-lations. Council on Foreign Relations. Accessed July 9, 2022. https://www.cfr.org/timeline/us-war-afghanistan.

Tully, Andrew. "Bush, Karzai Sign 'Strategic Partnership'." Ra-dioFreeEurope/RadioLiberty. Bush, Karzai Sign 'Strategic Part-nership', April 8, 2008. https://www.rferl.org/a/1058976.html.

"Two U.S. Army Rangers Killed in Anti-Isis Raid in Eastern Afghanistan." NBCNews.com. NBCUniversal News Group, April 28, 2017. https://www.nbcnews.com/news/world/least-2-u-s-service-members-killed-anti-isis-raid-n751826.

U.S. Department of State. U.S. Department of State. Accessed July 9, 2022. https://2001-2009.state.gov/p/sca/rls/pr/2005/46628.htm.

"U.S. Probe: Afghan Airstrike Killed at Least 33 Civilians." CNN. Cable News Network. Accessed July 9, 2022. http://www.cnn.com/2008/WORLD/asiapcf/10/08/afghanistan.us.airstrike/?iref=nextin.

"U.S.-Led Attack on Afghanistan Begins." History.com. A&E Television Networks, July 20, 2010. https://www.history.com/this-day-in-history/u-s-led-attack-on-afghanistan-begins.

"The U.S.-Taliban Agreement and the Afghan Peace Process." Stanford Law School. Accessed July 9, 2022. https://law.stanford.edu/2020/12/07/the-u-s-taliban-agreement-and-the-afghan-peace-process/.

"Ue Tae Titue Peace Peacebrief - United States Institute of Peace." Accessed July 9, 2022. https://www.usip.org/sites/default/files/PB183-Forging-Afghanistans-National-Unity-Government.pdf.

"United States Senate Select Committee on Intelligence." Accessed July 9, 2022. https://www.intelligence.senate.gov/sites/default/files/documents/CRPT-113srpt288.pdf.

"US Air Strike Wiped out Afghan Wedding Party, Inquiry Finds." The Guardian. Guardian News and Media, July 11, 2008. https://www.theguardian.com/world/2008/jul/11/afghanistan.usa.

"US Killed Aqis Deputy Emir, Shura Member in January Drone Strikes." FDD's Long War Journal, April 14, 2015. https://www.longwarjournal.org/archives/2015/04/us-killed-aqis-deputy-emir-shura-member-in-january-drone-strikes.php.

"US Military Strikes Large Al-Qaeda Training Camps in Southern Afghanistan." FDD's Long War Journal. Accessed July 9, 2022. https://www.longwarjournal.org/archives/2015/10/us-military-strikes-large-al-Qaeda-training-camps-in-southern-afghanistan.php.

"US-Taliban Afghanistan Peace Talks in Qatar Cancelled." The Guardian. Guardian News and Media, June 20, 2013.

https://www.theguardian.com/world/2013/jun/20/afghanistan-talks-taliban-qatar-cancelled.

Vanda Felbab-Brown, "Pipe Dreams: The Taliban and Drugs from the 1990s into Its New Regime," Brookings (Brookings, March 9, 2022), https://www.brookings.edu/articles/pipe-dreams-the-taliban-and-drugs-from-the-1990s-into-its-new-regime/.

"The War in Afghanistan: A Timeline." CBS News. CBS Interactive, December 1, 2009. https://www.cbsnews.com/news/the-war-in-afghanistan-a-timeline/.

Washburne, Mike, James Mitchem, A foreign Soldier, Mike, and Richard. "Operation Red Wings: The Darkest Day in History of Navy Seals." Spec Ops Magazine, April 19, 2022. https://special-ops.org/operation-red-wings-darkest-day-navy-seals/.

"What Does the Term 'Jihad' Mean?," Islam Ahmadiyya, accessed July 12, 2022, https://www.alislam.org/question/what-does-jihad-mean/.

"Whither the Taliban?," Foreign Military Studies Office Publications - Whither the Taliban?, accessed July 12, 2022, https://irp.fas.org/world/para/docs/990306-taliban.htm.

"Will Afghanistan Prosecute Kandahar's Torturer-in-Chief?" Human Rights Watch, October 28, 2020. https://www.hrw.org/news/2017/05/17/will-afghanistan-prosecute-kandahars-torturer-chief.

World News. "Karzai Says He's at 'End of the Rope' with Us over Afghanistan Massacre." World News, March 18, 2012. https://web.archive.org/web/20120319061242/http://worldnews.msnbc.msn.com/_news/2012/03/16/10722610-karzai-says-hes-at-end-of-the-rope-with-us-over-afghanistan-massacre.

"'Troops in Contact.'" Human Rights Watch, November 24, 2020. https://www.hrw.org/report/2008/09/08/troops-contact/airstrikes-and-civilian-deaths-afghanistan.

COMING EARLY 2023

At What Cost: Voices From the Battlefield of Afghanistan

Want to read more stories about what it was like to deploy to Afghanistan? In *At What Cost: Voices From the Battlefield of Afghanistan* you'll get to read more stories from troops who served in Afghanistan – including my own story - and learn more about the history of the war. Stay tuned for book two in the *At What Cost* series, available in early 2023.

Follow me on social media to stay tuned for more information on the forthcoming book release and more: @authorjjainsworth